Bond Men Made Free

Medieval Peasant Movements
and the English Rising of 1381

Bond Men Made Free

Medieval Peasant Movements
and the English Rising of 1381

RODNEY HILTON

METHUEN

LONDON and NEW YORK

First published in 1973 by
Maurice Temple Smith Ltd
37 Great Russell Street, London WC1
First published as a University Paperback in 1977 by
Methuen & Co. Ltd
11 New Fetter Lane, London EC4P 4EE
Reprinted 1980 and 1982

Published in the USA by
Methuen & Co.
in association with Methuen, Inc.
733 Third Avenue, New York, NY 10017

© *1973 Rodney Hilton*

Printed in Great Britain by
J. W. Arrowsmith Ltd, Bristol

ISBN 0 416 82520 6

Contents

Acknowledgements

I have been helped in writing this book by many different people, not least by my students on whom I have tried out some of the ideas contained in it. But it has also been read by a number of friends who have offered essential corrections and useful advice— Jean Birrell, Christopher Dyer, Christopher Hill and Zvi Razi. To all these helpers I dedicate this book.

Abbreviations

Annales	*Annales: économies, sociétés, civilisations*
Bloch	*French Rural History: Its Original Characteristics*, 1929 (French edn), 1966 (English edn)
CEcH	*Cambridge Economic History of Europe*
Dobson	R. B. Dobson (ed), *The Peasants' Revolt of 1381*, 1970
Duby	G. Duby, *The Rural Economy and Country Life in the Medieval West*, 1962 (French edn), 1966 (English edn)
EcHR	*Economic History Review*
EHR	*English Historical Review*
MGH	*Monumenta Germaniae Historica*
P & P	*Past and Present*
Powell	E. Powell, *The Rising in East Anglia in 1381*, 1896
PRO	Public Record Office
Réville	A. Réville and C. Petit-Dutaillis, *Le Soulèvement des Travailleurs en Angleterre en 1381*, 1898
RS	Rolls Series
VCH	*Victoria History of the Counties of England*

'We pray that all bonde men may be made ffre for god made all ffre w^t his precious blode sheddyng.'

From a petition by Robert Kett and his followers, at Mousehold Heath outside Norwich, 1549 (printed in *Kett's Rebellion in Norfolk; being a history of the great civic commotion that occurred at the time of the Reformation in the reign of Edward VI* by F. W. Russell, 1859, p 51). This clause, though late in date, epitomizes the chief desire of rebellious serfs throughout medieval Europe.

Introduction

Social classes which have played a crucial part in transform-
ations of human society inevitably attract the attention of
historians, who, more than most practitioners of the social
sciences, are primarily concerned with the analysis of change.
Consequently studies, at any rate by European historians,
have tended to cluster around the problems connected with
the feudal nobility, the bourgeoisie and the industrial working
class. The feudal nobility created institutions and a social
ethos in the tenth and eleventh centuries which set a stamp
on medieval and early modern societies long outlasting the
original conditions which gave rise to them. The bourgeoisie,
once it had grown out of the subservient role it had played in
feudal society, that is when it became an industrial rather than
purely a commercial capitalist class, contributed to Europe its
first genuine revolutions. The industrial proletariat has subsequently been the necessary social basis for the revolutionary
socialist movement of modern times, though the peculiar
nature of modern imperialism led to the staging of successful
proletarian revolutions in relatively backward sectors of the
now worldwide economy.

There is no need to emphasize the immensity of the volume
of literature devoted to these social classes, their economic
basis, their origin, their internal stratification, their outlook
and their aspirations. Recently, however, the most ancient
social class of all, the peasantry, has come to the front of the
stage as a leading actor in the drama of change. The contemporary peasantry of the formal or informal colonies,
which constitute the bulk of the so-called 'third world', is in
many areas involved in revolutionary struggles and forcing
its attention on the established powers. It is also a class
which, even where not engaged in revolutionary actions,
is still the centre of attention for those who would like to
see peasant societies 'modernized', 'industrialized', and so

transformed, if possible without experiencing the revolutionary process.[1]

The contemporary appreciation of the numerical importance of peasants and of the incredible resilience of peasant societies (for instance, under military attack by the most technically advanced modern state), is matched by a new appreciation of the long history of this social formation. Whatever we may think of the nature and the chronology of prehistoric tribal societies, there seems little doubt that peasantries were the basis of the ancient civilizations out of which most European feudal societies grew; and that the class of slaves, though economically and culturally of great significance at certain times and in certain sectors of the ancient world, was numerically inferior and of less permanent importance than the peasant producers. In fact, viewed from the standpoint of this most numerous class of rural society, the difference between late Roman and early medieval civilization may not have been all that easy to discern.

This book, however, is only about peasant movements in the middle ages, even though a wide-ranging comparative study including ancient, modern and contemporary movements would be of interest and value. Wide-ranging comparisons need to be based on a body of detailed work if they are not to be superficial. Good medieval studies of value have quite properly been confined to individual movements, so that it still remains worthwhile at this stage to investigate, on a comparative basis, the movements simply of the medieval period. Furthermore, it is the medieval peasantry which, until recently, has been the most thoroughly investigated of all peasantries in history. This is partly because for the historian of modern times the bourgeoisie and the proletariat

[1] Hence, rural sociology might be described as a growth industry. From the considerable material published, two students' readers have already been compiled: *Peasant Society, a Reader*, ed. J. M. Potter, M. N. Diaz and G. M. Foster, 1967; and *Peasants and Peasant Societies*, ed. T. Shanin, 1971. The period of greatest growth in publications about peasants seems to be the 1960s. Historians became conscious during this decade of the connexion between the problems of peasants today and the peasant past, as can be seen in the reports to the *Second International Conference of Economic History, 1962* (published 1965). *The International Institute for Labour Studies* (offshoot of the International Labour Office) began to organize conferences on peasant problems and the history of peasant movements in 1967.

have, as has been mentioned, tended to fill the stage. It is also partly because, compared with the sources for the history of the working population of the ancient world, the medieval peasantry is not too badly documented. There are of course many obscurities, but thanks to the pioneer work of a number of historians, such as Vinogradoff, Dopsch, Maitland, Sée and Bloch, and the more recent studies of Postan, Kosminsky, Duby[2] and others, we can have a fairly detailed knowledge of essential aspects of peasant life—the size and composition of the peasant holding, the crops grown, consumed and sold, the rents paid and the legal and social status of the different strata within the peasant class.

The peasantry is referred to here as a 'social class', which implies a definition in terms of its role in the process of production and its place in the social distribution of property and incomes. This definition will be discussed more fully in Chapter 1. At this point it must be emphasized that a necessary condition for the existence of the peasantry as a class of small-scale agricultural producers has always been the existence of other classes who, to put it crudely, live off the surplus product of peasant labour. This involves the peasantry in a wide network of relationships with these other social groups, relationships which inevitably generate antagonism. Antagonism is inseparable from peasant movements, since even the most pacific result in the development of forms of organization—protective or aggressive—for the promotion of peasant interests, and ultimately of a separate peasant self-consciousness.

Historians of medieval society have recognized that peasant revolts were an important feature of it. But they have not all accepted that such movements were, in Marc Bloch's words, as 'natural to the seigneurial regime as strikes are to large-

[2] e.g. P. Vinogradoff, *Villainage in England*, 1892; *The Growth of the Manor*, 1905; A. Dopsch, *Economic and Social Foundations of European Civilisation*, 1923–4 (German edn), 1937 (English edn); F. W. Maitland, *Domesday Book and Beyond*, 1897; H. Sée, *Les classes rurales et le régime domanial en France au moyen-âge*, 1901; M. Bloch, *French Rural History*, 1929 (French edn), 1966 (English edn); M. M. Postan, innumerable articles, but especially, 'Medieval agrarian society in its prime: England', *CEcH* I, 1966; E. A. Kosminsky, *Studies in the Agrarian History of England in the Thirteenth Century*, 1956; G. Duby, *The Rural Economy and Country Life in the Medieval West*, 1962 (French edn), 1968 (English edn).

scale capitalism'.[3] Bloch's remark occurs at the end of a paragraph outlining the 'long and tragic chain' of peasant risings from the ninth century to the summer of 1789. Other writers have suggested that peasant rebellion was not so much a natural and inevitable feature of the seigneurial regime as a symptom of its general crisis—indeed of the crisis of the whole society of medieval Europe—between the fourteenth and early sixteenth centuries. A few examples from the writings of influential or typical historians of this period will illustrate the point.

Eileen Power, one of the most eminent of medieval economic historians, though referring to the peasant rebellion in late tenth-century Normandy, thought that the twelfth and thirteenth centuries were on the whole free of these disturbances. It was not until after the middle of the fourteenth century that peasant rebellions multiplied until they began to 'assume the proportions of a "green revolution"'. The phrase 'green revolution' suggests perhaps that the author was influenced by the stirrings of peasant political consciousness, especially in the Balkans, during the period of revolutionary upheavals in the 1920s.[4] More recent writers also tend to emphasize the connexion between peasant movements and the social crisis of the later middle ages. In one of those attractive but scholarly general histories of civilizations which have been produced by French historians in recent years, Michel Mollat refers to peasant and other social revolts of the fourteenth and fifteenth centuries as 'explosions of misery and anger', the consequence of the 'difficult times' which all the countries of Europe were experiencing at that time.[5] In another popular but scholarly general work the English historian, Daniel Waley, characterizes the period—in conformity with the general trend in economic history research—as one of economic setback. Popular unrest was one of the by-products of these economic difficulties.[6] Finally, a leading

---

[3] Bloch, p 170.   [4] *Cambridge Medieval History* VII, 1932, p 738.
[5] *Le moyen âge*, ed. E. Perroy (*Histoire générale des civilisations*, III, 1957), p 489. In the work written by M. Mollat in collaboration with P. Wolff (*Ongles bleus, Jacques et Ciompi*, 1970) revolts are still seen as the outcome of the late-medieval crisis, though social tensions are seen, too, as the consequence of the so-called expansion period of the thirteenth century.
[6] D. Waley, *Later Medieval Europe*, 1964, p. 107.

authority on the medieval peasantry, Georges Duby, has re-inforced this general interpretation of peasant rebellion as specifically related to the social and economic tensions of the late middle ages. In his great survey of the medieval rural economy he recognizes, as a general principle, that tumultu-ous resistance by peasants to exactions occurred in all medi-eval centuries. But, in fact, Duby's discussion of peasant revolts as a phenomenon of the medieval west is placed in a section connected with the changes of the fourteenth century, and the reference to earlier movements is illustrated simply by the revolt of the Pastoureaux in France in the middle of the thirteenth century.[7]

It is, of course, not unreasonable to connect movements of rebellion among peasants and other lower classes with stresses in the medieval social order that showed themselves in various ways during the fourteenth and fifteenth centuries. Do we not associate popular upheavals at all times with periods of economic, social and political crisis, when existing social relationships are subject to strain and questioning? Are we not frequently presented with interpretations which suggest that the medieval social order in its heyday (whenever that was) before the period of crisis was characterized by an organic balance between functional social groups whose members recognized their place and did not seek to step be-yond it? However, since the view that there was a relationship between social discontent and social crisis is undoubtedly in-fluenced by our experience of the upheavals of the twentieth century, let us not forget that industrial capitalism in its expansion phase was by no means exempt from strikes, riots and rebellions. It would seem not unreasonable, therefore, to survey the whole of the medieval period to see what evi-dence there is of conflicts inherent in peasant society. This will not necessarily be a rewarding task, for as is well known the documentary evidence for any aspect of early medieval life, particularly before the tenth or eleventh century, is scanty. The problem is worst of all for those wishing to investigate the activities of an illiterate section of the population which en-joyed low prestige in the eyes of those who put pen to parch-ment. These considerations, in fact, already begin to suggest

[7] Bk IV, chap. 3, i.

one reason for the emphasis on late medieval movements, that they occur in a relatively well-documented period.

Now if we follow Marc Bloch's suggestion that peasant revolt was a necessary feature of the social relationship in the rural seigneurie—an institution which lasted virtually throughout the medieval epoch—it does not mean that we must simplify medieval social history to the extent of denying that important, indeed critical, changes took place during those centuries. Naturally historical change was at a much slower tempo than it was during the centuries which have seen the emergence of modern industrial capitalism and latterly of socialist economies. Nevertheless we can fairly distinguish three main phases of development during the millennium 500–1500, as they affected the peasants, though certainly within these three phases there were many other patterns of change. In any case it is not suggested that the categorization of these three phases should provide much more than a useful framework or setting for consideration of the life of the peasants. We say 'not much more', because this tripartite subdivision is not simply superimposed on the facts. It is a recognition of distinct though broad phases of social evolution.

The first phase is that of the feudalization of western European society, roughly between the sixth and the tenth centuries. This period begins with the establishment of the barbarian successor states on the collapsed political system of the Roman Empire. There was substantially within it, nevertheless, a continuity of the basic social relations which characterized the late Empire.[8] It is a period of considerable complexity of political evolution, and yet one during which territorial aristocracies hierarchically linked by ties of vassalage between the greater and lesser elements, established their control over the rest of society. These men were the indispensable social basis for the emerging princely and monarchical powers which defined the forms of state organization. Their control was expressed, of course, in their monopoly of the

[8] This seems to be generally accepted by most historians of ancient and early medieval Europe, e.g. F. Lot, *The End of the Ancient World and the Beginning of the Middle Ages*, 1927 (French edn), 1931 (English edn); Dopsch, *op. cit.*; A. H. M. Jones, *The Later Roman Empire*, 1964; L. Musset, *Les invasions: les vagues germaniques*, 1965. Only some English historians cling to a theory of English exceptionalism.

means of coercion, for this ruling landed class was itself the armed power. It was also expressed in the regulation of jurisdiction at high and low levels, from the courts of kings, dukes and counts where the conflicts within the upper ranks were judged, down to the lower courts where greater and lesser lords and their officials judged the peasants, most of whom were either completely unfree in the eyes of the law or so dependent in various ways on their lords that, if they were free, their freedom was a formality and meant virtually nothing.[9] In this phase, the agrarian economy was producing very little surplus beyond that necessary to support the power, and rather primitive status distinction, of the landed aristocracy. Production for the market was low, rents tended to be in labour or in kind, there was little money in circulation and, since upper-class incomes were in produce rather than in cash, there was little effective demand for the luxury commodities of international trade. The urban element in western European life was, therefore, necessarily small. Lords and peasants constituted the overwhelming majority of the population.[10]

The second phase, from the eleventh to the early fourteenth century, is characterized by a considerable growth of population, expansion of the cultivated area, some technical progress and a remarkable development of production for the market. The necessary basis for this market production was, of course, an increase in the surplus product of agriculture—surplus, that is, to the subsistence needs of the basic producers. Undoubtedly this was made possible in part by increased technical efficiency, but improved organization and increased pressure by lords to transfer more of the surplus, in one way or another, from the producer to themselves was even more important. The two problems, in fact, must have been interdependent to some extent: demand for rent sometimes stimulated peasant production, and at other times depressed it.

[9] Among the innumerable books about early European feudalism, reference may still be made to F. L. Ganshof, *Feudalism*, 1944 (French edn), 1952 (English edn), and M. Bloch, *Feudal Society*, 1939–40 (French edn), 1961 (English edn). See also R. Boutruche, *Seigneurie et féodalité*, I and II, 1959–70.

[10] The essential reference work for trends in the medieval agrarian economy is the 1966 edition of *CEcH* I.

Although lords participated in market production in their demesnes, it would seem that the bulk of the agricultural commodities which were offered for sale in village markets, in country towns and in cities were produced by peasants in search of money to pay for rents, taxes, judicial fines and industrial products. The money paid by people in towns and elsewhere for peasant products eventually found its way into the hands of the landed proprietors, the ecclesiastical hierarchy, the possessors of jurisdictions, the governments and ultimately of course the merchants who provided the goods and services which these recipients of cash incomes demanded. The provision of these goods and services, though bringing great profit to merchants, also expanded urban populations of artisans, retail traders, industrial entrepreneurs, not to speak of a substantial element of unskilled labourers, servants and other poor people whose exact functions are seldom recorded. These increasing populations, reaching the hundred-thousand mark in some of the bigger Italian towns, and twice that number in thirteenth-century Paris, were largely recruited from rural immigrants.[11] This immigration reflected not only the attractive power of the towns, but a rural over-population which was becoming acute by the end of the thirteenth century, and which was shown by the large number of village families trying to live on smallholdings too inadequate to support them. All these factors—involvement in the network of a monetary economy, immigration, urban and rural poverty, demands for rents, tithes and taxes by landowners, church and state—produced considerable social upheavals and generated a sense of uncertainty.

The third phase, covering the fourteenth and fifteenth centuries, is no less enigmatic, in spite of increased documentation, than the earlier phases of medieval social evolution. It is a period when, initially, the tensions of the previous age seemed to be reaching breaking point, and when a series of plagues caused a drastic, though unevenly distributed, reduction of the European population. There continues to be much

[11] On European town populations in general see R. Mols, *Introduction à la démographie historique des villes d'Europe du XIVe au XVIIIe siècle*, 1954–6. The latest contribution to a debate about the size of Paris is by B. Geremek, *Acta Poloniae Historica*, 1968.

dispute among historians and demographers about the scale of the mortality in the third quarter of the fourteenth century, ranging from as little as twenty to more than fifty per cent.[12] There is less dispute about some of the main results of the mortality. Wages went up, as did the prices of industrial goods, and rents fell, together with prices of agricultural commodities. More land became available, there were fewer poor smallholders, and the provision of livestock in peasant agriculture, which had reached a dangerously low level at the end of the thirteenth century, was markedly improved— partly because more pasture was available. There was, however, not a little social dislocation, especially in the urban and industrial sectors of the economy, owing to the decline of older (especially luxury) industries and a shift of industrial activity and markets to new areas. The woollen textile centres, for example, in Flanders and central Italy, suffered severely, but English woollen textiles expanded and captured the Baltic market; other new centres of production of cheaper cloths developed in northern Italy, around Lake Como for instance, and in southern Germany, as at Nuremberg. It was not until the last quarter of the fifteenth century that a population recovery began, and with it a new phase in European development.[13]

The three evolutionary phases which have been briefly sketched are described here primarily in terms of economic and social factors. These, though basic, are insufficient in themselves for an understanding of the general character of the successive epochs. It is true, however, that these factors were the most important for the peasants who are our main concern. Even so, forms of political organization and religious life also played an important part in the response of the peasants to the changing circumstances of their lives. Reference

[12] E. Carpentier, 'La peste noire', *Annales*, 1962; P. Ziegler, *The Black Death*, 1969. A recent author, J. F. D. Shrewsbury, in *A History of the Bubonic Plague in the British Isles*, 1970, advocates the lower figure, but writes as a bacteriologist without first-hand knowledge of the documentary evidence.

[13] Disputes about whether the European economy was stagnant or not in the later middle ages seem likely to go on for some time. For a taste of the controversy see R. S. Lopez, H. A. Miskimin and C. M. Cipolla in *EcHR*, 1962 and 1964, and A. R. Bridbury, *Economic Growth: England in the Later Middle Ages*, 1962.

has been made to the burdens of state taxation and jurisdictional fines as additions to the demands which landowners made for rents and services. These additional burdens were, of course, the necessary by-products of the growth of the apparatus of government, ranging from the lesser principalities of dukes and counts to the great feudal monarchies, such as England and France. They were caused mostly by the increasing expenditure of the ruling classes on war, feasting and display, but also by the increased costs of administration —facts which hardly escaped the taxpayers. But since this is not a general history of medieval Europe, political factors affecting peasant rebellion will be considered in direct connexion with the individual movements.

Similarly, we cannot here consider the whole development of the church, its hierarchical organization, the role of the religious orders, or the complex relationship of the church with secular society, but these matters will enter into the consideration of individual movements. It is important to emphasize at this point that the vital problem of the social consciousness of the peasants is inextricably bound with our understanding of popular religion, the relations of the people with the official ecclesiastical hierarchy, and with the heretical sects which become so important from the twelfth century onwards. Many of the thoughts and feelings of peasants must have derived from pre-Christian or non-Christian sources. The church necessarily, even consciously, absorbed into its own ritual and activities at parish level many of the propitiatory rites, animistic practices and forms of sympathetic magic which strictly speaking had nothing to do with the Christianity of Rome, of the schools, or of the diocese. Such elements in the peasant mentality were essentially connected with the routine of agricultural production and as such were not apt to enter into the expression of peasant political or social aspiration. It was, so it would seem, the non-pagan element in Christianity which affected peasant thoughts and feelings at the political level. Peasants, like other poor people in medieval society, were concerned not merely with the comforts of the sacraments but with the historical example of the early church, whose leaders were people more like themselves than the landowning abbots and bishops who were presented to them as the representatives of the Apostles. The relationship, however, between evangelical heresies and peasant discontent is by no means clear, particularly as such heresies were often complicated by elements of eastern dualism or by anticipations of a millennium which tended to appeal to propertyless and urban elements rather than to peasant landholders.

In the chapters which follow I aim to demonstrate that peasant society in medieval Europe, from the Dark Ages to the end of the fifteenth century, like peasant societies at all times and in all places, contained social tensions which had their outcome in social movements, some on a small and some on a large scale, some peaceful and some violent. Those which resulted from the very nature of the peasant economy are considered first. No apology is made for describing the basic features of medieval peasant society, for it is the beginning of understanding. But to develop understanding it is necessary to be historically specific, and to locate each movement in its context.

In this book, therefore, I have attempted to describe the growing complexity of peasant movements. Without becoming involved in a general history of social discontents, I have tried to show how peasant movements relate to those involving other social classes and therefore to the changing society of medieval Europe. The division between early and late movements may seem a little artificial, as indeed any attempt to classify and interpret a mass of historical evidence is bound to be. It might also be objected that to refer to the German peasant wars of the early sixteenth century only in passing is carrying traditional definitions of what is 'medieval' and what is 'modern' to ridiculous lengths. A reason for this omission is that the German peasant wars are too big a subject to treat as an appendage, and this reason (apart from the linguistic inadequacies of the author) applies also to the history of the eastern European peasantry.

One of the principal difficulties facing a historian who attempts to describe movements of growing complexity, varying character and apparently random distribution over a wide area, is to present a coherent picture to the reader. It is all too easy to be dominated by the complexities.

Therefore I have chosen a 'problem oriented' approach to the subject. This sort of approach can easily become dry and abstract, and so I have attempted to make a reasonable balance between description and analysis, between the abstract and the concrete. Since one of the main objects of this book is to place the English Rising of 1381 in its European context, the approach which I have chosen requires some justification. The events of 1381 were intensely dramatic and ran their course in a comparatively short space of time. They seem to invite a narrative treatment. And indeed a number of excellent narrative histories of the English rising have been written. Nevertheless, in order to make comparison between the English and the European experiences more systematic, I have avoided this type of treatment, apart from giving at the beginning of Part II a very brief outline chronology of the main events of the English rising.

In order to lead up to the discussion of the English rising in terms of the general problems posed by the events, I attempt to deal with the main problems of the later medieval European movements in a similar way. Obviously some description of events is necessary, but this is contained within an analysis which focuses on the following issues. What were the longer-term and immediate causes, economic, social and political? What was the social composition of the rebel forces? Where did their leaders come from? What allies did they seek? How did they organize themselves? What were their aims? What were their beliefs? These problems are common to all of the movements to be considered, European and English. They are also problems which cannot be understood other than on the basis of a general understanding of the nature of medieval peasant society.

Such in general are the justifications for placing the English rising of 1381 into its European context. There are other reasons of a more specific character. It has usually been thought sufficient by the historians of the English rising to relate the outburst to those discontents and aspirations of English peasants, artisans and townsmen which seemed to be mounting during the course of the fourteenth century and especially after mid-century. Naturally these matters must bulk large in any analysis which attempts to make sense of the events and the rebel demands in 1381. Yet there are not a few aspects of the English rising which cannot be adequately appreciated other than in connexion with the social and ideological tensions of Europe as a whole. For example, if it is conceded that such powers of mobilization and organization as the peasants showed in 1381 need to be understood in terms of a century of past struggle at village level in England, those earlier struggles need to be seen as part of a continental movement. It will be shown that the movement for the establishment of rural communes in Italy and France from the eleventh century onwards led to gains of greater political advantage than were ever made in England. We shall see that this greater political sophistication may have been to an important degree the consequence of a relatively advanced participation by peasants in production for the market. Nevertheless, the knowledge of this background alerts us to the operation of similar, though less developed, factors in English movements. The claim for the fixity of rents and services on the grounds of having once been privileged tenants of the crown, so important in twelfth-century England, is revealed as an archaic element in the situation when we realize that precisely this issue was at stake in tenth-century Italy. At the same time it is realized that the erosion of ancient privileges in changing conditions always produces explosive situations.

Another feature of the 1381 uprising, whose importance has often been minimized, is its ideological content. We shall deal with this in detail later in the book. Here it is sufficient to remark that the ideas enunciated by the leaders of the rising, especially those critical of the church's role, could not simply have sprung from the heads of Tyler, Ball and Straw. Yet we are always told that there was no heresy in England before Wycliffite Lollardy. Whether this is really so or not, it is clear that in the absence of evidence of truly radical thinking in England (as distinct from the traditional social criticisms by orthodox preachers) we must look wider to critical or heretical thinking in France, Italy, Germany and elsewhere, and to its subversive social and political implications.

It is also relevant to consider the problem of success and failure in 1381 with our thoughts on comparable issues in

Europe. Like the Jacquerie, the 1381 rising was over in a few weeks. In this it differed from other movements such as that in maritime Flanders, or the social banditry of the Massif Central, or the war of the Catalan *remensas*. We shall argue that the quick defeat of the English rebels did not necessarily mean that their cause was entirely lost. All the more reason for thinking this if we regard it as part of a European movement in which peasant communities were to be pitted against State, church and nobility for two or three centuries to come, as they had been for the two or three previous centuries.

PART I

General Problems of Medieval Peasant Societies

1 The Nature of Medieval Peasant Economy

We have reaffirmed that peasants were primary producers in ancient, medieval and modern civilizations, and that they fulfil this role still in many contemporary societies which have not been industrialized. It might therefore be supposed that the definition of this class must be so broad as to be of little use as a tool of historical or social analysis. Furthermore, it might be felt that types of food production, even in Europe, are so varied that they could hardly be carried on by people with sufficient common characteristics to be identified as members of the same class. Yet clear characteristics of such a class, distinguishing it on the one hand from tribal food gatherers and pastoral nomads, and on the other from capitalist or collective farmers and agricultural wage labourers, can be seen to have existed over a very long period of time, in many different countries and in states with widely differing political systems.

A peasant economy is one in which the large majority of the population consists of families who cultivate crops and rear animals on their individual holdings. The primary function of production in the family holding is to provide the subsistence needs of the family itself. But a society composed of nothing but peasants is, if not inconceivable, absent from the historical record. Peasant societies were not the most primitive. They emerged from older societies, organized tribally, which had already in late-prehistoric times evolved ruling clans, possessed slaves and had long contained industrial specialists, such as metal workers and potters, not to speak of specialist intermediaries with the unseen world of the gods, that is, priests. Peasants had to support aristocracies, priests, craftsmen, merchants and others who were not agricultural producers. Consequently peasant holdings had to produce more than the subsistence needs of the peasant

family, the surplus being transferred directly or through the
market to these other social groups.[1]

The peasants of medieval Europe had a varied historical
and geographical background. At first glance it might be
thought that the main dividing line would be between those
living in the territories of the former Roman Empire and
those living beyond the imperial frontiers. But the social
structure of the so-called 'barbarians' was by the fifth century
becoming not unlike that of the dying Empire, and the features
which distinguished late Roman from 'barbarian' society
were mostly to be found among the middle and upper classes
rather than among the peasants. More important was the
distinction between peasant communities living in different
natural conditions.[2] Food production in the Mediterranean
zone was different from that in northern France or England,
or that in mountainous areas contrasted with that of the
plains, or that on the Atlantic seaboard with that of Slavonic
eastern Europe. In the Mediterranean areas, in parts of
south-western France and in the Rhineland, early medieval
societies inherited and extended the vineyards of the Roman
world. In the Alps, the Apennines, the Pyrenees and the
Pennines there was inevitably a greater emphasis on pasture
than on arable land. In the hard continental climates of
eastern Germany, Poland and Russia rye was the predominant cereal crop, while in England cereal production
could be diversified with such spring-grown crops as barley,
oats and legumes.

In spite of these widely differing physical environments,
there was a basic similarity of social structure in the rural
communities of medieval Europe. This arose from the simple
fact that in a subsistence economy, and in the climatic conditions of most parts of Europe, the most easily and cheaply
produced foods were derived from cereals. Although some
peasants still used the hoe to till the soil, plough cultivation
was widely adopted and this required the use of draught

[1] See Daniel Thorner's report to the 1962 Economic History Conference
(Introduction, n. 1) 'Peasant economy as a category in economic history';
A. V. Chayanov, *The Theory of Peasant Economy*, 1925 (Russian edn),
1966 (English edn); Eric R. Wolff, *Peasants*, 1966.

[2] C. T. Smith, *An Historical Geography of Europe before 1800*, 1967, especially chaps. 4 and 5.

animals, especially oxen. Other domesticated animals such as pigs, goats, sheep and poultry provided milk, cheese and meat. Peasant agriculture therefore was mixed arable and livestock farming in which grazing land for the animals was as necessary as cultivable land for the sown crops. Inevitably the balance between arable and pasture could vary considerably, according to differences in natural conditions, demographic pressures, and even cultural traditions.

The size of the peasant holding was largely determined by the labour force employed on it. This was nothing less than a family labour force, and yet at this point we face considerable obscurities of the evidence. By the thirteenth century, or even earlier, the normal family in most parts of western Europe was not the extended family consisting of all the descendants of common great-grandparents—or beyond— with their wives and children living together.[3] Instead, we often find grandparents, the married eldest son and heir with his wife and children, together with the unmarried members of the second generation. If the grandfather were active he might run the holding; or he might have made way for the heir, but still live on the holding. On the death of the grandparents, the family would become a two-generation nuclear family until the pattern repeated itself with the maturity and marriage of the heir. There may have been some exceptions in the Balkans, or in mountainous parts of France, where the so-called *communautés taisibles*,[4] that is large joint families continuing to live on the ancestral holding, were found as late as the eighteenth century. But if such family groupings were exceptional in and after the thirteenth century it does not follow that this was the case in the early middle ages. In the badly documented era from the sixth to the tenth or eleventh century some peasant households might have been much bigger and more cohesive than they were in the central middle ages. A family group at Corbon in France in the ninth century occupying a seventy-five-acre

[3] This is the inescapable conclusion from the examination of the abundant manorial documentation of the thirteenth century.

[4] Bloch in *CEcH* I, pp. 280–81, writes about early patriarchal families; for the later *communauté taisible* see Bloch, pp 164ff., and a perceptive discussion by E. Le Roy Ladurie in *Les paysans du Languedoc*, 1966, pp 162–8.

holding provides an example: it consisted of two brothers and their wives, two sisters and fourteen children.[5] Perhaps even more important, some early peasant households may have contained one or two slaves.[6] This may be one of the reasons why the average size of the peasant holding in the ninth century was so much bigger than it was in the thirteenth, up to one hundred acres of arable as against twenty or thirty.

Another feature of peasant life common to most European countries was the association of peasant families in larger communities, hamlets or villages. There were areas of dispersed settlement where individual holdings were some distance from one another. These were common amid hilly country where the terrain was broken up and where patches of cultivable land were small and scattered. They might also be found in the newly colonized woodland and waste, where single pioneering families from old settled areas were starting up fresh cultivation, or even in the spaces between older-established, nucleated settlements. But life in a closely organized community was the norm, and the basis for this had existed for centuries.[7] As historians investigate the history of settlement in detail, it becomes clearer that, in spite of the newly created villages during the era of population expansion between the eleventh and thirteenth centuries, the basic settlement pattern was already established, not merely in Roman times, but in the pre-Roman iron age, even in the late bronze age. The evidence for this is, of course, archaeological. It implies that late prehistoric communities in Europe, however small, were settled rather than nomadic, and consequently were cultivating cereal crops as well as grazing herds and gathering the fruits of the extensive woodlands.

The existence of settled agriculture in prehistoric times has even been established for Germany, where the economy was

[5] G. Duby, *The Rural Economy and Country Life in the Medieval West*, p 383 (Document 20). But the Polyptyque of St Germain-des-Prés from which this evidence comes also suggests a predominance of nuclear families on the estate among the tenants. Independent households may have been more like that at Corbon.

[6] The Anglo-Saxon law codes assume that the free non-nobles known as *ceorls* possessed slaves.

[7] The distribution of dispersed and nucleated settlement is discussed in C. T. Smith, *loc. cit.*, and in Bloch, chaps. 1 and 2.

once supposed to have been that of pastoral nomadism as late as Caesar's days.[8] Detailed studies, based on archaeological and place-name evidence, of such regions in France as Burgundy, Auvergne and Picardy have shown that the expansion of population in the middle ages was from the existing established settled areas created by the Celtic populations of Roman and pre-Roman Gaul.[9] Even in England, where, according to an old school of thought, the Romanized Celts had been killed or had fled before the Anglo-Saxon invasions, more and more evidence of settlement continuity from Roman and even pre-Roman times is being discovered.[10] And, as one would expect, there is even stronger evidence for the continuity of settlement from prehistoric to medieval times in Italy, in spite of the political upheavals and economic fluctuations experienced during the Republic, the Empire and the barbarian invasions.

Of what significance are all these discoveries for our appreciation of the characteristics of the medieval peasantry? It is that the basic organisms of peasant communities—the family holding, the hamlet, the village—were deeply rooted, and had had many centuries to evolve institutions, common practices and a consciousness of their own interests. It is also that, however ancient were the ruling aristocracies, peasant communities were even older. And given the tendency of aristocracies to be eliminated and replaced by conquest, peasant communities had a more continuous existence.

The solidarity of peasant communities is a well-known fact of medieval social history, at any rate from the twelfth century onwards. It showed itself in many ways, most strikingly of course as a measure of defence against outsiders, invaders or oppressors. This, then, will be one of our themes, but we may at this point ask whether this solidarity existed *only* as a

---

[8] A. Dopsch, *Economic and Social Foundations of European Civilisation*, 1937, strongly criticizes theories of German primitiveness. The problem is more temperately discussed by E. A. Thompson in *The Early Germans*, 1965.

[9] e.g. A. Déléage, *La vie rurale en Bourgogne au moyen-âge*, 1941–2; G. Fournier, *Le peuplement rural en Basse Auvergne durant le haut moyen-âge*, 1962; R. Fossier, *La terre et les hommes en Picardie jusqu'à la fin du XIIIe siècle*, 1968.

[10] D. B. Harden, ed., *Dark Age Britain: Studies presented to E. T. Leeds*, 1956.

function of outside pressure. Some historians have insisted that this was so, suggesting that villages and other peasant communities only found their self-consciousness insofar as they were organized for service by their lords, for the payment of tithes by the church or for the payment of taxes by the king or prince and his officials. To some extent this view was formed in the course of ideological conflict between historical schools. Early twentieth-century historians such as Maitland, Sée and Dopsch[11] reacted against the interpretations of their predecessors who had mingled late-medieval evidence with the writings of Caesar and Tacitus to support the view that early Germanic society was free, egalitarian and based on the communal control, if not ownership, of the arable land. The evidence is scanty for the early history of village communities, whose existence is either reflected only in the records of the landowners of the state, or is archaeological and therefore limited as regards juridical or institutional aspects. The archaeological evidence certainly suggests that not only Celtic society in pre-imperial Europe was highly aristocratic but so was Germanic society at the time of the collapse of the western Empire.[12] But a peasantry dominated by aristocratic clans is not necessarily devoid of forms of practical cooperation among the peasants which would provide the basis for a common self-consciousness. Practical cooperation would vary in intensity according to the agricultural system, of which unhappily we know little before the relatively well-documented period beginning with the sporadic survival of estate records in the ninth century.

The agricultural systems of peasant communities in late medieval and early modern times have been studied and categorized in great detail.[13] In flat or gently undulating country with good soils there were, surrounding the big nucleated village, open fields in which the strips of land that made up individual family holdings were intermixed, and over which, once the grain was harvested, village gleaners could

[11] Works cited in Introduction, n. 2.
[12] Jan Filip, *Celtic Civilization and its Heritage*, 1960, pp 101–7; J. J. Hall, *Celts and Gallo-Romans*, 1970, p 181.
[13] To Bloch add the bibliographical information in R. Dauvergne's supplementary volume to *Les caractères originaux de l'histoire rurale française*, 1956; also E. Juillard *et al.*, eds, *Structures agraires et paysages ruraux*, 1957.

first work and subsequently village animals graze, with no distinction being observed between one man's land and the next. Beyond the arable fields lay the woodland and waste, available to the village community for gathering timber, nuts and fruits, chasing rabbits and hare, and giving extra grazing to their animals. Even if each family privately determined the use to which to put its garden or other enclosed plot within the village area, it had to observe a common routine of sowing and fallowing in the open field. It had to agree on the rules governing gleaning and concerning the number and type of animals grazing on the stubble, and concerning access to the commons. This was the practical basis of village common action, which did not, of course, exclude internal disagreements. These could arise from disputes over the possession or ownership of the arable or over the numbers of animals permitted on the commons, especially when common lands were reduced as the expansion of population caused an increase of the land under the plough.

There were many variations of open-field agriculture. Not all were characterized by strict rotational schemes, where year by year spring-sown crops followed those sown in winter and the spring-sown area was fallowed. Nor were peasants' holdings always distributed evenly over the main divisions of the arable, as in the case of the regular rotational schemes. Even so, communal regulation of grazing on the stubble and of access to the commons was necessary. It was less important in those agrarian systems where holdings, whether scattered over the village area or concentrated in the vicinity of the homestead, were enclosed and therefore not available for common grazing. But even enclosed villages usually had stretches of common wood and waste to which access had to be regulated. Furthermore, villagers also exercised jealous control of the acceptance of outsiders to their community. Even where the actual forum for these decisions was the court of the lord of the village, it seems normally to have been the villagers as much as, if not more than, the lord who operated the controls.

The distribution of different agricultural systems in different parts of Europe was determined partly by natural conditions and partly by the speed of historical evolution. The

Mediterranean countries, though (for the most part) potentially less fertile than much of northern and central Europe, were more densely settled and—very important—more urbanized. The cultivation of the soil near to cities had been geared since ancient times to olive and vine production, which does not involve communal practices (such as controlled grazing) and where individual enclosures predominated.[14] Further away from the cities there was grain cultivation and in the mountains a primarily pastoral economy. But over most of Europe the principal contrast of rural life was the enormous disparity between the huge uncultivated areas of waste, wood and mountainside, and the small cultivated patches around the human settlements. Where the wood and waste was most abundant, systems of cultivation tended to be more loosely organized than the formal system already mentioned. Although there might be continuously cultivated garden patches around the homes, cultivation within the great wastes was shifted from spot to spot as land was won from the scrub for a few years and then allowed to relapse. Varieties of this type of shifting cultivation are found widely scattered from the Pyrenees to the Celtic highlands of Britain, even in early modern times;[15] but it was in these more backward areas that it persisted. On the plains and in the valleys, as population grew, shifting cultivation had to give way to the various forms of rotation within a limited arable area, and up to the mid-fourteenth century the amount under the plough tended to expand at the expense of wood and waste. Compared with the early medieval period, therefore, there now had to be an increasingly careful supervision of grazing rights, and control by the village community was strengthened, while factors such as the development of market production strengthened certain elements among the peasantry.

The peasant community was not a community of equals. The stratification of peasant communities, moreover, was at least as old as the earliest records which we have of them.

[14] Articles by Philip Jones in *CEcH* I and *Second International Conference of Economic History*; P. Torelli, *Un comune cittadino in territorio ad economia agricola*, 1930; E. Sereni, *Storia del paesaggio agrario italiano*, 1961.

[15] C. Higounet, *Le comté de Comminges*, 1949, pp 448–9; H. L. Gray, *English Field Systems*, 1915, chap. 5; C. S. and C. S. Orwin, *The Open Fields*, 1957, p 38.

This suggests that such polarization of fortunes as there was between the village rich and the village poor could not simply have resulted from competition in production for the market, important though this factor was from time to time in generating social differentiation. In the ninth century in villages owned by wealthy monasteries in the region of Paris there were immense differences in the sizes of peasant holdings.[16] Some recently arrived tenants had minute holdings of less than an acre which they probably cultivated with the hoe or the spade; others had some 12 acres of arable; others twice that amount. These better-off tenants must have cultivated their land using a plough drawn by a team of oxen. In Picardy, on another church estate where the population was much sparser than in the Seine basin, most of the tenant holdings contained about 30 acres of arable land, but some had 50 acres or more, and others as few as 20 acres.[17] The situation was further complicated by the fact that in heavily populated areas not one but two or three peasant families had to live off a single holding. This applied not only to the Paris region but to northern and central Italy as well.[18]

The social stratification of the peasant communities, already marked in the ninth and tenth centuries, did not diminish in later centuries. It probably continued to reflect the same basic factors, which were the possession by some peasant families of one or even two plough teams, a full holding in the village arable and full grazing and usage rights in the commons, and by others, the smallholders, the possession of little more than the power of their own arms with which to work their inadequate plots, and to earn the rest of their keep by working on the lands of the rich. We can see this stratification right across the English counties in Domesday Book of 1086, where at least one-third of the peasant population were smallholders. By the end of the thirteenth century this proportion, in parts of south-eastern England, was over a half.[19]

[16] C. E. Perrin, 'Le manse', *Annales*, 1945.

[17] W. G. Coopland, *The Abbey of St Bertin*, 1914, p 19.

[18] P. Jones, *CEcH* I, p 354, and 'An Italian Estate 900–1200', *EcHR*, 1954, p 26.

[19] Domesday smallholders, R. V. Lennard, *Rural England 1086–1135*, 1959, chap. 11; thirteenth-century smallholders, E. A. Kosminsky, *Studies in the Agrarian History of England in the Thirteenth Century*, 1956, pp 216, 223, 296ff.

Similar figures are to be found in Picardy, Flanders and Namur. In Bavaria at the same period the majority of peasant families were living on holdings of under ten acres of arable. Italy, too, had its impoverished smallholders and well-to-do farmers living in the same village, the contrasts being the greater where population pressure was high, as in Tuscany.[20] It was not until after the series of mid-fourteenth-century plagues which struck most of western Europe and which reduced the population drastically that the high proportion of poor cottagers was reduced. The basic division continued, however, between the owners of plough teams and those who had to hire themselves out to live.

The internal stratification of peasant society, during the greater part of the medieval period, was strictly limited. The market for agricultural commodities was relatively too small to permit large-scale commercial enterprise. Even had the market possibilities been greater, the technical level of medieval agricultural production, transport and distribution all contributed to preventing the scale of production from growing beyond the limits of a holding which could be worked by a family with at the most one or two hired hands. To advance far in the world, a peasant family would not enlarge the scale of production, but would simply acquire additional landed property worked by other peasant tenants. The profits from the extra land would consist of the rents paid by the tenants. Various profitable seigneurial rights, additional to landed rents, might also be acquired. Such enlargement of property holdings on the basis of the profits of peasant production was unlikely, though not impossible. But it would mean that the successful peasant family would move into another social group, that of the landowning lords, and would assume a completely different life style. Such social advancement was not unknown, but it was very rare.[21] As we have

[20] Sixty per cent of peasants in the Paris region had a cottage and one acre or less of land; one-third of the holdings in a number of villages in the county of Namur were under 3 acres, another third between 3 and 10 acres; elsewhere in the Low Countries most peasants had not more than 6 to 8 acres. G. Fourquin, *Les campagnes de la région parisienne à la fin du moyen-âge*, 1964; R. Fossier, *op. cit.*; L. Génicot, *L'économie rurale namuroise au bas moyen-âge*, I, 1943, and articles in *Etudes Rurales*, 1962–3; P. Dollinger, *L'évolution des classes rurales en Bavière*, 1949; P. Jones, *CEcH* I, pp 424–5.

[21] A piquant example of a peasant who tried but failed to acquire

suggested, it was economically difficult. Furthermore, the social barriers against penetration into even the lowest ranks of the landowning aristocracy were very great—and intentionally so. The gentry and the nobility regarded peasants as different creatures from themselves, almost as a different race. It was not until early modern times, when the traditional structures of medieval society began to disintegrate, and when the market demand for agricultural products vastly increased, that an effective way forward, other than through absorption into the gentry, was open to the richer peasants. This was, of course, through the development of capitalist farming on the basis of the employment of wage labour and the application of a considerable capital investment to the agricultural enterprise. But the conditions for the effective development of capitalist agriculture were those which spelled the end of peasant society—however long-drawn-out the agony might be—and do not concern us here.

In the middle ages, then, poor smallholders and richer peasants were, in spite of the differences in their incomes, still part of the same social group, with a similar style of life, and differed from one to the other in the abundance rather than the quality of their possessions. There were others, too, who belonged to peasant communities, although fulfilling different functions from the occupants of agricultural holdings.

First, we must mention the craftsmen. Every rural society needed workers in wood, leather, metals and pottery, since objects made of these materials were essentials for agricultural production and for daily living. Most peasants were probably able to repair, and even to make, many necessary tools, but some specialists were essential. The most important was the smith working in iron;[22] he made or repaired the iron parts of ploughs and carts, shoed horses and oxen, made or sharpened sickles, scythes, axes and knives, and provided hooks and nails for buildings. The ironsmith's forge was a focus of village life, and, over and above this, the mysteries of his craft gave him an almost magical prestige. The carpenter, though less ubiquitous, was also a key man in an

lordship over his fellow peasants is in R. H. Hilton, ed., *The Stoneleigh Leger Book*, Dugdale Society, 1960, p xxxiv.
[22] L. Febvre, 'Une enquête; la forge de village', *Annales*, 1935.

agricultural community, whether he practised as a general
and relatively unspecialized worker in wood, or whether he
concentrated on certain lines of work, such as the making of
ploughs, or carts, or mill wheels and gears. The skills of carpenters were also indispensable in house-building, for (except
in areas where stone was easier to come by than timber) most
peasant houses were timber-framed.[23] Building workers in
general, however, whether carpenters, masons, plasterers,
thatchers or tilers, tended to be migratory rather than established members of a particular community.[24] Potters, too,
were for the most part much on the move, and their kilns
set up on the clay seams were not necessarily in or near places
of habitation. Occasionally, however, when good seams
occurred near villages, we find those communities becoming
specialized centres, such as Potters Marston in Leicestershire.[25]

One of the important characteristics of the medieval rural
craftsman, which brings him to the very centre of peasant
life, was the fact that he usually had some agricultural land
as well as his workshop. Smiths in the Sussex villages which
belonged to the estate of the Bishop of Chichester possessed
holdings of four acres attached to their smithies and had to
acquit their rent by providing shoes for the lord's horses,
mending the ironwork on the lord's ploughs and grinding
the lord's scythes and sheep-shears.[26] Other craftsmen whose
work was closely geared to agriculture would normally have
holdings which were often, though not inevitably, small.
Miners, smelters, charcoal-burners, glaziers and suchlike
specialists working in the forests, some of whom were rather
further removed from normal agricultural life, also possessed
agricultural land which helped them to live during off-
seasons.[27] Spinning was such a common by-occupation of

[23] L. F. Salzman, *Building in England down to 1540*, 1967; F. W. B.
Charles, *Medieval Cruck Building and Its Derivatives*, 1967.
[24] G. P. Jones, 'Building in stone in medieval western Europe', *CEcH*
II, 1952; P. Wolff and F. Mauro, 'L'âge de l'artisanat' (*Histoire générale
du travail* II), 1959.
[25] H. E. J. Le Patourel, 'Documentary evidence and the medieval
pottery industry', *Medieval Archaeology*, 1968.
[26] W. D. Peckham, ed., *Sussex Custumals*, Sussex Record Society, 1925,
e.g. pp 48–9, 82.
[27] J. R. Birrell, 'Peasant craftsmen in the medieval forest', *Agricultural*

peasant women that it was hardly regarded as a specialized craft. These spinsters, however, were often working on yarn brought to them from towns. In some rural areas, especially in the later middle ages, other textile processes such as weaving and fulling developed to the extent that the craftsmen's products reached an international market and the villages became as much 'industrial' as agricultural. This occurrence is found as far apart as East Anglia, the Low Countries, southern Germany and northern Italy.[28] Nevertheless, the village craftsmen tended to identify themselves with the peasant communities to which they belonged.

The craftsmen with smallholdings, the smallholders lacking industrial skills who worked on lords' and richer peasants' lands were, we have argued, integrally part of the peasant class. Another group in the rural communities which also formed part of the peasantry were the altogether landless wage labourers, distinguishable from the smallholders, though often merging into that group. They were always a minority. Had they been a majority, this very fact would have implied the end of the peasantry, since the essence of peasant society is that the basic form of productive labour within it is that of the peasant family living on its own holding. Nevertheless, the wage labourers were an important element. They did not constitute a completely homogeneous group, but one important section consisted of the permanently employed workers on the demesne or home farm of the lords. These included ploughmen, carters, oxherds, shepherds and dairymaids, living in. In the early middle ages these people were slaves, while later they were often chosen from among the younger sons and daughters of servile peasant families. Even when not working on the demesnes, some of the younger members of peasant families might hire themselves out, in addition to working on the family holding. Some of the wealthier peasant families, like the lords, had farm servants living in. Apparently, too, there was a group, not large, of wage workers who possessed no land of their own, but did not live in with their employer—whether lord or well-to-do

History Review, 1969; I. Blanchard, 'The miner and the agricultural community in late medieval England', *ibid.*, 1972.
[28] E. Carus-Wilson, 'The woollen industry', *CEcH* II, 1952.

peasant. Such persons lived in wretched shacks on the edge of the commons rather than in the centre of the village where the homesteads of full members of the community were grouped. While it is impossible to say *how* they lived for most of the year, their labour was essential at certain times, especially in summer and autumn, when the nucleus of the permanent servants on the demesne or richer peasant holdings did not suffice for the haymaking and the harvest.

Since it was the solid central core of landholding families which constituted the social centre of gravity of the peasant class, one would expect the interests of this group to determine the prevailing assumptions of the whole class, though one cannot expect to find a clearly articulated expression of these assumptions as the peasants were illiterate. To cease to be illiterate, a peasant's son had to be 'put to letters', which meant entering the clerical order and adopting a completely new set of ideas. However sympathetic a medieval cleric may have been to peasant aspirations, we cannot assume that he could accurately express them. It is therefore a question of piecing together the fundamentals of peasant ideology from fragmentary expressions of opinion, or from demands made from time to time, or from formulations of accepted custom.

For most of the period with which we are concerned a primary feature of the peasant outlook was a deeply rooted sense of family property rights in the peasant holding, and the various appurtenances which made it a viable economic unit—such as claims for common pasture and other customary usages. With this naturally went the conviction that the family's right in the holding was hereditary. While this included all members of the family, the sole right of the eldest son to the inheritance is frequently found, especially in the later middle ages, and it would seem that normal inheritance customs in earlier times envisaged that all the sons, if not all the daughters as well, had a right of succession.[29] This right could be granted by all members of the family remaining to work on the holding, apart from those who left the group through marriage (in western Europe, the women). It could also be fulfilled by the holding being divided among the heirs,

[29] L. Verriest, *Institutions médiévales*, 1946, pp 14–35, 133; G. Duby, *La société dans la région maconnaise aux XIe et XIIe siècles*, 1953, pp 48, 51.

as was often the case during periods of population expansion and when profit could be made by production for the market; this led to uneconomic fragmentation, so that the inheritance by a single heir (primogeniture or ultimogeniture) seemed desirable to keep the family holding intact. Inheritance by one heir was also encouraged by lords who found they could more easily collect rents and services from a single tenant.

Some historians have tended to minimize the deep sense of hereditary family right in the peasant holding, but the circumstances under which there may well have been a weakening of this feeling were temporary. E. A. Kosminsky emphasized the undoubted fact that in the thirteenth century when the market for land—stimulated by the market for agricultural produce—was very brisk, holdings tended to be broken up. One would find the messuage place of a holding, that is the site of the central homestead, being sold separately from the arable land, just as the crofts and curtilages normally attached to the messuage would be detached and sold off. And many were the cases of dealings in acres, half-acres, even quarter-acres, in the common fields. In such circumstances, continuous possession of a holding by the same family over many generations would be exceptional in practice, though it might still be an object of peasant aspiration.[30] Another factor leading to the impermanence of the family control of the holding has been studied by R. Faith, who has discovered that during the period of a collapse of population in the century after about 1350, inheritance customs tended to disintegrate as peasant families, stimulated by unusual land abundance, moved from village to village in search of better and cheaper land.[31] Nevertheless, both the market conditions and the extreme population pressure of the second half of the thirteenth century, and the sudden relaxation of population pressure after 1350, covered a relatively short period of time, and took place under peculiar circumstances. However strong were the external forces making for the dissolution of the family holding as the basic unit of rural society, it was always being re-created. Perhaps the best example of this

[30] E. A. Kosminsky, *op. cit.*, p 224.
[31] R. Faith, 'Peasant families and inheritance customs', *Agric. Hist. Rev.*, 1966.

process is the way in which whole peasant communities in France re-emerged on the depopulated sites of devastated villages in the immediate aftermath of the Hundred Years' War.[32]

A strong sense of family right also implied the consequential attitude that the family should be able to devote all of its labour to the cultivation and maintenance of the holding. This feeling lay behind the objections to the acquittal of rent obligations in the form of labour services on the lord's demesne, though other factors, such as the equation of forced labour under the coercion of the lord's bailiff with serfdom or slavery, were involved as well. Linked with the wish to keep the family labour on the family land was a belief that the product of that labour should remain in the possession of the labourers for their subsistence and to provide, by the sale of the surplus, for such extra needs as could be satisfied only by exchange.

We have already seen that to a greater or lesser extent, according to the nature of the agrarian system, peasant families were bound to cooperate with one another. This involved mutual arrangements for sharing the natural resources beyond the cultivated arable which was separately appropriated by each family. These arrangements were strengthened by an attitude to nature which reappears frequently in peasant movements of all sorts. It is clear that men felt that the woods containing the resources which were available to the huntsman and the gatherer, and the rivers with their fish, should not be the individual property of any person, lord or not. This attitude was of a piece with those other attitudes already described which arose from the feeling that the family should control its own labour resources and enjoy the whole product of that labour. In the same way, the game should go to any huntsman who could take it, and the fish to any fisherman who could catch it—a view no doubt strongly reinforced by the chronic shortage of protein in the peasant diet.

This brief consideration of fundamental peasant attitudes has necessarily involved references to those who by the nature of their social position stood in the way of the achievement of

---

[32] F. Braudel, ed., *Villages désertés et histoire économique*, 1965, pp 153–90.

the natural goals of the peasant communities. Medieval peasants were quite capable, in economic terms, of providing for themselves without the intervention of any ruling class. In this they differed from ancient slaves, and from modern wage workers who have to work on the means of production owned and possessed by others in order to gain their living. But medieval peasants, for the most part, though possessing their holdings, did not own them. Large-scale land ownership by the church and the lay aristocracy was a characteristic of the later Roman Empire on the eve of its dissolution in the West.[33] This was hardly at all modified as a result of the Germanic settlements, before and after the invasions. The German tribal aristocracies simply fitted into the existing estate structure. Outside the boundaries of the Empire, primarily in Germany, though little is known about property distribution, it would seem that the private ownership of land was well established though probably not as firmly rooted or on as large a scale as in imperial territory.

As we shall see, landownership was not the only basis for the power of the European aristocracy over the mass of the peasantry. Jurisdictional control backed by armed force was also necessary. Nevertheless, it was within the physical context of the estates, composed of a varying number of manors or lordships, that lords and peasants met. It was here that rents in money or in kind were paid to the lord's agents, and on the lord's home farm or demesne that rent in the form of unpaid labour service was performed. It was by virtue of birth or residence in the manor that the peasants had affixed to them the various disadvantages of their status. It was here that they were judged for the whole range of offences which they might commit in contravention of the lord's rights. Finally it was to the soil of the manor that those of them who were of servile status were bound from birth to death. The landed property of the aristocrats varied considerably from place to place and over time. Manorial structures were by no means homogeneous: in some, the demesne worked by servile labour might be all-important; on others there might be no demesne, so that the lord's income would be derived entirely from dues of

[33] A. H. M. Jones, *The Later Roman Empire*, chap. 22.

various sorts paid over by the tenants. Some estates comprised
dozens of manors, including scores of villages, forests and
stretches of wild country. Others consisted merely of one
manor which supported a lord of meagre status, perhaps not
even the only manor in the village. But, whatever the variations, the essential fact was that it was on the manor that the
surplus product or the surplus labour from the peasant holding, whether realized in cash or in kind, was transferred to the
ruler from the ruled.

While recognizing the great social significance of the landowning aristocracy, and the economic importance of their
large estates, it would be wrong to think that every acre of
cultivated land, forest or waste was included within the
boundaries of some royal or aristocratic estate. Obviously,
we have no comprehensive early surveys which would enable
us even to guess at the distribution of landed property
between various classes. England's Domesday Book in 1086
is the first document that makes this possible. Nevertheless, it
seems certain that there was, in the early middle ages, a
considerable amount of landed property, whose owners had
no landlord and were subject only to the jurisdiction of the
church and the State. These holdings were known as *allods*,
and although some could be of considerable size, many were
small-scale peasant properties. As the big landowners extended their estates by purchase, or more often perhaps
by pressure, they made considerable inroads into allodial
property which they would either take over entirely, or
probably more often absorb into their estate as dependent tenancies still occupied by the formerly independent
owner.

The absorption of allodial property was an important feature
of the development of feudalism and of serfdom. Unfortunately, the usual form in which allodial property entered
the historical record was at the moment when it was converted
into a dependent tenancy, that is, in the charter recording its
surrender to the landowner (usually an ecclesiastical corpora-
tion) who was acquiring it. From such and other evidence it
would seem that there was a good deal of allodial property
in Germany, as well as in various parts of France, namely, the
Bordeaux region, in the north-east and in Burgundy, to

mention only a few regions.[34] There was almost certainly a considerable amount of allodial property in Anglo-Saxon England on the eve of the Norman conquest, in spite of the rapid growth of the big estates in the tenth and eleventh centuries. But allodial property was wiped out by Norman law which recognized only dependent tenures, all held 'mediately', or immediately, from the king.

The gradual erosion of allodial property, especially small-scale peasant allods, implied an increase in the scope of aristocratic landownership and a reduction of the independence of peasant communities. There was, however, a trend in the other direction, operative particularly from the eleventh century onwards. This trend was the consequence of increasing population, increased production for the market, and firmer and more ambitious political organization by the aristocracy and the ruling kings and princes. It involved a response by landowners to the search by peasants for more land, which took the form of attempts to direct this land hunger towards the colonization of forest, scrubland and marsh. The best known aspect is the expansion of German colonization in central and eastern Europe. Lay and church magnates obtained grants of land, or took part in movements of conquest in sparsely settled, wooded areas. Then they put into the hands of special agents the recruitment of peasants from the Rhineland and the Low Countries to take up new holdings and, in effect, create new village settlements. It was not exclusively a German movement, though it was associated with aggressive moves by Germans into Slav territory, thus creating immense problems for the future. At the same time, Slavonic princes organized similar colonizing ventures. Furthermore, there were still many forest, marsh and waste areas in west Germany, in France, in England, and even in Italy, which were filled up by the overflow from crowded villages in old settled areas. The point about both movements is that peasant colonists tended to be offered land on favourable terms of tenure (mainly free status), on low fixed money

[34] For example, R. Boutruche, *Une société provinciale en lutte contre le régime féodal*, 1943, showed how important allodial property was in western France, subsequently reinforced by Duby for the Maconnais. See also Verriest, n. 29 above.

rents and with no labour services, together with a degree of local autonomy.[35] Thus, while some allod-holders were surrendering family land to the aristocracy, other peasants acquired—if not entirely free and independent tenures— holdings which were less closely controlled by landlords than those in the old settled villages.

The creation of free tenures for colonizers and the survival of allods, important though they were, did not deprive European society in the middle ages of its essentially aristocratic character, which remained its principal social aspect during the whole medieval period and beyond. Some attempt must therefore be made to describe the characteristics of the landowning aristocracy. These are difficult to define, except at length, because the aristocracy was never at any time or in any place an entirely homogeneous class, and because it changed considerably during our period of interest. It will be necessary to simplify, and to do this, if possible, without falsifying.[36]

An essential aspect of the medieval aristocracy, at all times, was that it was a hierarchy, not a class of equals. In the sixth century, as in the fifteenth, the members of the upper ranks of the aristocratic hierarchy, few in number, interrelated by family ties and owning immense stretches of landed property, dominated not only the rest of society but also the rest of the aristocracy. They usually also dominated the state, whether its apparatus was primitive or sophisticated, and in spite of frequent attempts by rulers (whose social origins are normally in this upper stratum) to find a political counterpoise to them. The rest of the landowning aristocracy, outside the ranks of these great magnates, included families of considerable wealth and influence, as well as lesser landowners whose resources were not all that much greater than some of the richer peasants. It should not be imagined, however, that the aristo-

[35] An example of a privileged village, founded in 1180, striking for its revealing name and the terms of tenure, was Forest in Hainaut. L. Verriest, *Le régime seigneurial dans le comté de Hainaut du XIe siècle à la révolution*, 1956, pp 48–51.
[36] There is a large bibliography on this subject. G. Duby, 'La noblesse dans la France médiévale', *Revue Historique*, 1961; L. Génicot, 'La noblesse dans la société médiévale', *Moyen Age*, 1965; K. Leyser, 'The German aristocracy from the 9th to the early 12th century', *P & P*, 1968.

cratic hierarchy was one of gentle gradation from great to not so great, and so down to the lesser gentry, for the cleavage between the mass of local notables and the few really powerful families was very sharp indeed. This was the case in the sixth century when the barbarian successor states were dominated by a few great families, a fusion of the old Roman senatorial aristocracy with the noble clans closely related to the ruling Merovingian and other Germanic tribal dynasties. It was the case with the *Reichsaristokratie* of the Carolingian Empire in the eighth and ninth centuries, a small group of families with property and influence in both Neustria and Austrasia contrasting sharply with the regional notables. It is seen in twelfth-century France with the contrast between the dukes, counts and greater châtelains on the one hand and the lords of single villages on the other, and in late medieval England with the dominance of the great dukes and earls, most of them related to the royal family, over the mass of county gentry.

The social cleavage between the magnates and the rest of the aristocracy was a disparity of wealth and power, but it did not mean a dissociation of the members of different aristocratic strata. For another permanent characteristic of this hierarchy of nobility was that members of it were bound together vertically by ties of loyalty, support and dependence sometimes described by the term 'vassalage'. Landownership was realized as power and wealth by virtue of the loyalty and toil which men contributed in return for land. The toil of the peasant, of course; the loyalty of the lesser lords who were rewarded for their armed support either by land or by movable wealth which ultimately came from land. The ties of lord and vassal go back far, being found among the early Germans before the creation of the barbarian successor states to Rome, in the form of the relationship between warrior leader and noble follower or companion, and found also in the Roman Empire as in other ancient civilizations in the relations between the great men and their clients. The 'classic' form of the relation between lord and vassal in feudal Europe was that which involved the vassal's doing homage and swearing an oath of fealty to the lord, in return for which he received a fief (*feodum*) from the lord, which was normally a landed estate. The vassal's subsequent obligations included military service in the lord's host, garrison duty in his castles, attendance at his court to give advice, or—in case of litigation—declaring custom in company with other vassals, and monetary aids when the lord was in need. The lord's obligations included support for the vassal's legitimate interests and aspirations, fosterage and military training of his sons, guardianship of his heirs and their land, if they were minors. The military aspect of this relationship (knight service for a fixed period from a specified amount of land) has been over-emphasized, and later forms of fealty and reward, such as grants of money incomes in return for military and political loyalty in the fourteenth and fifteenth centuries, could express the same sort of lord–vassal or lord–retainer relationship.[37]

If the economic and social distinction between the great landed magnates and the rest of the aristocracy was a persistent feature over most of western Europe in the middle ages, there were some important developments, in the course of which relationships between the various aristocratic strata changed considerably. One of the most interesting was the rise in social prestige of the knights.[38] Another was the spread of jurisdictional power over the peasants—downwards from the magnates to lesser members of the aristocracy. Another was the change in the composition of the aristocracy due to the growth in the power of the state, and consequently the importance of its patronage for those who served it.

Knighthood and aristocracy in the middle ages have been closely associated, and even regarded as inseparable. This popular impression, however, is justified only from about the middle of the twelfth century onwards. While it is true that adult males among the medieval nobility, early and late, regarded themselves not merely as rulers but as warriors also, it should be remembered that, in the early middle ages, *all* free men were regarded as having an obligation of military service. Working peasants—such as were free—were not normally suitable for military activity, partly because of the

[37] B. D. Lyon, *From Fief to Indenture*, 1957.
[38] For knights see Duby, *op. cit.* in n. 36; and on 'The diffusion of cultural patterns in feudal society', *P & P*, 1968; Sally Harvey, 'The knight and the knight's fee in England', *P & P*, 1970.

nature of their work, and partly on account of their slender resources. Fighting, and particularly fighting on horseback, had become a professional occupation by the middle years of the eighth century, although in times of crisis the peasant militia might be used—as Aelfred of Wessex used it to resist the Danish invasions at the end of the ninth century. The nobility, of course, continued to regard fighting, not so much as a profession but as a natural part of their life.

The knights of the post-Carolingian period, those who were called *milites* in the Latin writings of the ninth to eleventh centuries, were busy enough in the many petty wars of those centuries of political collapse and piecemeal reconstruction. They were needed by the lords, but they were not regarded, as yet, as the lords' social equals. At best they were small landowners, at worst landless mercenaries, living in their lord's retinue, at his court or in his camp when he went to war. Then, at slightly different periods in various countries, their social, if not their professional military role, began to change. In parts of France by the eleventh century, they were beginning to be more highly valued than in earlier years, while in England and the Empire their rise cannot be dated before the middle of the twelfth century.

Various converging factors led to this social up-grading. Economically, some, if not all, of the landowners from whose ranks the knights were drawn were improving their position. This is an observed phenomenon in England in the century after the compilation of Domesday Book (1086) when the landed property of the average knight doubled or tripled in size. The church which had once tended to regard knights as men doing the devil's work, that is, of spoliation of the lands of the church and of the church's tenants, began consciously to recruit them for the work of God, from the end of the tenth century onwards. God's work was the attempt to promote the truce of God and the peace of God for periods of time during which lords and their knights would swear to respect the lands of the church and of the poor.[39] This did not solve the problem of knightly banditry, so the church's tactic was extended to canalize the warlike activities of the

[39] H. E. J. Cowdray, 'The peace and the truce of God in the 11th century', *P & P*, 1970.

knights against the external enemy, the Moslems of Spain
and Syria and the pagan Slavs of eastern Europe. Knighthood
began to acquire the odour of sanctity, and finally it became
not only holy, but fashionable, when courtly literature, culminating with the Arthurian romances of Chrétien de Troyes
in the last quarter of the twelfth century, chose as its hero the
ideal knight who was not only endowed with military prowess
but mixed as an equal with kings, dukes and counts. By 1200,
kings, dukes and counts were proud to undergo the initiation
ceremony by which the apprentice knight (the esquire)
entered the order of knighthood fully fledged.

Another aspect of the social advancement of the middling
and lesser landowners was the acquisition by them of jurisdictional control over the lower classes of rural society.[40]
Even when the Frankish monarchy had seemed most powerful, in Charlemagne's day, the counts, in theory the appointed
officials of the king-emperor, had in practice been chosen from
among the leading landowners of the district over whose
court they presided. When the central power disintegrated,
earlier in France than in Germany, the power of the counts
remained and they continued to exercise public jurisdiction
on their own account. Similarly, ecclesiastical landowners
to whom the king-emperors had granted rights of immunity
from royal judicial and fiscal officials, provided they exercised these powers as royal representatives, were continuing
to do so as private individuals within their immunities. In
both cases these judicial rights had to be devolved still further,
to castellans and to lay ecclesiastical advocates—often one and
the same—who began to rule their subjects within their
lordships as the counts had once done within their counties
as imperial officials. A lord's right of command (the *ban*),
provided he could enforce it physically, became generally
recognized even at the level of the knight. And since, by the
twelfth and thirteenth centuries, customary rents from land
were becoming devalued, lords at all levels had every in-
centive to improve their cash incomes by exploiting the rights

[40] G. T. Beech gives good local examples in *A Rural Society in Medieval
France: the Gâtine of Poitou in the 11th and 12th Centuries*, 1964. See also
J. Richard, 'Châteaux, châtelains et vassaux en Bourgogne aux XIe et
XIIe siècles', *Cahiers de civilisation médiévale*, 1960.

of the ban in the form of judicial fines, tolls, fees payable by peasants for enforced use of the lord's mill, oven or winepress. This was an evolution most characteristic of France and the western Empire. In England a strong monarchy prevented the development of exempt areas of private jurisdiction at a high level (such as judging 'pleas of blood', that is, those which demanded the death penalty). But there was, nevertheless, a parallel evolution of seigneurial jurisdictional power in the strengthening of the lords' control over peasants in the manorial courts.[41] In Italy the peculiar characteristic of development, from the eleventh century, was the move of the lesser nobility of the countryside (especially in Lombardy) into the towns, where they became identified with mercantile interests without losing interest in their country property. The higher nobility retained an even greater interest in its rural base, to the extent of dominating urban politics—except where the urban bourgeoisie proved too strong, as in Florence.

A third important element in aristocratic evolution, giving a further twist to the outlook and internal composition of the landed ruling class, from the twelfth century onwards, was the emergence of a ministerial function as the channel of entry into the landed aristocracy. This was an aspect of the increase in the power of the state, or to be more precise in the power of rulers such as the kings of France or England, or the territorial princes of Germany, or the dukes and counts who were theoretically the French king's vassals. Rulers trusted men of the lesser nobility[42] more than they trusted the great nobles as agents who would carry out their will without hesitation. These royal servants fulfilled these requirements, having no interest in the separatist politics of the higher nobility, though as agents of the ruler they had ample opportunities, in the roles of judges, tax collectors and farmers

[41] In England the thirteenth century was a great period for the acquisition by lords of minor jurisdictional powers (S. Painter, *Studies in the History of the English Feudal Barony*, 1943) but the late thirteenth century *Quo Warranto* pleas show that, compared with men of baronial status, only a few knights successfully acquired these powers.

[42] In Germany many members of the ministerial class were of servile origin, but even they, because of their function, eventually entered the class of nobles. R. W. Southern's 'The Place of Henry I in English History', *Proceedings of the British Academy*, 1962, shows the process operating in England.

of crown lands, to acquire more land of their own, and so ascend the social hierarchy.

All these aspects of changing patterns among the European nobility—the increased prestige of knighthood, the spread of private jurisdiction, the use of ministerial office as a means of social promotion—seem to imply an evolution in a single direction, that is, the relative enhancement of the influence of the lesser nobility. This undoubtedly happened. In many ways the lesser nobility was more efficient than the great magnates in managing its estates, in producing for the market and in controlling administration and politics at a local level. The political influence of this group increased from the thirteenth century onwards, but, although its relative position improved, it did not cause the disintegration of the territorial or political position of the higher nobility. That class generally seems numerically to have contracted, but in so doing the individual families concentrated more land and more lordships in their own hands. The contrast between the immense wealth of individual magnate families and that of the rest of the aristocracy remained.

An important element in the medieval landowning aristocracy remains to be considered: in any European country during the middle ages a large proportion of landed property was owned by the church. In the late Empire the church was already endowed with enormous landed estates. In the west these estates were mainly in the possession of the bishops, especially the Bishop of Rome, who had estates within the boundaries of twenty-five *civitates* in Italy, as well as other properties in Sicily, Africa and Greece.[43] Monasteries as yet did not enjoy a comparable popularity with those in the east, but foundations and endowments multiplied from the sixth century onwards. The landed possessions of bishops, cathedral churches and monasteries were so enormous that only the temple endowments in ancient Egypt were at all comparable in previous epochs. It is true that the church estates did not grow gradually over the course of time. Periods of lavish endowment were sometimes followed by periods of indifference or even hostility. Cathedral churches and monasteries seem to have been immensely rich by the

[43] A. H. M. Jones, *op. cit.*, p 781.

end of the Merovingian period in the early eighth century, partly because of the enthusiasm of the early Frankish nobility for their new religion and its promise of salvation—which gifts might have been thought to buy—and partly because of lands which wealthy Roman aristocrats brought to the church as they entered its hierarchy as bishops and abbots. Following on this there was a period of spoliation of church lands, to provide fiefs for warriors, during the course of the eighth century. There was a pattern of alternate endowment and deprivation which tended to repeat itself. In tenth-century England, for example, after the defeat of the Danes, monastic bishops such as the keen, businesslike Aethelwold of Winchester got many landowners to give land to the church, which their sons at the turn of the century were attempting (in the face of anathema) to regain.[44] Aristocratic families in all countries tended to regard land given to the church as still in part theirs, and treated the church lands as a reservoir on which they could draw in order to reward followers or extend their own estates.[45]

Other factors besides fluctuating aristocratic generosity operated. As the church, especially the monasteries, acquired more land, its way of life tended to be more assimilated to that of the lay landowners, and become further removed from the aims of the most influential of the western rules, that of Benedict of Monte Cassino (*c.* 525), summed up in the three words 'Poverty, Chastity and Obedience'. Successive reform movements, such as that of Cluny in the tenth century and Cîteaux at the end of the eleventh, aimed at re-creating a monastic order which would eschew the preoccupations of the laity with wealth and power. But the greater the spiritual prestige of the new orders, the more the wealthy laity sought to win salvation after death by endowing these worthy causes, and the more involved in the world the monks once again became. By the thirteenth century, monasteries not only were recipients of lay benefactions, but actively entered the land and commodity markets, buying land to enlarge or round off

---

[44] D. J. V. Fisher, 'The anti-monastic reaction in the 10th century', *Cambridge Historical Journal*, 1952.
[45] See the old but useful article, 'The proprietary church' by U. Stutz in G. Barraclough, ed., *Medieval Germany*, II, 1948.

their estates, accumulating cash by selling wool, grain or wine, and using their cash reserves to lend money to the chronically embarrassed nobility, usually on the security of land. By this time, since the monastic orders' spiritual prestige was considerably diminished, they were replaced by the friars, especially the Franciscans, as the objects of lay esteem.[46]

The position of the religious in aristocratic society was nevertheless unshakeable. Together with the bishops, cathedral chapters, collegiate churches and other church landowners, the monks owned substantial proportions of the landed estates of most European countries, in some cases nearly half the total. The higher clergy, whether monastic or secular, tended to be recruited from noble families and to remain closely associated with aristocratic lay society. Bishops and abbots, besides being landowners, had extensive powers of private jurisdiction which were exercised through lay agents, and they were to be found alongside dukes, counts and barons in the courts of kings as prominent political advisers.

It must have been of great importance for the European peasants in their relations with the landowning ruling class that a substantial proportion of that class consisted of church-men. For these persons supposedly embodied the principles of the religion in which all believed, controlled the administration of the sacraments without which men could not achieve salvation, and (being the overwhelming majority of the literate members of society) were the formulators of the received ideas about social and political obligations. The peasants themselves could not read, but there was no lack of people to instruct them, from their own parish priest, through the wandering preachers of all kinds, to the learned men who were appointed to preach in the public places in important centres in which country people as well as the townsmen congregated. All these preachers exhorted their audiences to be diligent in all the necessary practices of their religion

[46] European monasticism has an immense literature. The English reader will find in D. Knowles's four volumes a history of English monasticism with a good deal of information about the European background: *The Monastic Order in England*, 1949; *The Religious Orders in England*, I–III, 1948–59. But English readers should also use the great work of the learned (if a little prejudiced) G. G. Coulton, *Five Centuries of Religion*, 1923–50.

and to observe the moral code promulgated by the church. In addition, they explained in simple terms what was the nature of the society in which men lived. Before the twelfth century the law and the power of authority were frequently interpreted as being God's punishment on mankind for its sins. With the stabilization of the feudal states and the relative peace which enabled local and long-distance commerce to develop, Europe was ripe to accept the ideas of such ancient philosophers as Aristotle who presented political institutions as the natural consequence of man's social being—'man is a political animal'. But whether the catastrophic or the natural interpretation of the origin of human institutions was accepted, the ultimate cause was God and consequently the established order at any given time was divinely sanctioned. Medieval thinkers and preachers did not attempt to disguise the fact that human society was stratified. They adapted and repeated a very ancient classification of the different social orders, which as it happened more or less fitted the realities of early medieval society—the well-known division of men into those who pray, those who fight and those who work.[47]

One of the earliest medieval expressions of this concept is found in the translation by King Aelfred of Wessex of Boethius's *Consolations of Philosophy* (*c*. 890). Though it became fairly common, the theory had some limitations as a description of reality. It made no allowance for the merchants and other members of urban populations, although these could hardly be ignored, especially from the eleventh century onwards. Later medieval analyses did accommodate these growing complexities, but a central feature of the theory is found in all later formulations: the social order as depicted was unchangeable, for it was divinely ordained. This belief is clearly expressed (*c*. 1025) by one of the earliest of medieval churchmen, Adalbero, Bishop of Laon, to enunciate the theory in some detail. Naturally, he puts the clergy first, and exalts their role, but gives no indication of social distinction within their ranks. He then comes to the laity whom he divides as between the nobles and the serfs:

[47] A useful summary of these ideas with bibliography is in J. Le Goff, 'Note sur société tripartite', *L'Europe du IXe au XIe siècle*, Polish Academy of Sciences, 1968.

In the first rank of the nobles are the king [of France] and the [Holy Roman] Emperor; the rest of the nobles have the privilege of not having to submit to the constraint of any outside power, on condition that they abstain from crimes which royal justice represses. They are warriors, protectors of churches, defenders of the people great as well as small, and in doing this they assure their own security. The other class is that of the serfs, a miserable race which owns nothing that it does not get by its own labour. Who can calculate the toil by which the serfs are absorbed? Their long journeys, their hard labours? Money, clothing and food – all are provided by the serfs. Not one free man could live without them. . . .These three groups exist together, they cannot be put apart. The services rendered by one are the condition for those of the others. Each in turn is charged with the support of the whole. This triple assemblage is as one, and so the law may triumph and the world enjoy peace.

It will be noticed that Adalbero in this description assumes that all who are not noble are serfs. This presents us with a problem and, at this point, an opportunity to discuss one of the most burning issues of medieval peasant movements, the search for freedom. The problem is that record sources do not confirm Adalbero's simple division of the laity, and yet one cannot dismiss his remarks as being, therefore, of 'no interest'. In different parts of Europe, as has already been indicated, considerable numbers of peasant allod-holders could not by any stretch of the imagination be termed 'serfs'. Furthermore, many tenants on lords' estates, while not being independent proprietors like the allod-holders, were still free in the eyes of the public law. On the other side, we have seen, too, that the by no means inconsiderable class of knights was not yet admitted into the ranks of the nobility. Yet Adalbero equates warrior with noble.

His classification, though inaccurate, is by no means eccentric. In the first place, there seems to have been in parts of the Low Countries, not far from the Laonnais in north-eastern France, and precisely at this time, an equation of free with noble status.[48] Small allod-holders were being subordinated to private jurisdictions, and the juridical status of knights was as yet dubious. Contemporary opinion—of those who drew up charters for the ruling group—seems to have been that anyone subject to private jurisdiction or unable freely to dis-

[48] L. Génicot, *L'économie rurale namuroise au bas moyen-âge : la noblesse*, 1960.

pose of his own land could not claim to be free; and that those who were free in this sense were noble. This concept of the nobility of the free men, the *liberi homines*, was perhaps a fleeting phase reflecting the disappearance of an ancient social stratum. It also poses the whole problem of the shifting meaning of important terms of social classification at a moment of rapid social change.

To return to Adalbero, his other assumption (that all the basic agricultural producers were servile) while not by any means reflecting reality, may reflect his impression of the social tendency of the time, which was towards the enserfment of the peasantry. Adalbero's depiction of the tripartite division of medieval society is, then, no less than a statement of the social theory common throughout the middle ages, but the way in which he expressed that theory was peculiar to him and his time. King Aelfred, for instance, makes no reference to the servility of the workers, whom he thinks essential for a kingdom, alongside the prayers and fighters. Nor does Abbo of Fleury, writing on the same subject about a quarter of a century earlier than Adalbero. For him, the cultivators are simply those who 'sweat over the tilling of the soil and in various rural crafts'.

Who and what, then, were the medieval serfs?[49] As a general definition, we may say briefly that they were those peasants who were not only dependents of other men, in the sense that they were tenants of land which they did not own, but those who were restricted by law in various ways as to freedom of movement, freedom to buy and sell land and goods, freedom to dispose of their own labour, freedom to marry and found a family, and freedom to leave property to their heirs. Some historians have attempted to narrow the definition so that only those without free status in public law should count as serfs. There is some justification for this view in terms of legal definitions current in some parts of western Europe, such as France, but, since there were so many peasants not officially designated 'serfs' who were as dependent and controlled as the many who were, this narrow

---

[49] M. Bloch, *Mélanges Historiques*, I, 1963, contains his articles on medieval serfdom. There are important criticisms of some of Bloch's views by L. Verriest in *Institutions Médiévales*, 1946.

legal definition is unhelpful. In any case, the terminology used by medieval people was itself ambiguous. In late thirteenth-century England 'villeins' were regarded as unfree, whereas at the end of the eleventh century they were regarded as free. Some peasants in midland England who, in 1280, were called 'villeins' in some documents were called 'serfs' in others.

By the beginning of the twelfth century the servile peasantry of western Europe was fairly homogeneous as to conditions, obligations and rights. But this vast body of serfs was of diverse origins, and these were not entirely obliterated by the simplifying pressures of the post-Carolingian processes of historical evolution. One source of medieval serfdom undoubtedly came from the slavery of the ancient world and the Dark Ages. Another was the process of commendation by which free peasants deliberately entered into dependence for the sake of security. Another was the imperceptible attribution to the free tenants of big estates of the conditions of tenure of the unfree so that they became indistinguishable. Another was the use by lords with rights of private jurisdiction of these forms of control to subject once free men to their power.

Slaves in the antique sense, that is human beings who were the chattels of others, had not disappeared. Sources of slavery existed for many centuries. Many were war captives. The word 'slave' is in fact a medieval word derived from 'Slav', for the early medieval slave-trade was largely supplied by German invaders of Slav-occupied territory on their eastern frontiers. Others were sold into slavery, often by their relatives. Some were made slaves as a punishment for infringements of the law. But although the church did not condemn slavery as such, it forbade Christians to enslave other Christians. As this prohibition took effect, the sources of slavery diminished. Slavs became Christians. The Moslem enemy was not so easily defeated as to provide an abundant supply of slaves. But, in any case, there were not many opportunities for the profitable use of slaves *en masse*. Even as early as the first century, some Roman estate owners had been providing their slaves with holdings of land, from which they and their families were able to find a living. This practice continued in succeeding centuries. In consequence, slaves provided with holdings, or *servi casati*, owing labour-service obligations on the lord's home farm, were probably more numerous than domestic slaves without land. Even so, they were a minority of the total peasant population. On the big estate of the monastery of St Germain-des-Prés, near Paris, at the beginning of the ninth century, only 120 out of the 2,800 tenant families were slaves.[50] Their position as regards size of holdings, rents and services was hardly distinguishable from that of the tenants who were not slaves, those known as the *coloni*. This was partly because the tenant population had mingled. Slave holdings were subject to heavier obligations than free holdings, but by the date of the document which tells us about this estate, free families were occupying slave holdings and vice versa.

Domestic slavery lingered on in some areas suprisingly long. In England at the time of Domesday Book, some nine per cent of the recorded population were slaves, and these were not *servi casati* but oxherds and ploughmen on the demesne farms.[51] However, they were soon to be given small-holdings which, in addition to providing a natural wage, enabled them to house a family. A similar situation was found on estates in Bavaria.[52] Here, too, the *servi cotidiani* were obliged to do heavy work on the demesne, but were given small-holdings which they cultivated for themselves. These English and German slaves were Christians, and are not to be confused with the Moslem and pagan domestic slaves found in Italian urban households during the whole of the middle ages.[53]

Many of the slaves to whom we have referred, even when provided with holdings and so assimilated into peasant life, were not given their freedom; but another group of slaves was manumitted, and constitutes a further contributory stream to medieval serfdom. Manumission made a slave into a serf rather than a free man. These freedmen, who have various designations, such as *collibertus*, *aldio*, *litus* and *laet*,

[50] P. Petot, 'L'évolution numérique de la classe servile en France du IXe au XIVe siècle', *Le Servage*, Société Jean Bodin, 1959.

[51] M. M. Postan, *The Famulus: The Estate Labourer in the XIIth and XIIIth Centuries*, Economic History Review Supplement, n.d., 2, pp. 6ff.

[52] P. Dollinger, *op. cit.*, pp 265ff.

[53] C. Verlinden, *L'esclavage dans l'Europe médiéval*, I, 1955; I. Origo, 'The domestic enemy: eastern slaves in Tuscany' *Speculum*, 1955.

cannot be estimated numerically, but it is clear from references in charters and law codes that they were an important
element in the rural population. On manumission they normally remained in the patronage, protection, or *mund*, of
their former owner. Consequently, they owed him fealty and
various obligations or recognition payments, such as: a perpetual annual tax, a portion of the inheritance at death, a
marriage tax, and, if already a tenant, a continuation of
customary rent obligations. It must be assumed that, in the
Dark Ages as later, manumission was paid for by the freedman. In this way a meritorious act was doubly rewarded, and
the freedman still remained very much at the lord's disposal.

All the same, freedmen and slaves who acquired landed
holdings may be regarded as being in a better position than
domestic slaves had been. Serfdom was a 'step up' from
slavery. There were those, however, who stepped down. These
were free men who commended themselves to the powerful
in return for protection, and surrendered their independence
and even their land, if they had any, to become dependent
tenants. Salvian, a monk from Marseilles, in the fifth century
succinctly described an early phase in the depression of persons of free status. Those suffering from pillage or from the
demands of the tax-gatherer 'had to seek shelter in the landed
estates of the rich whose tenants they became. . . all these
people who settled on the big estates underwent a strange
transformation as if they had drunk of Circe's cup, for the
rich began to treat as their own property these strangers. . .
real free men were transformed into slaves.'[54] In later centuries,
when monasteries were among the wealthiest landowners,
many poor men who commended themselves to the great, did
so to the religious bodies, those surrendering their persons
and their land being persuaded that they were coming under
the protection of the patron saint of the monastic house concerned. Such men were particularly common in France,
Germany and Italy. Their obligations were not necessarily
heavy, sometimes consisting merely of an annual payment in
recognition of dependence—in money or sometimes in wax
for the church's candles.

It may well be that the greatest numerical contribution to

[54] Quoted by J. Le Goff, *La civilisation de l'occident médiéval*, 1964, p 51.

the medieval servile class came from none of these categories. It will be remembered how few slaves there were on the St Germain estates as compared with the *coloni*. This last class bears the name that was given to the mass of the peasantry in the Roman Empire who, by the fifth and sixth centuries, though still legally free, were the close dependents of the estate on which they had their holdings. To quote the Code of Justinian: 'Although *coloni* seem to be free in condition, they are nevertheless counted as serfs [or slaves, *servi*] of the land where they were born.'[55] In spite of the lapse of time, it seems probable that the tenants referred to as *coloni* in the estate documents of the ninth and tenth centuries, of which there are many other examples besides those of St Germain-des-Prés, are not dissimilar in character from those referred to in Justinian's code. Nor was the Parisian basin the only area where it was becoming difficult to distinguish the *coloni* from the *servi*. The same situation is found in other parts of France, in the Low Countries and in western Germany. There were some striking variants. The conditions of early urbanization in central Italy and the Lombard plain pro-duced an evolution of peasant tenures which anticipated some later developments further north. England, on the other hand, acted later than France over the enserfment of the *villani*, the counterparts of the continental *coloni*.

The assimilation of tenants into a common pattern of de-pendence did not mean the elimination of local and national variations. One would not expect this to happen in Europe, whose communications were poor and where regional cul-tural identities were so strongly marked. What is surprising is not that such peculiarities should exist, but that there should be so many common features of dependence over a wide area. These common features are found, by the thir-teenth century, in England, and in most parts of France, western Germany, Spain and in many parts of Italy. In most cases the peasants who were subject to these widespread forms of obligation were regarded as unfree in terms of public law, and were excluded either entirely, or as regards their relations with their lords, from the courts of public law.

[55] M. Bloch, *Mélanges Historiques*, I, p 434 and n. 5; A. H. M. Jones, 'The Roman colonate', *P & P*, 1958.

This was the situation with regard to English villein or customary tenants by the end of the twelfth century. There were, however, some peasants whose forms of obligation seem indistinguishable from those of the English villein or the French serf, but who were not strictly speaking unfree in the eyes of the law. Nevertheless, they were so closely controlled by the customary law of the estate or lordship in which they lived that their freedom was unreal. Indeed, the fact that they had obligations which were shared by persons of indubitably servile status put them at considerable risk as regards the remnants of a free condition which they enjoyed.[56]

The main purpose of these various rules of dependence was to ensure that peasant families were kept on the holdings, and to guarantee for the lord the payment of rent and the performance of services. The three most common obligations, often used as a test of servility, were: a restriction on marriage outside the lordship, other than with the lord's permission; the right of the lord to take part or the whole of the tenant's chattels at death, thus emphasizing that an unfree person had no rights of ownership in property; and the payment of an annual tax, the *capitagium* or *chevage*, as a recognition of the tenant's perpetual subordination to the lord. Other obligations included: the payment of tallage, or *taille*, an arbitrary—frequently annual—levy; unpaid labour service on the lord's demesne land; the obligation to grind corn at the lord's mill (and at his alone), for a payment of part of the grain, together with a similar obligation with regard to the lord's oven and winepress. The sons of dependent tenants were not allowed to be put to school without permission, in case they should find a means of escaping from the lordship by taking holy orders.

The medieval peasantry was strongly tainted with these aspects of serfdom, the inevitable by-product of the power of lords on their estates and of their fear that, in conditions where there was an abundance of unoccupied land, their tenants, without whose labour their landed property was valueless, might escape them. But peasants were not universally servile, even when the pressure of lords was most intense. Furthermore, just as there were conditions which made for successful

[56] R. H. Hilton 'Freedom and villeinage in England', *P & P*, 1965.

enserfment so there were other conditions which favoured peasant freedom. Thus, when the English law had, by the end of the thirteenth century, accepted the doctrine that traditional customary villein tenure was servile, there was still a very substantial number of free tenants—impossible to measure exactly but possibly between one-third and one-half of the whole peasant population. Documentary evidence makes impossible even such rough calculations for countries other than England, but it is unlikely that free tenures, in most western European countries, were substantially fewer than in England; in some areas, such as northern and eastern Germany and central and northern Italy, they may have been present in even greater numbers. The significance of free tenure and status must not, of course, be mistaken. Marc Bloch asked: 'In social life is there any more elusive notion than the free will of a small man?'[57] Many free men were landless labourers or smallholders whose poverty made them as dependent on the lords and the well-to-do peasants as unfavourable legal conditions would have done. Nevertheless, given equal amounts of land, the free man was likely to be less heavily burdened than the unfree, and to be obliged to convert less of his surplus product into rent, judicial payments and seigneurial dues of one sort and another. But what provided the best protection for peasants, rich and poor, free and unfree, was the strength of common action in the local communities. This, as we shall see, was the starting point of the peasant movements—non-violent and violent—and enabled peasants to make and to hold gains in a world otherwise dominated by the armoured men on horseback.

What this implies, of course, is that when we speak of peasant movements we normally refer to common action in pursuit of aims which are specific to peasants as a class. On the one hand, we are not concerned simply with attempts at individual self-improvement, as in the case of families which accumulated land, livestock, and other movable goods and cash. Neither are we concerned, on the other hand, with peasant participation in social, political or religious movements whose aims were determined by other social classes. As we shall see, especially when we come to consider the peasant

[57] M. Bloch in *CEcH* I, p 268.

movements of the later middle ages, problems arise here, since in the first place few (if any) social movements reflect exclusively the interests of one class, and because a class may pursue aims which are common to other classes, as well as those aims which are exclusive to itself. However, no concerted action by peasants in association with other social groups can count as 'peasant movements', unless aimed at some shift in the position of the peasants as a class. Hence, although popular crusades with mass peasant participation should be studied for their contribution to peasant self-consciousness, they should not necessarily be classified as peasant movements. Some movements were obviously direct confrontations between lords and peasants over the proportion of the surplus product of peasant labour which should go in rents, services or taxes. Others appear as movements of social, religious or political protest, and it is these which present the greatest problems of analysis, because it is in such movements that the mingling of class interests is most likely to be found.

2 Early Movements and their Problems

The evidence for peasant movements during the middle ages is, surprisingly, still only at the collection stage. Such as it is, it is very unevenly distributed chronologically. The unevenness of the distribution does not necessarily reflect an unevenness in the incidence of these movements, of course. The survival of evidence is quite accidental for most aspects of medieval life, depending not only on the preservation of records from careless storage or deliberate destruction in the middle ages but in the subsequent centuries as well. No one would expect the survival of much evidence from the early medieval centuries, when in the first place people did not keep many written records, and when the few that were kept risked destruction in the course of havoc wreaked by invasion and internecine war. However greatly the spoliation of monasteries in England and Gaul by the Viking invaders may have been exaggerated, for instance, it *did* exist and was directed against the most important record-keeping institutions then in existence.

These difficulties over sources must be constantly borne in mind as we interpret the evidence we have about peasant movements. Further work will undoubtedly disprove some of our hypotheses, but hypotheses are none the less necessary as a means of ordering scattered fragments of information. Scanty though the evidence may seem to be, it does not entirely defy interpretation and, for the historian, among the most important attempts at interpretation which must be made are those which illuminate change over time.

In examining the evidence for peasant movements with these considerations in mind, elements of change and elements of permanence contrast with each other. Let us consider the elements of permanence. If we accept, with Bloch, that peasant revolts are inseparable from the seigneurial regime, and if we also accept that, whatever changes may have occurred, the basic features of the lord–peasant relationship within the rural seigneury persisted during the whole of the medieval period, then we would expect similar forms of conflict to recur during the whole period. Nevertheless, great changes also occurred, though they did not lead to the destruction of the seigneurial regime or of the peasant communities without which it could not have existed. The European population grew and then declined. Society became more urbanized, and commerce penetrated to the most backward regions. Social, political and religious orthodoxies were challenged, and heresies became the basis for mass movements. Governmental machines were elaborated, and tax-gatherers reached further and further down the social scale to raise cash. Public jurisdictions took over from private jurisdictions, and industries penetrated the countryside.

These developments could not but affect the character of peasant movements. Nevertheless, throughout the medieval period, early and late, we find examples of elementary types of protest recurring with little change. Such protests became proportionally less and less frequent and were, so to speak, swamped by other movements which responded to new elements in the social situation. On the whole, the more elemental movements with the simplest demands were at village level, while the movements affected by the new developments in medieval society tended to be regional in scope, and generally to have wide horizons which were extended not merely beyond the village but beyond purely social aspirations. In later movements, however, many of the simplest elements of the earlier movements were still present; more complex elements were added rather than substituted.

The earliest elements in peasant protest were the direct consequence of the peasants' attempts to devote as much as possible of the family's labour to the cultivation of the holding, and to keep for the disposal of the family as much as possible of the product of that labour. Already in 800, a capitulary of Charlemagne briefly summarizes an order aimed at preventing the members of the household on royal estates from withdrawing from due services—an enigmatic order which might refer to permanent farm servants rather than dependent tenants.[1] No ambiguity, however, arises in the Edict of Pitres (864), which condemns *coloni* on royal and ecclesiastical estates for evading carrying services, threshing and other manual works.[2] Fortunately, these laconic indications in the administrative or quasi-legislative decrees of the Frankish kings can be illustrated from other documents concerning particular places and events. No historian can say with certainty whether such examples are typical or exceptional, but the evident unease of Frankish kings, as expressed in the capitularies, suggests that the situation of conflict was widely recognized.

How this situation fits in with economic and social development during the Carolingian, and even pre-Carolingian periods, is difficult to say. Many historians see the epoch as one in which the slave labour force on the great estates was diminishing in quantity. Possibly it was also showing signs of unmanageability. At any rate, as early as 643, an edict of the Lombard king, Rothari, refers to conspiracies of slaves (or serfs) under the leadership of freemen, leading to attacks on landlords' property.[3] If slaves were diminishing absolutely in numbers, and at the same time were being given holdings which converted them into servile tenants rather than full-time unfree farm or domestic workers, it is conceivable that landlords would press for an alternative supply of labour in the shape of unpaid services rendered by free, as well as unfree, tenants. Some such services may have been customary for centuries, but a decline in the availability of slave labour, and an increase in landlords' needs for produce (related perhaps to the increase in organized military activity) could well lead to demands beyond the norm. Such, perhaps, were those extra boon services demanded—as if as a favour, in fact under pressure—by agents of the royal demesne as well as by private landowners which were disapprovingly referred to in the second capitulary of Mantua at the end of the eighth century.[4]

It is in this context that we may see, in the first place, a

---

[1] *MGH Capitularia*, I, ed. A. Boretius, 1883, p 81, sec. 31.
[2] *ibid.*, II, eds A. Boretius and V. Krause, 1897, p 323, sec. 29.
[3] *MGH Leges*, IV, ed. G. H. Pertz, 1868, pp 67–8.
[4] *MGH Cap.*, I, p 197, sec. 6.

minor conflict at the beginning of the ninth century on the manor of Antoigné, belonging to the Abbey of Cormery near Tours, a daughter house of the greater and more ancient Abbey of St Martin. There is no question here of slaves but of *coloni*, and the complaint was of services and rents being demanded beyond what their ancestors had customarily rendered. The only evidence for this complaint is a written act by Pepin I, King of Aquitaine, one of the sons of the Emperor Louis the Pious and grandson of Charlemagne. The act says that the *coloni* appeared before the king, but that their claim on the basis of custom was defeated on the production by the abbot's agent of a 'description' of customary obligations drawn up by the abbot's predecessor, twenty-seven years earlier, in 801. As is well known, this was a period when the drawing up of such documents, sometimes called 'polyptiches', was commonplace. They were regarded not merely as private estate documents to remind landowners of what their tenants owed them, but as legally binding in public law. Their very existence is an indication of a situation of conflict which landlords presumably wished to stabilize at the point which was most favourable to themselves—namely, a peak period in the demand for labour services.[5]

Another conflict, rather better documented, occurred at the end of the ninth century in northern Italy. The interesting fact about this affair is that in spite of the considerable differences between the agrarian arrangements of the Loire valley and of the region of Lake Como there should be so many similarities in the fundamental issues involved. The Italian conflict was between the abbot of the monastery of St Ambrose, Milan, and some forty servile tenants from four villages on the shores of the lake which were part of the manor, or *villa*, of Limonta.[6] We have four documents, spaced over some seventy years, the first being dated 882 and the last 957. They are printed in rather old collections of charters and have not been critically edited, but the outlines of the story are clear. Sometime between 840 and 855, the

[5] L. Levillain, ed., *Receuil des actes de Pépin I et de Pépin II, rois d'Aquitaine*, 1926, p 44, No. 12.

[6] G. Porro Lambertenghi, ed., *Codex Diplomaticus Langobardiae*, Monumenta Historiae Patriae XIII, 1873.

Frankish Emperor Lothar gave Limonta and its villages to the Abbey of St Ambrose, the manor having presumably been part of the imperial estate, and possibly even at one time part of the estates of the Lombard kings whom Charlemagne had deposed in 774. In 882 the case is first recorded as being discussed at Limonta before a formidable array of judges and notaries. The abbey's tenants admitted that they were not imperial freemen or *aldiones*, though in making the disclaimer the implication is that this had at one stage been put forward.[7] They did, however, state that when the manor was part of the imperial estate they were only obliged to pay a rent and a due, named the *aldiaricia*. In particular they denied any obligation to do the service of gathering and pressing olives in the abbey's groves and transporting the oil once made (to Limonta, or even to Milan). Their claim was defeated on the oath of *arimanni*—local nobles of Lombard descent—who said that the services concerned had been rendered in Lothar's time.

The remaining documents show continuous pressure against the tenants by the monastic lord. In July 905, the tenants admit their servility, the obligation to do the disputed services, the payment of an annual rent of seventy shillings-worth of silver pennies, one hundred pounds of iron, thirty hens and three hundred eggs, and the service of transporting the abbot and his retinue by boat on the lake. These obligations were committed to writing as evidence. Another document whose date is doubtful but may have been contemporaneous, shows the Archbishop of Milan attempting to moderate the abbot's demands. The archbishop's arbitration indicates that further demands had been made under the threat of distraint of the tenants' animals. These included services of making lime and threshing grain, together with an humiliating insistence on cutting the hair short as a mark of servility. These dues were apparently abandoned by the abbey, but additional dues were now added to those already listed, that

[7] In discussing this affair, C. Violante puts it in the general context of the improvement in the conditions of persons of genuinely servile status (*servi prebendarii*) rather than treating it as an attempt of free peasants to avoid serfdom. (*La società Milanese nell' eta precomunale*, 1953, pp 85–6.) He does not say that the Limonta tenants were *servi prebendarii* and as Bloch has shown, the elevation of slaves and the depression of free men both contributed to the formation of the medieval servile class.

is, twelve measures of wheat and thirty pounds of cheese. Finally, an abbey document of 957 shows the maintenance of all previous demands with, in addition, the payment at the time of the vintage of a portion of the wine made by the tenants. This obligation appears for the first time, with the concession by the abbot and his monks that it should be considered as a boon granted by the tenants rather than an exaction because of their condition.

Apart from the straightforward evidence given by these documents about the conflict over the level of rents and in particular labour services, there is an additional element of interest. The increase in services is alleged by the tenants to have taken place at a change in lordship. This is to be expected. Respect for custom was strong throughout the middle ages, so that lords often accepted a customary level of rent when conditions might have justified (or at any rate made easy) an increase. At a transfer of ownership, custom, if not breached, could be weakened. Such transfers of ownership in the early middle ages, when kings and nobles were endowing monasteries in the hope of heavenly reward, frequently led to pressure for increased services by the new ecclesiastical owners. Kings and nobles tended to be peripatetic and preoccupied by wars and politics. Monks, permanent residents on their estates, paid closer attention to profit and the tenants suffered the consequence. The times of the previous owner, especially if he had the magical prestige of king or emperor, became a golden age of freedom and prosperity. Such situations repeated themselves. In twelfth- and thirteenth-century England, for example, the kings granted away considerable proportions of the crown lands, sometimes to churchmen and sometimes to laymen who deserved rewards or who could provide ready cash, and so we find situations which were very similar to those at Limonta.

The nearest analogies are those cases in the thirteenth century which concern manors in England of the so-called ancient demesne of the crown.[8] They had a special status in law, in that if a manor had been part of the crown estate

---

[8] For ancient demesne, see P. Vinogradoff, *Villainage in England*; R. S. Hoyt, *The Royal Demesne in English Constitutional History*, 1950; R. H. Hilton ed., *The Stoneleigh Leger Book*, Dugdale Society, 1960.

in 1066 and thus written down in Domesday Book (1086), and had subsequently been granted by a king to a vassal or a monastery, the tenants had a remedy in law if the new lord tried to increase the rents and services beyond those obtaining when the manor was in the hands of the crown. There is no evidence for the application of these special rules before the thirteenth century. The most plausible explanation for this protection is that the king was still entitled to tax the alienated demesne, and did not want the tenants' capacity to pay diminished by increased exactions from the new lord. However this may be, tenants quickly appreciated the possible remedy, since the thirteenth century generally was an age of rising prices, rising rents and demands for increased labour services. Just as the Limonta tenants may have claimed to be imperial *aldionnies*, so the English tenants claimed to be villein sokemen of ancient demesne and tried to produce evidence of a favourable situation before the change of lordship.

It will be remembered that the main change in condition that the peasants of Limonta complained about was the addition of labour services to obligations which were alleged previously to have been in the form of rent, probably in money but possibly partly in kind. Parallel cases in thirteenth-century England illustrate this hostility to a form of obligation which deprived the peasant of the free disposal of his and his family's labours. A Staffordshire case also emphasizes the grievance arising from a change in lordship from the king to a private person.[9] Wednesbury had once been part of the crown estate and had been given as part of an exchange to a family from among the local gentry named Heronville. A long-drawn-out dispute (1272–1307) between the tenants and the lord showed the very considerable gap that existed between the two parties as to what should be paid for an individual peasant holding of about twenty-five acres of arable land with normal appurtenances. The tenants appealed to custom as far back as the reign of Henry II (1154–89), saying that they had been accustomed to pay a fixed rent of five

---

[9] *Staffordshire Historical Collections*, VI, i, 1885, p 60; *ibid.*, IX, 1888, pp 7, 17. For discussion see R. H. Hilton, 'Lord and peasant in Staffordshire in the middle ages', *North Staffordshire Journal of Field Studies*, X, 1970.

shillings a year, with tallage proportionate to the size of the holding when the king tallaged the rest of his demesne, and attendance at the lord's court twice a year, unless a dispute about land was being tried in which case they were prepared to attend at three-weekly intervals. The lord, on the other hand, claimed that these peasants must, when appropriate: undertake the duties of reeve or tithing man; plough and harrow the lord's arable in spring; make the lord's hay and reap his corn; pay a toll to him when they brewed ale, and pay for the pasture of pigs, he also claimed 'merchet' on the marriage of a daughter and 'leyrwite' if she was found to be unchaste, and an exceptionally heavy 'heriot', or death duty; and, finally, arbitrary tallage and three-weekly attendance at court. Apart from the different character of the obligations, those claimed by the tenants were characteristic of common-law free tenure, while those claimed by the lord were characteristic of servile tenure or villeinage.

If the disposal of the peasant family labour resources was an issue found, at different periods during the middle ages, at the heart of many conflicts, another feature of the peasant economy, and indeed of the peasant mentality, led from time to time to clashes between lords of the soil and working peasant families. Peasant families appropriated arable land— or rented it from landlords—from which they satisfied their own subsistence needs and those of society's non-producers in castle, manor house or town. As far back as we have written records in Europe, this appropriation was individual, which does not mean that it had been so always. But beyond the arable, especially before the population pressures of the thirteenth and early fourteenth centuries, lay stretches of rough grazing, of woodland, mountains, streams and rivers. Even though these might be included in such-and-such a great man's title deeds, they were thought of by peasants as a sort of public domain where all men might pasture beasts, hunt animals and fish—not, of course, for sport but as the necessary adjunct to cereal production on the arable part of the holdings.

What seems to have been one of the fiercest and most bloody of early conflicts between lords and peasants took place over this issue. The evidence for the peasants' war in Normandy in

996, at the beginning of Duke Richard II's reign, is not at all abundant. The first reference to it is in the chronicle of William of Jumièges,[10] who was writing nearly a century later, but who is usually regarded as sober and reliable. According to him, a sudden and widespread movement of discontent throughout the duchy among the peasants (*rustici*) was organized on the basis of the rejection of established rights and the assertion by the peasants that henceforth they would live as they pleased. The phrases are vague, and the only particular manifestation of peasant self-assertion mentioned by the chronicler is that they intended to exploit at their will the woods and the rivers, presumably for pasture, timber and fish. Subsequently the peasants' movement was highly organized, and involved the election of delegates from regional gatherings to a general assembly. These moves were then suppressed by the duke's uncle, Raoul, Count of Evreux, with the utmost ferocity. There is a good deal more detail about it in the poet Wace's rhyming chronicle, *Roman de Rou*, written in the mid twelfth century.[11] Our difficulty is that although this work may be based on authentic tradition, Wace may, for poetic effect, have added to the tenth-century grievances some others that he knew existed in his own day. For instance, he slightly augments, in paraphrasing, William of Jumièges' words about the peasants invading the woods and the fisheries: 'And so we can go to the woods, cut down trees and take what we want, take fish from the fish ponds and game from the forests—we'll have our will in the woods, the waters and the meadows.' Wace also puts strong words in the mouths of the peasants about a variety of jurisdictional oppressions which have a twelfth-century ring to them, as well as attributing to the peasants words which, though referring specifically to the organization of resistance to the lords, have an egalitarian implication, 'we are men like them'.

Quarrels over access to common rights continue well beyond the early middle ages. Conflict between lord and peasant on this issue was often latent rather than open. When

[10] A. Duchesne, ed., *Gesta Normannorum Ducum*, 1619, Bk V, chap. 2.

[11] Hugh Andresen, ed., 1879; partly reprinted as an appendix in L. Delisle, *Etudes sur la condition de la classe agricole en Normandie au moyen-âge*, 1851.

wood and waste were abundant in relation to the demands of
the rural population there was little strife, although records
of agreements between lords and peasant may have come at
the end of an unrecorded period of conflict. Rural communities in northern Italy seem to have been sufficiently well
organized by the twelfth century to get concessions of hunting
rights from their lords—as in 1179, when the Bishop of
Bergamo allowed his peasants of Ardesio and Valle to hunt
freely as individuals or in groups, provided they handed over
to the lord the bears they might capture.[12] This contrasts
strongly with the stringent laws in England, where kings
reserved big game, such as deer, in the forest for themselves,
and allowed the lords to monopolize the hunting of smaller
game, like hare and rabbit, in their own lordships. In view of
the shortage of meat in the peasants' diet at this period, it
might well be thought that the popularity of outlaw ballads
(such as those later tales of Robin Hood) reflected not only
an interest in the adventures of these rebellious men living
outside settled society in the wilds, but also some Utopian
vision of free communities of hunters eating their fill of a
forbidden food. As we shall see, demands for access to natural
resources figure in later revolts, such as that in England in
1381 and in the German peasant war of 1525.

Concepts about free communities, free status and tenure
and the equality of man have been encountered already in
considering reasons for conflict between lord and peasant,
such as rival claims to men's labour or to rights over woods,
waters or pastures. In our consideration of these simple and
basic issues in the earliest period of peasant demands, the
desire for freedom emerges clearly, and like other simple requirements which we have considered, is continuously present
in peasant movements, sometimes more and sometimes less
strongly. As early as the year 800, a Frankish capitulary,
probably directed to the bailiffs of the royal estates, refers to
fugitives from the manors who fraudulently claimed to be
free.[13] We have already seen that in the Limonta case there
were hints that at some stage in the conflict (probably before

[12] P. S. Leicht, *Operai artigiani agricoltori in Italia dal secolo VI al XVI*,
1946, p 97.
[13] *MGH Cap.*, I, p 92, sec. 4.

the date of the first documented hearing of the case) the serfs may have claimed the rights of imperial freemen. The problem was put explicitly in a constitution of the German Emperor Otto III (996–1002), and probably alludes to the situation in Italy. The constitution refers to the way in which, on both lay and ecclesiastical estates, persons of servile status were slipping into freedom because of the difficulty experienced by their lords in regularly exercising control over them. Already, of course, in northern Italy the development of commerce and urbanization was leading to a brisker movement of population than was to be found in rural areas characterized mainly by a subsistence economy. Some estates, especially those of the church, were tending to disintegrate. Peasants were finding opportunities for self-improvement by production for the market and were pressing for, and obtaining, improved terms of tenure. It was in these circumstances that the emperor attempted, as a minimum measure, to lay down that serfs should at least acknowledge their dependence by an annual recognition payment to the lord of one penny a year. The emperor firmly stated that ecclesiastical serfs in particular should never be free, even by their lord's manumission.[14] But he seemed to be fighting against a powerful tide. The history of peasant freedom is marked by many advances and retreats during the course of the middle ages, and in spite of the emperor's stern words this would seem to be a phase when lords were on the defensive.

The acquisition by serfs or slaves of the advantages of freedom was by no means a straightforward motive of peasant movements, in the sense in which we are interested, that is, organized attempts by peasants to change their economic, social or political status. Freedom, then as now, was a concept that acquired significance only in specific contexts, in terms of concrete gains or losses. As already indicated, it occurs as an accompaniment, sometimes no doubt a necessary accompaniment, to striving for other goods or against other evils. The context in which freedom for servile peasants was gained was not always one of struggle, or at any rate of social struggle. It has, for instance, long been one of the commonplaces of the history of Europe during the central period of the middle ages

[14] *MGH Constitutiones*, I, ed. L. Weiland, 1893, pp 47ff.

that freedom was an almost automatic by-product of seigneur-
ially directed colonization of new land during a period of
population growth. Freedom, it has been put at its crudest,
was an aspect of the development of real estate. This aspect of
the growth of agrarian free tenures and peasant free status is,
of course, one which cannot be ignored. What matters for us
is the way in which human beings realized these ends not only
in the context of available land and population pressure, but
in the context, too, of their historical relationship with other
social forces: lords, kings, popes and townsmen.

The offer of free status and tenure to tempt colonizing
peasants to clear virgin land is a well-known theme of medieval social history. The offer was made, of course, by landowners seeking to realize the value of their property. But it
should not be imagined that freedom proffered from above
was the only freedom to be had in the twelfth and thirteenth
centuries. It was also demanded, and fought for, and won
or bought, by peasant communities consciously organizing
themselves to this end, and their organizational effort is as
significant for the history of the medieval peasants as such later
and better known episodes as the French Jacquerie or the
English rising of 1381. However, the significance is different.
The struggle for village charters in the earlier period was part
of the peasant reaction to the economic expansion of the period
when the development of production for the market made the
wealthy peasants who benefited from it socially and politically ambitious, and their demands and achievements were
a straightforward reflection of the potentialities of the situation,
primarily economic. By the fourteenth century the atmosphere
changed, not merely because of a changed economic conjuncture, but because of the introduction of an ideological element
which, instead of being confined to the clerical intelligentsia,
was now spreading to other social groups.

For the moment, however, we are concerned with the
movement for village enfranchisement, strongest as a peasant
movement in twelfth- and thirteenth-century France—
though presaged in Italy as early as the last quarter of the
eleventh century. What were the main features of the movement? Each case, of course, has its own individual character-

istics, resulting from the special circumstances in which it developed, but on the whole these were movements which aimed to obtain from the lord of the village a charter granting, at least, exemption from various exactions and fixed rather than arbitrary obligations, and at most an element of autonomy in the running of the village community. Freedom of personal status was frequently demanded, or understood on the basis of the privileges enjoyed by the beneficiaries of the charter. The similarities with a contemporaneous urban communal movement are evident, and indeed the two are at points difficult to distinguish, since some of the supposedly urban communes were as much agricultural communities as trading or industrial ones.

The development of the rural commune in Italy well illustrates that, though in general the movement is to be understood ultimately as the response of the peasant population to the development of the market, the way in which each situation developed was determined by a complex of other historical conditions. No more need be said about the precocity of northern Italy as far as the development of trade is concerned, than that even in the eighth century there existed a Po valley trade in which agricultural produce was exchanged, first for Venetian salt, then for goods of eastern provenance that came through Byzantium. This commercial development was uneven, in that areas remote from trade routes and towns remained primitive. To begin with, it was the estate owners who were the chief beneficiaries of market production, though the development of peasant money rent in the tenth century indicated clearly that villagers as well as lords eventually became involved.

This increasing peasant activity suggested to some historians that the communal movement was a direct reflection of the weakening of the feudal estate owner in the face of increasing prosperity among servile peasants. Others stressed rather the action of free peasants, with their ancient claims to joint control of the common lands of the village and their military role in the defence of fortified villages (*castelli*) in times of danger from outside invaders and internal anarchy.[15]

[15] R. Caggese in *Classi e comune rurali nel medioevo italiano*, 1907–9 and G. Salvemini in 'Un comune rurale nel secolo XIII: Tintinanno', *Studi*

These explanations are not mutually exclusive. In Italy, as elsewhere, early medieval rural society was by no means homogeneous; peasant servility was widespread especially on big estates; but allod-holders and free leaseholders, the *livellarii*, constituted a significant proportion of the working population of the countryside. In the Veronese and perhaps in other areas, the bigger villages were occupied mainly by freemen, whereas the smaller ones, especially those owned by church landowners, were manorialized.

There seems little doubt that control of village commons provided an important early focus for the development of self-administrations in northern Italy. References to village commons are found in documentary sources from the ninth century. The parishes, or *pieve*, of the Verona district were not simply ecclesiastical but also economic and military communities, exercising their exclusive claims over the common woods, pastures and meadows, and over such resources as lime, stone and timber. Their existence can be traced back to the tenth century, but it is worth noting that by the twelfth century, membership must have been confined to well-to-do peasants. At Caprino, for instance, would-be associates (*consorti*) of the community had to pay an entrance fee (*entratica*), and contribute a substantial meal consisting of a hundred loaves, two shoulders of pork, two cheeses and a measure of wine.[16] In the Padovano at the beginning of the twelfth century, two villages in the Sacco district, Rosaria and Melaria, formed a commune which disposed of its own common lands and elected its own officials (*marici*)—to be joined a decade later by the other villages of the district. The active elements in this communal organization seem to have been free small proprietors who were not subjects of the Bishop of Padua's manor of Sacco, a property acquired at the end of the ninth century from the king. These free commoners or neighbours (*vicini*) are found in control of the common lands and pastures some forty or fifty years before the formation of the commune. They were even able to exclude the

Storici, 1901, argue the first case. The counter-case is to be found, *int. al.*, in A. Checchini, 'Comune rurali Padovani', *Nuovo Archivio Veneto*, 1909.
    [16] L. Simeoni, 'Il comune rurale nel territorio Veronese', *ibid.*, 1921.

bishop and the tenants of his domain from enjoyment of these common rights.[17]

But control by a village community of common lands and rights was only a beginning, though perhaps an educative beginning, to forms of autonomy. The management of the commons was after all so closely linked with the rhythm of a peasant economy that it could well suit a lord's convenience that communities under his jurisdiction should look after the allocation of their own pasture rights. More authentic signs of peasant gains in a society whose lords and peasants were often in conflict are to be found in charters embodying concessions made by lords, whether under pressure or for cash. Such was a charter given to the tenants of Nonantola by the abbot of that place in 1050, which promised not to imprison them without legal process and not to beat, slay or despoil them, or destroy their houses without legal process. The Abbot of Monte Cassino, in a charter in 1079, granted his tenants of Castello Suio a reduction of the labour element in their rent, abolished death duties, commuted military service into a money payment and guaranteed to respect both hereditary and acquired property.[18] Since in the Veronese in the tenth century (before communes were thought of) lords of villages could not sell the commons, took fixed rather than arbitrary rents and allowed villages free alienation of land and the right to elect their own officials, it might be thought that the tenants on the big monastic estates had been singularly unfortunate. It is possible, however, that the modest autonomy rights in the Veronese were thought a necessary concession in return for peasant garrison duty in the *castelli*.

It was in the late eleventh and twelfth centuries that the village communal movement got under way in the Veronese. In 1091 the *vicini* of Biondo on the cathedral estate induced the chapter to agree that they should elect their own *gastaldo* (reeve) and exercise a limited right of the jurisdiction previously in the hands of the lord. Attempts by lords to increase dues payable—as happened particularly in the twelfth century—led to resistance, to the stabilization of existing obligations and to refusals to provide hospitality to the lords and their retinues. Proposed transfers of jurisdictions over villages

[17] A. Checchini, *op. cit.*   [18] P. S. Leicht, *op. cit.*, pp 87ff.

from traditional (especially ecclesiastical) lords to new feudatories were objected to, and for substantial payments, sometimes more than 1,000 lire, the villages obtained the jurisdictions for themselves, not infrequently together with the lords' rights in common lands and fisheries.

Rights were often obtained by stages, the reward of repeated pressure at opportune moments. By 1195 we find that the village of S. Giorgio delle Pertiche, a *castello* in the diocese of Padua, was held of its overlord for a fixed and perpetual rent in grain and for garrison duty, and that it governed itself and was entitled to two-thirds of the profits of jurisdiction in the village court. By 1223 there was a commune of S. Giorgio in association with a group of other villages. Each village had its own elected headman, the *rector*, while in S. Giorgio itself, as headquarters of the joint commune, were a *podesta*, together with tax-collectors, supervisors of the commons and other shared officials.

More obvious and quickly-achieved gains were made by the tenants of the Abbot of St Ambrose, Milan, at Origgio.[19] In 1228 the abbot had in his hands the rights of 'low justice' ('high justice' being held by the city commune), the nomination of the *podesta*, and the exercise of various seigneurial rights, such as control of sales of wine and timber, control of land alienations and so on. The village community administered the commons, chose many of its own officials (subject to the abbot's approval), had the right to half the profits of jurisdiction and paid the dues owed by the tenants in a single lump sum. By 1244 it would seem a group of nominees of the village community (two of whom were priests) had taken over all the abbot's jurisdictional rights (his *honor et districtus*) and were paying a consolidated farm rent for his other dues. This situation emerges from the terms of a lease which was terminable—and did terminate. For a time the abbot even lost the right to confirm the popularly elected officials, though this was recovered by the 1270s.

In 1228 the majority of Origgio's inhabitants were *rustici*, and distinguished from those inhabitants who were not subject to the abbot's full jurisdictional powers, such as the local

[19] R. Romano, 'L'abate di Sant' Ambrogio e il comune di Origgio', *Rivista Storica Italiana*, 1957.

feudal nobles, the free tenants, the clergy and the notaries. But many of the *rustici* were in fact *livellarii*, leaseholders holding by fixed rents in kind. The market in land, the market in agricultural products and the mobility of the village population made the division between *nobiles*, *liberi* and *rustici* less significant. What mattered now was the division between the village rich and others, between those with holdings of 30 to 50 acres and those with less than 10 acres.

In the urbanized environment of north Italy, many villages whose economy rested on agricultural production became large enough to have the appearance of towns. This was partly because they became the market centres of the region and because, to serve the agricultural population of the village itself and of its market area, a number of industrial craftsmen and small retailers joined the village community. Bassano on the Brenta river was a community of vine cultivators which together with the adjacent settlement of Margnano was referred to as a commune as early as 1175. Its mainly servile population were originally subjects of the Ezzelini, or da Romano, a notorious feudal family of northern Italy whose power disappeared in the late thirteenth century under the pressure of the church and the urban communes. Owing to Bassano's strategic importance and the existence of a castle on the hill between Bassano and Margnano, it was eventually much disputed between the communes of Vicenza and Padua. But already in 1175, in addition to the agriculturalists, there were various craftsmen, traders and notaries, and in the second half of the thirteenth century these were even organized into guilds. Once the Ezzelini had been expelled, the commune elaborated its institutions on the model of the nearby towns. The perhaps unnecessarily elaborate structure now consisted of three councils, the general assembly, or *arengo*, a big council of a hundred, a smaller one of forty, four consuls and a *podesta*. It even had its own militia, a schoolmaster and a group of clergy. The community was large and complex enough to need some form of institutional apparatus, and it is interesting to note that control of the common lands of ancient origin continued to be one of the commune's most important concerns. These common lands had become pieces of property rather than jointly enjoyed rights. They included

woods, meadows, pastures, islands in the river, arable and
even shops, and were leased out by the *podesta* or put up to
auction.

Having extricated themselves from feudal control, whether
of the Ezzelini or of the Bishop of Vicenza, Bassano was
eventually taken over by the commune of Padua (1268) and
absorbed into its *contado*. The replacement of the old feudal
nobility by the urban communes was an important development for the Italian peasantry. It could bring gains, such as
the abolition of serfdom and expanded market opportunities.
It also had a negative side—its subjection to city fiscality,
military service and other burdens, and, not least, the appropriation by rich individuals of the precious commons which
had been the nursery of rural communal autonomy.[20]

France, too, had its rural counterpart to the urban communal movement. The charters which were granted between
1160 and 1250 in the Macon region of Burgundy (rather late
as compared with other parts of France) illustrate some of the
ambiguities of the movement. Six of these charters were to
towns, such as Cluny (1162–72), and four were to villages,
such as St André-le-Désert (1188), but the terms were virtually the same. They were on the whole granted by lords as
wielders of jurisdictional power over the areas concerned
rather than as landowners giving concessions to tenants.[21]
And although there was an element of pressure from below,
it was not as strong as in some villages in the Parisian basin.
Lords, it seems, were not unwilling to grant the concessions
so as to attract new inhabitants. The terms of the charters,
were, however, fairly characteristic of concessions which had
already been obtained elsewhere, sometimes as the result of
sharp conflict, sometimes by the offer of large sums of money
to financially embarrassed lords.

The principal features common to both urban and village
charters were: fixed judicial fines in the lord's court; no arbitrary arrests; regularity of court procedure; reduction of
military obligations; abolition or regularization of the *taille*

[20] G. Fasoli, 'Un comune Veneto nel duecento: Bassano', *Nuovo
Archivio Veneto*, 1934.

[21] G. Duby, *La société dans la région maconnaise aux XIe et XIIe siècles*,
1953, pp 599–611.

(the seigneurial tax); no *mainmorte* (death duty); freedom of testamentary disposition and inheritance; a fixed instead of an arbitrary marriage tax; a fixed rent instead of the lord's monopoly of wine-selling in the period after the vintage (*banvin*); fixed instead of arbitrary payments to the lord on the alienation, by sale or otherwise, of property; and immigrants to obtain personal freedom after a year-and-a-day's residence. The confusion between the urban and rural aspect of this movement in the Maconnais is emphasized by the fact that even villagers who enjoyed the new franchises were to be known as *bourgeois*.

The famous charter of Louis VII of France granted in 1155 to Lorris, near Orleans, which was borrowed by innumerable urban and rural communities, illustrates the strong rural element in the movement for enfranchisement, or, what is equally significant, the strong commercial element in those rural areas where a claim for franchises was strong.[22] The second clause of the charter refers to the abolition of tolls on the grain and wine produced by the inhabitants for themselves; clause 15 abolishes labour services except the carriage of the king's wine to Orleans by those owning horses and carts; clause 22 abolishes the custom by which farmers who cultivated their land by plough had to give a measure of rye to the king's agents at harvest time; clause 23 limits the fines imposed for the accidental straying of horses and other animals into the royal forest; clause 31 refers to men from Lorris with vineyards, meadow and other land which they held from the local Benedictine community.

There are enough references in the Lorris charter to wine, that cash crop *par excellence*, to make one realize that these peasants who were pressing for chartered privilege must have been already deeply involved in the developing market economy. Early pressures for charters of enfranchisement, rural as well as urban, came from the important wine-growing district whose 'capital' was the cathedral city of Laon. Laon's burgesses were vineyard-owners as well as traders, and they were engaged in a particularly bitter struggle with their lord the bishop over their demand for a commune, a struggle

[22] M. Prou, *Les coutumes de Lorris et leur propagation aux XIIe et XIIIe siècles*, 1884.

which eventually resulted in the granting of a charter (1134), but which had had its violent moments, leading to the killing of the bishop in 1112.[23]

More interesting from our point of view is that during the course of the twelfth century between thirty and forty villages in the Laonnais and a group of five in the nearby Soissonnais had tried to achieve chartered privileges analogous to those of the urban communes, and nearly half of them were successful. Their case was all the stronger in that they bargained collectively rather than individually. One charter, for example, was sold to four villages, with Bruyère at their head. Another was obtained by a group of six led by Crandelain on the domain of the church of St Jean-de-Laon. Cerny and seven associated communities formed another group of chartered villages.[24] These, no doubt, were those peasant communities whose members according to a local chronicler were so involved in a commercial economy that they normally raised loans (presumably from Laon money lenders) on the security of the vintage to come—and found themselves in difficulties when the harvest failed. It is unlikely that they were always in these financial difficulties. Chartered privileges cost money and they must have bought them from the profit on wine sold to merchants from Flanders and even England.[25]

One would-be collective rural commune in the Laonnais was unsuccessful. A group of fourteen villages south of Laon which belonged to the bishop, led by the community of Anizy-le-Château, bought a charter modelled on that of the town from the king during a vacancy of the bishopric in 1174. Three years later they were crushed by force by the knights of the new bishop, a warlike member of a local noble family. For political reasons, royal protection ceased, and the most that came out of it was a minor concession to one village, Anizy-le-Château—that is the abolition of servile death duties and marriage fees (*mainmorte* and *formariage*).[26]

It would be a mistake to underestimate the scale of this

[23] Described by C. Petit-Dutaillis, *Les communes françaises*, 1947, pp 85–92.

[24] *ibid.*, pp 13, n. 2, 46; A. Luchaire, *Les communes françaises*, 1911, pp 81ff.

[25] R. Doehaerd, 'Laon capitale du vin au XIIe siècle', *Annales*, 1950.

[26] Petit-Dutaillis, *op. cit.*, pp 128–9.

movement for peasant emancipation. Between 1177 and 1350 there were some 280 enfranchisement charters in Lorraine, mostly similar to the famous charter granted to Beaumont-en-Argonne by the Archbishop of Reims in 1182, and therefore involving some degree of local self-administration. In a much shorter space of time in the Paris region (1246–*c*. 1280), nearly 60 villages got charters, mostly involving the abolition of the three main signs of servility (*mainmorte, formariage* and *taille*). In Picardy during the course of the thirteenth century about 120 villages got charters which gave them precise juridical privileges and the right to a village *échevinage*, that is, the village's own court, both judicial and administrative. Another hundred or so villages got lesser forms of privileges giving some control over the exercise of village customary practices. In fact, one village in ten in Picardy, by the beginning of the fourteenth century, enjoyed some degree of chartered privilege.[27]

Enfranchisement was won by a combination of mass pressure and offers of cash. Marc Bloch has described in detail the two cases of Rosny-sous-Bois, a village east of Paris which the King of France gave to the Abbey of St Geneviève, probably in the early 1160s, and of Orly, a village near Paris owned by the canons of Notre-Dame-de-Paris.[28] Both were cases of prolonged struggle, at Rosny from about 1180 until 1246, and at Orly from the 1240s until 1263. At Rosny it was a question of whether the villagers were serfs or freemen. The Abbey of St Geneviève, backed by the king, denied that the tenants were the free descendants of colonizing peasants. The tenants financed representations to the papal curia in Rome and even got sporadic backing from some of the popes. In the end they won their enfranchisement, but only by admitting their previous servility and by paying 60 *livres* of silver a year for their freedom.

[27] C. E. Perrin, 'Chartes de franchise et rapports de droit en Lorraine', *Moyen Age*, 1946; G. Fourquin, *Les campagnes de la région parisienne à la fin du moyen-âge*, 1964, pp 160–73; R. Fossier, *La terre et les hommes en Picardie jusqu'à la fin du XIIIe siècle*, 1968, pp 708ff.
[28] See Vol. I of Bloch's *Mélanges Historiques* for articles on both cases. One of them has been published in translation ('From the royal court to the court of Rome: the suit of the serfs of Rosny-sous-Bois'), in S. L. Thrupp, ed., *Change in Medieval Society*, 1965.

The Orly affair concerned the disputed right of the canons to tallage the villagers for their own financial benefit, that is, not simply acting as the collectors of royal tallage for the king. The peasants played their cards awkwardly, for they began by offering to buy out the canons' right to tallage for 2,000 *livres* (an enormous sum which they would probably raise from a Parisian financier). Having failed, they denied that they ought to pay tallage, and in 1252 the peasants were imprisoned by the canons. They were released only in order to appear before a royal commission of enquiry which decided against them; the commissioners were the Bishops of Paris, Orleans and Auxerre. It was not until 1263 that they were enfranchised on condition that they paid 60 *livres* a year as a composition for an arbitrary tithe payment. The enfranchisement covered over 600 persons from Orly. It is worth noting that other chapter tenants, two thousand in all, were backing them and that they were able to use a Parisian bourgeois as their intermediary.

The issue is interesting in that it seems to have been the arbitrary and unexpected character of tallage which provoked reaction. It was heavy when it was levied, but it was not levied often. Peasants preferred to pay a fixed annual sum, and, in the long run, probably to pay more. The issue continued to be a live one on the Notre-Dame estate. The serfs of Bagneux refused to pay, in 1264, and were backed by the non-servile peasants of the village, the *vileins* who no doubt realized that resistance to servile dues was in their interests, since there was a tendency for *vileins* to be assimilated to the condition of the serfs. Another village, Itteville, also refused to pay tallage in 1268, and when the chapter's agents seized their goods the peasants sounded the tocsin, gathered together, and took back their goods by force. In both of these villages the tallage was subsequently commuted for a fairly low annual sum.[29]

We have seen French peasant communities, under the leadership of the village rich, engaged in trials of strength with their lords. They were partially successful. But we must remember that, if the growth of production for the market strengthened some of the peasants, the thirteenth-century

[29] G. Fourquin, *loc. cit.*

nobility as well as the royal power were by no means feeble. When faced by a common front of crown and noble land-owners, the peasants were defeated. When they made gains they paid heavily—and often for rather minor gains at that. In 1248, the Parisian Abbey of St Denis freed its tenants in six villages from the main servile obligations, but still insisted on the subservience due to it as the patron of these new free men. Since it retained its rights of jurisdiction, it had power to emphasize this role as patron. Furthermore, the villagers paid over 1,700 *livres*. The next year another rich Parisian abbey, that of St Germain-des-Prés enfranchised the inhabitants of three of its villages, but provided that they should neither form nor join a commune without permission. Quite a number of the tenants' obligations to the abbey were maintained yet they had to pay 1,400 *livres*.[30]

French and Italian peasant communities led the way in the struggle for charters of enfranchisement. Some historians regard their activities as secondary to the urban struggles. Henri Pirenne thought that the village movements simply imitated the urban initiative.[31] There may be something in this view. However, without ignoring the likely priority of movements for charters of independence by urban communities, it would perhaps be best to regard both urban and rural movements as being generated in the conditions of an economic development whose predominant feature was the growth of production for the market, and consequently the acquisition of wealth and self-consciousness by the leading producers and traders. No wonder, in this case, that the spearhead was in the most advanced regions of western Europe. In other regions the movement assumed other forms and the gains were less spectacular.

In England, peasant movements during the greater part of the period of economic expansion were defensive rather than aggressive. It is true that there may have been a shortlived

[30] For comments on the financial gains made by the lords from the sale of privileges see Duby, Bk III, chap. 3. The French kings were also well aware that money could be made by offering enfranchisement to well-to-do peasants, at a price. M. Bloch, *Rois et serfs—un chapitre d'histoire capétienne*, 1920.

[31] H. Pirenne, *Economic and Social History of Medieval Europe*, 1936, pp 72–3.

period when some peasants were making inroads on the
lords' positions—in the middle of the twelfth century. The
circumstances, though interesting and worth further investigation, are obscure. It seems that after the Norman Conquest
of England there was a considerable increase in the exploita-
tion of the peasantry, revealed rather in Domesday Book
evidence of increased farm rents in money taken from the
manors than in detailed evidence of any increase in particular peasant obligations.[32] The legal position of the English
peasantry at the time of the Conquest and in the first few
decades of the Norman occupation seems to have been analogous to that of the peasants in the western lands of the Franks
a century earlier. The majority of cultivators were of free
condition in the eyes of the public law; those who were
tenants on lords' estates were nevertheless also subjected to
the customary law of the estate, which involved real restrictions on their freedom, including the obligation to do labour
services as part of their rent.[33]

Though the number of real slaves was appreciable, except
in the eastern part of the country, it was declining. By the
second half of the twelfth century slaves as a class had virtually
disappeared.[34] On the other hand, the majority of the peasants on the big estates, the villeins or customary tenants, were
more and more tightly bound by the imperatives of the landlord economy, and were beginning to be regarded as servile
by the public courts.[35] Sokemen and other free tenants preserved their relative independence insofar as they were not
absorbed in the domanial economy. Paradoxically, their
numbers may even have increased at the same time as the
manorial villeins were being treated as serfs. The chief reason
for this increase in free tenants was that the newly colonized
land in forest, fen and upland was often offered on free terms
of tenure.

[32] R. Weldon Finn, *Domesday Studies: the Eastern Counties*, 1967.
[33] See the pre-Conquest statement of estate custom, called Rectitudines
Singularum Personarum, in D. C. Douglas, ed., *English Historical Documents*, II, 1953, pp 813–16.
[34] M. M. Postan, *The Famulus*, Economic History Review Supplement,
n.d., 2, p. 11.
[35] For what follows, see R. H. Hilton, 'Freedom and villeinage in
England', *P & P*, 1965.

This was, in fact, a general trend. There is some evidence, however, from the estate surveys of the mid twelfth century that a temporary reaction by the landowners to increased market production, and to the increased volume of money in circulation, was to reduce the size of their demesnes, to lease out portions of those demesnes for money rent, and to commute some peasant labour services for money. Interpretation of this trend is made somewhat difficult, because during the fourteen or fifteen years of civil war in mid-century some peasant tenants may have been able to take advantage of the disarray of the landowners. At any rate, there are indications that some tenants obtained permanent commutation of labour services and the status of free tenants by a combination of pressure and purchase. But this pressure seems to have been individual rather than collective, and indeed, throughout the twelfth and thirteenth centuries and beyond, the trickle continued of individual manumissions of well-to-do villein tenants who were prepared to pay quite considerable sums of money for their freedom.

This did not mean that English peasants did not eventually organize themselves collectively. Most of the evidence for such actions comes from the period of the lords' later counter-reaction to these few peasant gains of the mid twelfth century. If participation in wider economic activity during the twelfth and thirteenth centuries had enabled peasant communities in Italy and France to undertake aggressive action, in England it was eventually the lords who took the most effective initiative. By the last decades of the twelfth century they were expanding and reorganizing their demesnes, and instituting a body of professional agents to supervise them instead of the traditional farmers (*firmarii*), the local men who had taken the demesnes on lease for a fixed rent. The new bailiffs, in order to make as much profit as possible, had to pay special attention to labour requirements. Peasant labour services were needed for expanded production, but to control an unpaid and therefore unwilling labour force, lords and their agents needed legally sanctioned coercive powers. Hence there was an inevitable pressure to reduce peasants to the uniform condition of unfree villeinage, unprotected by the royal courts. Furthermore, there were other aspects of social status which brought in a financial profit through the manor courts, which lords, in a period of rising prices, could not ignore. It was against this pressure that the collective actions, for which we have abundant evidence in the thirteenth century, were organized.

Conflict between lords and peasants in England sometimes began in a similar way, for example, by opposition to the collection of tallage.[36] This attempt to tallage arbitrarily seems to have sparked off a village revolt at Mears Ashby, Northamptonshire, in 1261, and a second at Harmondsworth, Middlesex, in 1278, though other grievances subsequently appeared in both places—the right to buy and sell land in Mears Ashby, and the payment of merchet at Harmondsworth. But other issues could just as easily be the *casus belli*.

In England, because of the persistence of labour as part of rent (and its servile associations) the attempt to exact rents fully frequently led to common action. This was, apparently, at the root of a conflict between a lord and tenants at Rempston, Northamptonshire, in 1247, while the collective refusal to do services was frequent on the estates of Ramsey Abbey at the turn of the century and the entire body of villeins at Newington, Oxfordshire, refused to do mowing services in 1300. In the last case, the villeins were also reported to have taken a collection of fourpence a head for their own purposes —almost certainly to set up a fund to fight their case by one means or another.

The collective aspect of protests very frequently shows itself (quite apart from accusations of conspiracy) in the hiring of a pleader to present a case against the lord in the law courts. Many of the cases which come to light are to be seen only through the standard formulations of plea and defence in the records of the courts; and unfortunately less formal records tend invariably to reflect the lords' rather than the peasants' side of the story. But one such record, a satirical Latin poem from Leicester Abbey, shows clearly that peasant actions were concerted. The legal record, which also survives, names thirty peasant plaintiffs from the village of Stoughton who pleaded mainly against labour services. The poem reveals that the

[36] R. H. Hilton, 'Peasant Movements in England before 1381' in E. Carus-Wilson, ed., *Essays in Economic History*, II, 1962.

ringleader was the village reeve, and that the peasants clubbed together to hire a pleader, who supposedly advised them against going through with the action. At the last moment they lost their nerve and went home. This last incident is quite untrue if the legal record is to be believed, for the case was pursued through two sessions of the royal court, until the peasants admitted their servile condition, one by one. The poem concludes by saying that the great men of the village had been humiliated and the rich made indigent. The reeve, of course, usually came from the wealthiest element among the village population. The leadership of peasant movements by the village rich in this period is confirmed in this poem.[37]

The nearest approach by English village communities to the continental achievement of a charter of enfranchisement was the legal definition of fixed custom, though it must be admitted that when matters came to court the lords tended to be more successful than the peasant litigants in having their version of custom accepted. However, as has already been shown, the tenurial conditions on manors of the ancient and even of the existing demesne of the crown were sometimes stabilized to the advantage at any rate of the upper stratum of the village population (sometimes known as 'villein sokemen'). Thus in 1292 the king responded favourably to a petition from the tenants of the manor of Costessey, Norfolk, when they complained about arbitrary tallage, restrictions on the land market and enforced service as reeve or rent-collectors.[38] On the ancient demesne manor of Stoneleigh in Warwickshire the villein sokemen enjoyed security of tenure, paid a money rent, and virtually no labour services, as well as having guaranteed rights of commons. However, even these most privileged members of the community owed frequent suit to the manor courts, and were restricted in buying and selling land. In addition, they owed heriot from their holding at death, paid pannage for the pasture of pigs, had to grind their corn at the lord's mill, and were bound by other customs of a quasi-servile character.[39] Until well

[37] The poem is printed in R. H. Hilton, 'A 13th-century poem on disputed villein services', *EHR*, 1941.
[38] Vinogradoff, *op. cit.*, p 435.   [39] *Stoneleigh Leger Book*, pp. 100–108.

into the fourteenth century, English peasant communities, though by no means quiescent, did not make an inroad into seigneurial privileges comparable to those of the French and the Italians.

There was another interesting symptom of peasant self-assertion, that was (so far as one can see) unlinked with the frequent battles over labour services, tallage, and villein status which constituted the main issues in the rural social struggle. This was the development of a limited form of self-government through the enactment and enforcement of village bylaws.[40] It was one of the contradictory features of medieval agrarian society that, although men were organized in a strict hierarchy, of which everybody was very conscious, the primitive level of communication and the character of the agrarian economy meant that at the peasant level some element of self-government was inevitable. Hence, the manor court, the expression of the private jurisdictional control by the lord, depended for its working on the activity of the suitors to the court, drawn from the peasant community. The court regulated affairs in the lord's interest and punished offenders against those interests. It also punished offenders against community interests, those whose animals trespassed on their neighbour's land, for example, as well as those who trespassed on the lord's demesne. The system of punishment in these courts, before the advent of the bylaw system, emphasized the overriding power of the lord. Offenders were 'amerced': they paid money in order to have the lord's mercy in respect of the offence.

The bylaw system grew up within the framework of the manor court. It was mainly concerned to regulate the gathering of the harvest, including times of reaping, entitlement to gleaning, pasturing of beasts on the stubble and so on, but it could cover other matters, such as blocking of ditches, repair of fences and harbouring of strangers. The original feature of the system is that the rules were made, not by the lord's steward but by the village community. In 1276 at Staines, Middlesex, an ordinance against strangers being brought in to glean was passed 'by the community of the whole village'.

[40] W. O. Ault, *Open Field Farming in Medieval England*, 1972. This includes an appendix of bylaws from 31 manors.

The 1290 autumn ordinance at Great Horwood, Buckinghamshire, was decreed 'by the whole homage and by the freemen'. In 1295, at Newton Longville in the same county, consent to the observance of the autumn statute was given by 'all the lord's tenants both free and customary'. Offences were punished, not by paying for the lord's mercy, but by paying a penalty, usually heavier than the traditional amercement. There were elected keepers of these ordinances, statutes or bylaws. The tribunal at which the offenders were presented was still the manor court, and although in quite a number of cases the penalties were paid into a parish fund, they frequently went to swell the profits of the manor court and became part of the lord's income. The bylaw system not only was permitted by the lords, but perhaps encouraged. There was nothing revolutionary about it, but it is interesting to note that this system begins when the evidence of litigation shows that peasants were standing up for themselves in response to attempts to worsen their conditions.

Local struggles for the stabilization of 'ancient customs' against landowners' attempts to increase rents and services are found in other regions which, like England, were relatively backward in applying pressure for communal franchises, either because of the relatively undeveloped state of the market or because of the stronger resistance of the lords. A case which resembles some of the contemporary English struggles is found in mid-thirteenth-century Normandy on the estates of the Abbey of Mont-St-Michel.[41] Our only evidence is a poem, written from the standpoint of the monks, about an attempt by the villagers of Verson, under the leadership of one of their number (*Osbert, vilein felon*) whom they had chosen as their representative. The poem is little more than an enumeration of the labour services owed to the abbey, which presumably the peasants were attempting to get reduced, to the disinheritance, says the poem's author, of St Michael himself. The poem is in celebration of the abbey's victory, and this may have been embodied in a schedule of 1247[42] which gives a new and detailed list of tenants, of holdings and of the

[41] Printed as an appendix to L. Delisle, *op. cit.*
[42] R. Carabie, *La propriété foncière dans le très ancien droit normand, I: la propriété domaniale*, 1943.

services owed from them. The obligations remained virtually unchanged until the beginning of the fifteenth century.

Declarations of custom could be in the interest of either lord or tenant. Only the examination of individual cases can determine this: both sides tended to appeal to custom and differed as to what customary practice was. Yet even when a particular fixing of custom favours peasant claims, it cannot be equated with the achievement of those communal franchises in France and Italy, which represented an element of transfer of power from lord to peasant community.

It is a remarkable feature of the old-settled lands of the Empire, mostly German-speaking, that there was no equivalent movement. As early as the twelfth century, as we have seen, colonizing German and Polish landowners, in the eastern territories beyond the Elbe, deliberately created villages whose inhabitants were offered, as bait, freer terms and conditions of life than in the western ones. The landlords' agents were authorized to offer holdings on free and heritable terms, to be held often for no more than money rents and church tithes. Superior jurisdictions and fiscal pressures were avoided and the agent himself, provided with a holding three or four times the size of the peasants', became in effect the immediate lord, presiding over the village court and taking a proportion of the fines. The legal code administered was often urban in origin, the system from Magdeburg being very common. Although such villages might to some extent reflect the peasant ideal, they came into existence as a result of seigneurial, not peasant, initiative.[43]

To the west of the 'colonial' lands, peasant success in Germany was largely achieved through the stabilization of custom as expressed in declarations, originally oral, but, from the thirteenth century onwards, increasingly in writing. They were usually referred to as *Weistümer*, though this term was mainly used in the districts of the middle Rhine, the Moselle valley and the Palatinate. Other districts had other names for essentially the same thing, such as *Rügen* in Saxony, *Dinghofrodeln* in Alsace, *Ehaftrechten* in Bavaria, or *rapports de*

[43] See *CEcH* I (2nd ed.), chaps 1 and 7, §4; *Cambridge History of Poland*, I, chap. 7, 1950, for outlines of this subject of which there is a considerable literature.

droit in such French-speaking parts of the Empire as Lorraine. They were most common in south-west Germany, Switzerland, Austria and the Tirol, areas of fragmented estates, nucleated settlement, open-field husbandry with a high degree of production for the market. These economic and social conditions were similar to those in Italy and France where more serious encroachments had been made on the power of the lords. It has been pointed out that the *Weistümer*, or their equivalents, were most numerous in the area where the peasants were later to be most strongly organized in the great peasants' war of the early sixteenth century.[44]

Declarations of custom were not always made, in the first place, in the peasants' interests. They were sometimes made on the initiative of monastic landlords as a move to relax the grip on their estates of the abbey's patron, known as *Vogt*, *avoué* or advocate. These noble patrons of ecclesiastical institutions are found all over the medieval world, and before the ecclesiastical reform movement of the eleventh and twelfth centuries they often had the disposal not only of the property but of the nomination to office of those abbots and bishops who owed their landed endowments to the piety of these noble families. Their grip continued to be strong in the Empire and they often exercised profitable jurisdiction over (and even took rents and services from) ecclesiastical tenants. Some *Weistümer*, then, were drawn up on behalf of the ecclesiastical owners in order to establish their own customary rights against the encroachments of the *Vogt*. In so doing they defined the level of peasant rents and services.[45] But many similar declarations of rights were sponsored jointly by village lords and representatives of village communities in which these were the only two interests involved and the advocate was absent. By the sixteenth century, when purely seigneurial ordinances began to replace the *Weistümer*, the known examples are very numerous, over 600 having been identified for Alsace alone.

In addition to the definition of rents, services and other

[44] G. Franz, *Geschichte des deutschen Bauernstandes*, 1970, p 58. There are examples in G. Franz, *Quellen zur Geschichte des deutschen Bauernstandes*, I, 1967. For Bavaria see also P. Dollinger, *L'évolution des classes rurales en Bavière*, 1949, VIII, iv.
[45] C. E. Perrin, *op. cit.*, and F. L. Ganshof, *CEcH* I, p 338.

obligations, the *Weistümer* (which vary considerably in content from village to village) record a considerable range of customary practices covering much of the social and agricultural life of the village. These include common rights of usage in woods, common lands and fisheries, inheritance customs, the sphere of action of the officials of the village, types of offence, forms of compensation for injury and so on. To have them recorded in writing, even though changing conditions could make them out of date and irrelevant, could be a considerable advantage for the peasant community. Nevertheless, they represent a lower level of peasant achievement than the charters which were acquired by many peasants in Italy and France, but which are hardly to be found to the east of the River Moselle.

At the end of the thirteenth century, the balance of forces between the peasants and their rulers varied a good deal from place to place. The two preceding centuries had seen considerable economic development in the spheres both of production and exchange. The power of feudal lords and monarchical governments had grown, due partly to the increasing size of the disposable agricultural surplus and partly to the development of more efficient methods of transferring the surplus from the basic producer to the lord. But in order to pay cash to lords and to political authorities, peasants had to sell produce on the market, and peasant agriculture, while retaining a subsistence basis, began to be commercialized. The market in agricultural goods was matched by a market in land. Stratification based on successful competition on the market was added to older types of stratification based on family size, traditional supremacies and physical power. Rich peasants built up sizeable holdings by spending their profits on land and by employing the village poor. They found that seigneurial restraints and jurisdictional rights hindered their development, and this is why the rich peasants took the lead in the fight for free status and local autonomy. But this did not happen everywhere, and even where some members of peasant communities prospered, there remained many landless labourers, poor smallholders, impoverished herdsmen, rural artisans and others whose lives were by no means idyllic. The rural poor, often the first to be affected by floods, droughts, famines, plagues and other natural disasters, were a force behind movements rather different from the slow encroachments on seigneurial power we have so far described.

3 Mass Movements of the Later Middle Ages

Apart from the remarkable—and seriously undocumented—Norman rising of 996, most of the peasant movements we have so far considered, which existed for the realization of basic class needs, were localized geographically and limited in scope. These were usually individual village movements aimed at altering the balance of the relationships between the peasant community and the individual lord, rather than transforming or abolishing those relationships. The most that was achieved—and it was not inconsiderable—was a form of self-government analogous to that of the urban communes under the leadership of the richer peasants, whose struggle came from the same source that gave strength to the towns in their struggle for autonomy, namely, production for the market.

The distinguishing feature of the peasant movements of the later middle ages is, however, their widened scope. Whole regions containing many villages are involved and aims are proclaimed, or are at least implicit in peasant actions, which subvert existing social and political relationships. This widened scope was undoubtedly partly due to the development of the machinery of state, as a result of which fiscal burdens, now quite as serious as the burden of rent, exercised an even and generalizing pressure over large geographical areas. This factor must be seen, of course, in the context of the breakdown of local isolation through the developed communications and trade, and through increasing scope of regional and national jurisdictions.

Another aspect of the wider horizons of later peasant movements is to be found in the realm of ideas and social mentality. Already in the twelfth and thirteenth centuries, or even earlier, there had been mass movements in which plebeians of town and country had played a partially autonomous role, but only partially autonomous because the aims of these movements were not specifically related to the condition of peasant or artisan. The ideological driving force of these movements was religious. At most, the movements were only imperfectly harnessed to the objectives of the church; often they deliberately ran counter to them. The former movements were embodied in the various crusades; the latter in the various mass heretical movements. What is important about them for the historian of peasant movements is first that they involved in their action and committed to their aspirations large numbers of peasants and other lower-class individuals; and second that they transcended the local and regional horizons within which the peasant movements with more or less clearly defined but limited class objectives of an economic and social type had so far mainly operated.

The people's crusades were comparable to some of the mass heretical movements not only because of their plebeian composition, but because of certain ideas common to both of them.[1] Although there seemed to be infinite variations on a few themes, the two basic ideas were the exaltation of poverty and the expectation of the end of the world. The pilgrimage to Jerusalem was a pilgrimage to the place of martyrdom of a redeemer who in life had had no property, whose followers had been equally poor, and who could best be approached by those with no or few worldly goods. Although the first crusade was preached in 1095 to an exclusively clerical and aristocratic audience by Urban II, the pope who was a monk of the most aristocratic of the religious orders, the Cluniac, it was first taken up as a mass movement by the poor. Peter the Hermit, the preacher from Amiens, was a man without property who had given away all his goods in alms. Before his leadership of the people's crusade he was known as a peacemaker, a man of charity, a man who saved women from prostitution not by driving them into nunneries but by giving them dowries. His crusade was a military failure, although to have got as far as Asia Minor was a fair achievement.[2]

[1] For much of what follows see P. Alphandéry and A. Dupont, *La crétienté et l'idée de croisade*, I and II, 1959. The most convenient general narrative of the crusades is by S. Runciman, *A History of the Crusades*, 3 vols, 1951–4.

[2] A point made by F. Duncalf, 'The peasants' crusade', *American Historical Review*, 1921.

Other popular armies, such as those following Walter the Penniless and the priest Gottschalk, foundered on the overland route through the Balkans. But before we accept the success of the army which took Jerusalem in 1100 as the apotheosis of chivalry and as being due to its aristocratic leadership, we must remember that it was the poor in that army, especially those from southern France, who were responsible for the pressure which forced the land-hungry lords to press on to the end,[3] though not before the most grasping had left the crusade to found such feudal states as the County of Edessa and the Principality of Antioch and others (such as Robert Curthose of Normandy) to idle their time in Mediterranean pleasure resorts.

By the end of the twelfth century the political and acquisitive character of the participation of kings and nobles in the crusading movement could have made the whole enterprise seem of little worth from the standpoint of religion. Alternatively, it could be said that only the poor could effectively perform the armed pilgrimage to the Holy Sepulchre. This was the expressed view of so well connected a writer as Peter of Blois, intimate of the court of Henry II of England.[4] More practically, it was expressed in preaching by Fulk of Neuilly and his master, Peter Cantor of Paris. But the fourth crusade of 1204, which simply achieved the conquest not of Jerusalem but of Christian Byzantium, revealed the cynicism of its highborn leaders. The next popular crusade, the children's crusade of 1212, in which a substantial element was drawn from the rural poor (shepherd boys and the like), was even persecuted by the Roman Catholic authorities and got no nearer to Jerusalem than did the barons in 1204.[5]

In spite of these failures, the people's crusades seem to

[3] This comes out clearly in the *Historica Francorum qui ceperunt Jerusalem*, by Raymond of Aguilers (English trans. by J. H. and L. L. Hill, 1968), esp. in chaps. 14 to 23. Note that the discovery of the holy lance, a turning-point in the battle for Antioch on the way to Jerusalem, was by Peter Bartholomew, a poor peasant from Provence (*pauperem quemdam rusticum Provincialem genere*) to whom and not to the clergy or the feudal potentates, St Andrew the Apostle is reported to have appeared in a dream.

[4] In *De Hierosolimitana peregrinatione acceleranda*, cit. Alphandéry and Dupont, II, *op. cit.*, pp 36–40.

[5] D. C. Munro, 'The children's crusade', *American Historical Review*, 1914.

have provided an important experience. Various reasons could be given for the involvement of the masses. The popular expectation of the millennium, whether it was to be the moment of the end of the world and the Last Judgement or alternatively the time of the coming of Antichrist, was widely current in the eleventh century and was associated with the pilgrimage to Jerusalem. If in the thousandth year of the Incarnation expectations were disappointed, it was hoped for again in 1033, a thousand years after the Passion. This expectation, too, was disappointed, but calculations and recalculations could and would always be made by those who hoped for the regeneration or the end of a rotten world. In addition, a more materialist explanation was given both by contemporary writers and by modern historians for the disorientation of the masses at the end of the eleventh century which predisposed them to go on the crusade.[6] This was caused, it was said, by diseases, bad harvest, famine, floods, drought and the rest of the natural disasters which from time to time afflicted the backward medieval economy. But the only evidence is that of the chroniclers and they were always inclined to look for portents of great events in natural phenomena, which they would tend therefore to exaggerate or to displace in time. Since dearths in medieval agriculture tended to occur fairly regularly—three or four times a decade— it would not be difficult to produce either natural or supernatural events which could be blamed for putting people into a turbulent frame of mind, as in the middle of the 1090s, when the masses prepared themselves for the crusade as if for a permanent emigration. At this, as at other times of mass enthusiasm, concepts of hierarchy tended to be blurred: the tripartite society must dissolve in the face of Antichrist.

A remarkable appendage to the people's crusades occurred in the mid-thirteenth century—an episode which seems to bridge the movements of pure enthusiasm for the freeing of Jerusalem with those to come, which aimed to free the unfree

---

[6] Guibert of Nogent's account of the famine of 1095 in northern France is frequently cited (from his 'Gesta Francorum Jerusalem expugnantium'; *Historiens des Croisades: Historiens occidentaux*, IV, 1879, p 141). If a socioeconomic foundation for these events is sought it may rather be found in the population pressure, also manifested in the contemporary assarting of waste and forest.

and the poor. In 1249, Louis IX of France, a monarch with
some popular prestige, had been captured by the Moslems
at Damietta in Egypt. This episode triggered off a popular
movement which at the outset seemed to have no other aim
than to deliver the Holy Land from the infidel and to free the
imprisoned king.[7] One of the best accounts of the subsequent
events and of the movements of the Shepherds, or Pastoureaux,
is by the contemporary English chronicler Matthew Paris.[8]
He was a monk of the Abbey of St Albans but in close touch
with the court of King Henry III. His information about the
Shepherds came to him from the king himself, who was in
turn given the story by a French monk of Sherborne Abbey
who had been a prisoner of the Shepherds. Practically every
detail in the story repeats the various elements found in most
of the subversive or heretical movements of the twelfth and
thirteenth centuries. Matthew Paris's details are corroborated
by other chroniclers,[9] though some of the more extravagant
accounts, in the excitement of denunciation, lack internal consistency and verisimilitude. The outside agitator—a necessary
figure for inquisitors and denouncers of movements of this
type—was an elderly Hungarian preacher, said by Matthew
Paris to have been the leader of the children's crusade forty
years before, and said by others to be a renegade Cistercian
monk. He preached without papal or episcopal authority
under the direct orders of the Virgin Mary, who had told
him that the Holy Land would be delivered not by the proud
knights of France, but by the humble and the simple, the
herdsmen of sheep and other animals. It was to these people
that he appealed, apparently with success, for without con-
sulting either their lords or their families, they joined this
preacher and were further reinforced by thieves, exiles,
fugitives and excommunicates. All took the cross, illicit marri-
ages were contracted, and laymen preached unlicensed by

---

[7] Detailed narrative by E. Berger, *Vie de Blanche de Castille*, 1895.
[8] *Chronica Majora*, RS, 1872–83, V, pp 246–53.
[9] A number of these are published in *MGH Scriptores*, XVI (Annales
Hamburgenses); XXIV (Chronica auctore Minorita Ephordiensi; Flores
Temporum); XXV (Richeri Gesta Senoniensis Ecclesiae; Anonymi
Chronicon Rhythmicum Austriacum; Baldwini Ninovensis Chronicon)
The Italian Franciscan, Salimbene, displays his prejudices in his *Chronica*,
II, ed. F. Bernini, 1942, pp 117–8.

the authorities. In particular they attacked in detail the various orders of the church for their characteristic sins: the Dominicans and Franciscans as vagabonds and hypocrites; Cistercians as greedy amassers of flocks and lands; the Benedictines for their pride; the canons for their secular lives; and the bishops and their officials for their pursuit of money. Nor was the Roman curia exempt from attack; the audience welcomed these attacks on the clergy.

A Franciscan writing to Adam Marsh, an English member of his order, said that the Shepherds aimed at the extirpation of the clergy, and then the uprooting of the religious orders. Next they would attack the knights and the nobles, so that when all rule was abolished the infidel could take over easily.[10] These remarks may have been due as much to the feverish imagination of the letter-writer as to any authentic record of the Shepherds' intentions. The letter begins by saying that the Shepherds' leader aimed to lead a crusade against the Saracens, but ends by recording that he perished by invoking Mohammed!

The movement seems quickly to have become more anticlerical than crusading in its aims and, after some success with the townspeople of Orleans and Bourges, was dispersed when the leader was killed. Clearly, it had been entirely plebeian in its composition, though not necessarily composed only of herdsmen. According to Matthew Paris, one of its leaders came to England and for a time attracted a following of 'herdsmen, ploughmen, swineherds and oxherds'. Herdsmen would very likely be the younger and more mobile of the rural population: the young peasants on the children's crusade had been mainly shepherds. It is doubtful, however, that we are entitled to call this movement a 'peasant movement', having aims specific to the peasant class. Its social radicalism is suspect, for the letter to Adam Marsh is hardly adequate evidence of a plan to subvert the social order, and in its early stages it had been looked on with favour by the Queen Mother of France, Blanche of Castile. Yet as a mass movement of the rural lower classes which involved an attack on the clergy —the pillar of the social order—it cannot be ignored, because, however strong was the religious impulse behind it, it must

[10] *Annales Monastici*, I (Burton), RS, 1864, pp 290–99.

reveal some form of discontent felt by the herdsmen with their world.

For the most part, religious enthusiasm for the crusades was acceptable to the papacy and the hierarchy, although that sniffer-out of heretics, the aristocratic Bernard, Abbot of Clairvaux, was already in the mid twelfth century suspicious of wandering hermits, such as Rodolph of Hainault, who sought on the eve of the second crusade to rouse the masses by presenting eschatological dreams.[11] There were, too, not a few heretical mass movements with a plebeian following which were contemporary with the crusading movement. They may have arisen from the same feelings of deprivation, disorientation and unease which provided suitable conditions for the success of the crusading preachers. They varied from place to place and from time to time in their tenets, their following, and their influence. At the beginning of the thirteenth century, two broad trends can be seen, with a good deal of overlapping between them. On the one hand, there were movements inspired by the dualist outlook, characteristic of the Persian Manicheans, the Paulicians of Asia Minor, and the Bogomils of the Balkans.[12] Members of these movements, of which the Albigensians of Languedoc are the best known, believed in two gods, a god of the spirit and a god of irreconcilable matter. Within this spectrum of belief, at one pole the believers were hardly Christian, though there were believers in Christ and his role who were affected by dualism. On the other hand, there were many movements, perhaps less sophisticated than the dualist, which were simply evangelical in inspiration and wished the church and the world to return to the simple poverty and equality of the age of the Apostles, and which looked to the authority of the Bible rather than to that of the church. Both types of movement criticized the wealth and power and political involvement of the existing church, and in varying degrees rejected the organized priesthood and the sacraments which the priests controlled. In so doing, whether they intended it or not, they would have undermined the entire social order.

[11] P. Alphandéry and A. Dupont, I, pp 174–6.
[12] S. Runciman, *The Medieval Manichee*, 1955; D. Obolensky, *The Bogomils*, 1955.

The Albigensian heretics, supported by elements among the Languedocian aristocracy as well as by a considerable body of persons in towns such as Toulouse and Albi, organized a parallel church to that of Catholic orthodoxy, within which bishops, 'perfected' members of the community, fulfilled a priestly role. This church was smashed by the Albigensian crusade at the beginning of the thirteenth century, a combination of papally backed orthodoxy, ambitious and territorially greedy barons from the overcrowded Île de France and the expansionist Capetian monarchy.[13] Dualists—'Cathars' (the pure) as they are sometimes called—continued to be active, especially in northern Italy. The main heretical inspiration was now that of the Waldensians, followers of a movement for evangelical poverty, founded around 1170, which in many respects was similar—apart from being outside the pale of the church—to the Franciscan Order. Waldensianism assumed many forms, suffered splits and internal rivalries, but was to continue as one of the most tenacious of the popular heresies of the late medieval world. Here we find reliance on the authority of the Bible; emphasis on the virtues of poverty, and therefore of the poor; an insistence on a direct relationship between God and man, so that priests and sacraments, confessions and prayers for the dead, and the intercession of saints, become irrelevant; an equality of men and women, and, in general, an outlook and behaviour which runs counter to current conceptions of hierarchy. The Waldensians contributed much to the thinking of the Hussites in Bohemia, and possibly to that of the English Lollards as well as some of the sixteenth-century reformers.[14]

The Order of Friars Minor founded by St Francis of Assisi only two or three decades after the beginning of the preaching of Peter Valdes, the founder of the Waldensians, made another important contribution to popular heresy, in spite of its initial orthodoxy and the continuing orthodoxy of most of its members. The insistence on the holiness of poverty and the cult of simplicity were hardly consistent with the highly

[13] A. Luchaire, *Innocent III: La Croisade des Albigeois*, 1905.
[14] Original documents illustrating the views of the Waldensians are translated in W. L. Wakefield and A. P. Evans, eds, *Heresies of the High Middle Ages*, 1969. This substantial volume contains a useful introduction.

organized and well-endowed international church, which, by the middle of the thirteenth century had a hierarchy, a central bureaucracy and a judicial and fiscal administration more elaborate than that of many secular states. The order became divided over the issue of the possession of property. Devices by which property granted to it was held in trust by the papacy did not satisfy the purists, known as the Spiritual, as opposed to the Conventual Fransciscans. The arguments began to turn on whether Christ himself lived in poverty, and they reached such a pitch that in 1323 Pope John XXII declared that the assertion of the poverty of Christ was itself heretical. By that time the Spirituals had been in a state of open warfare for many years with the rest of the order and with papacy itself. In the course of their struggle they had adopted and sponsored many ideas additional to that which exalted poverty. Some of them were openly revolutionary.[15]

These elaborations on the theme of the end of the world were, of course, hardly exclusive to the Spiritual Franciscans. As we have seen they were particularly potent from about the year 1000 onwards and played some part in producing the outlook which encouraged poor men as well as rich to embark on the armed pilgrimage to Jerusalem. The whole concept gained added definition in the writings of Joachim of Fiore, Abbot of the Cistercian monastery of Curazzo in Calabria and founder of the new order of Fiore. Joachim, inspired like many others by biblical prophecy, especially that in the Book of Revelation, divided human history into three ages, each of which progressed to a conclusion and constituted an improvement on the previous one. The first age, the age of the Father, covered the period of the Old Testament; the second, the age of the Son, corresponded with the era which began with the New Testament and was still continuing at the beginning of the thirteenth century when Joachim was writing; and the third age, the age of the Spirit, was due to begin in 1260 or thereabouts. Antichrist would appear at this time, and be vanquished by Christ. Antichrist would reappear at

---

[15] The bibliography on the Franciscans is enormous. For their heretical tendencies see H. C. Lea, *A History of the Inquisition in the Middle Ages*, 1888; D. L. Douie, *The Nature and Effect of the Heresy of the Fraticelli*, 1932; G. Leff, *Heresy in the Later Middle Ages*, 1969.

the end of the era of the Spirit, and again be defeated by Christ, when the world would end and the Last Judgement would occur.[16]

Joachim's scheme was much more intricate than has been indicated here, and was full of symbolism and pictorial-cum-geometrical illustration. Each of the three ages, for instance, was subdivided into seven, each with its own characteristics. But the important feature about Joachim and his disciples —many of them Franciscans, like Gerard of Borgo San Donnino and Peter John Olivi—was that instead of hungering after the past age of apostolic poverty and simplicity they created a scheme of historical inevitability, which could be, and frequently was, related to precise dates and named individuals. Furthermore, social and political doctrines of a subversive character entered into religious schemes additional to their theologically heretical content. Thus the famous inquisitor Bernard Gui, writing about heretical offshoots of the Spiritual Franciscans at the beginning of the fourteenth century, summarized their views as follows.[17] For them the rule of St Francis was as unchangeable as the Gospels. In addition to the 'carnal' church of Rome there was a 'spiritual' church, which they represented. At the end of the sixth age of the world—in which the world was at that moment—Christ would reject the carnal church. Antichrist would at this time persecute all the religious orders, so that only one-third of the Franciscan Order out of all of them would survive. From this surviving rump about a dozen poor and evangelical men-of-the-spirit would found the spiritual church of the seventh and final stage. Antichrist would die and the whole world would become good and benign. All goods would be held in common, all men would love one another under one shepherd. This golden age would last one hundred years, but through a failure of love, evil would re-enter society, so that Christ would come and usher in the day of the Last Judgement.

Such was one among many of the historical schemes which

[16] G. Leff, *op. cit.*, discusses Joachim and his followers. But see especially M. Reeves, *Prophecy in the Middle Ages*, 1969.

[17] There is a translation of a substantial portion of Bernard Gui's *Pratica inquisitionis heretice pravitatis* in W. L. Wakefield and A. P. Evans, *op. cit.*, pp 375–445. Cf., M. Reeves, *op. cit.*, p 25.

anticipated an age of the spirit before the Last Judgement. These schemes could be adapted to varying political and social ambitions, ranging from the revolutionary passions of outcast heretics to the calculated writings of literati making propaganda for the French or German monarchs, whom they cast in the role of the last Angelic Emperor.[18] It is the former which are our concern, and we shall examine one movement which shows the earliest influence of Joachite thinking on social discontents.

Northern Italy, which had seen the earliest emergence of the rural communal movement in the eleventh and twelfth centuries, was an area riven with social conflicts by the end of the thirteenth century. The dominating political force was the urban commune, sometimes ruled by a conciliar regime, sometimes by a despot, but always in the interest of an oligarchy composed of an upper class of merchants and land-owners from the city *contado*, the rural area under its jurisdiction. The communes had for the most part taken over the independent feudal jurisdictions of the old nobility over the villages, while the nobles had become part of the communes' ruling class. Villages became bound to the urban economies as suppliers of foodstuffs, as suppliers of labour for urban industry, as contributors to communal taxes, and as payers of rent to city dwellers. As we have seen, at Origgio, village communities contained many poor families. Common rights would be transformed into properties at the disposal of the ruling groups in the villages who leased them to the highest bidders.[19] It is not surprising that in these circumstances alternative ideologies to those of the rulers should find many adherents from Catharist dualism to Waldensian evangelicalism, even including in the 1280s a female Messiah.

One of these movements was founded in Parma in about 1260 by an illiterate popular preacher named Gerard Sega-

[18] One such was Jean de Roquetaillade, a Franciscan and a papal prisoner at Avignon in 1356. He forecast that the king of France would be chosen Roman emperor and would rule the world. N. Cohn, in his important book, *The Pursuit of the Millennium*, 1970, p 96, refers to Jean's *Vade mecum in tribulatione* as a 'vehicle for the new social radicalism'. It was hardly new or radical. See also J. Bignami-Odier, *Etudes sur Jean de Roque-taillade*, 1952.

[19] See above, pp. 78–9.

relli, whose followers called themselves Apostles.[20] Segarelli in starting his movement had no wish to found an order, or to exercise authority. And so, lacking discipline in a hostile world, the movement soon disintegrated in spite of a popular response to its preachers. Elements of it did continue to exist in the heretical underground, as witnesses in a major trial of followers of the movement testified at Trento in 1332. Their continuing success was apparently due to a broad social basis of support, not only in the Vercelli and Novara dioceses where they made their last stand, but in the towns and country districts of Brescia, Novara, Bergamo, Trento and Modena. While the majority of supporters were artisans, workers and peasants from the mountain and the plain (and amongst these, as in other heretical sects, a high proportion of women), there were also representatives of what we should now call the intelligentsia. Fra Dolcino, the outstanding leader of the Apostles before their military defeat at the hands of the Bishop of Vercelli and his crusading army in 1307, was the son of a priest; it was the rector of Serravalle who was punished by the Inquisition for sheltering Dolcino and his followers in 1304; a priest from Ticino, a canon, and some nuns, were accused at Trento in 1332, as were a surgeon and an apothecary.

Clearly, the movement was not 'pure' in either the religious or the social sense. Those who followed Dolcino were not all devoted to the anticipation of the *ecclesia renovata*, nor to the achievement of justice for the oppressed. Elements of feudal banditry by landowners like the Biandrate, who had been reduced to impotence by the communal governments of Novara and Vercelli, had become confused with the heretical underground of Patarins and Cathars (*Gazzari*) before the arrival of the Apostles. The situation was further complicated by struggles between the Guelf and Ghibelline political factions, not only in Novara and Vercelli, but also in Milan.

[20] For the Apostles and Fra Dolcino, see, in addition to works already mentioned by G. Leff and M. Reeves, F. Tocco, 'Gli Apostoli e Fra Dolcino', *Archivio Storico Italiano*, 1897; E. Anagnini, *Dolcino e il movimento ereticale all' inizo del trecento*, 1964; S. D. Skaskin, *Le condizioni storiche della rivolta di Dolcino*, 1955 (Soviet Delegation Reports to the Xth International Congress of Historical Sciences). Bernard Gui wrote about Dolcino: see W. L. Wakefield and A. P. Evans, *loc. cit.*, and an anonymous writer wrote the short history which is the chief evidence, 'Historia fratris Dulcini heresiarche', in A. Segarizzi, *Rerum Italicarum Scriptores*, IX, v, 1907.

Furthermore, the rural communes of the Valsesia had been in revolt during the whole of the thirteenth century, first against the territorial nobles, and then against the urban communes. It is not surprising that in this welter of conflicting interests, Dolcino and his Apostles should have made initial headway. What is surprising is that his following of more than 1,400 men and women should have remained sufficiently united for three years to fight a destructive battle in the foothills of the Alps against the Bishop of Vercelli, the urban communes and the nobility. In the end they were defeated partly because to survive they had to become organized for spoliation themselves and so lose the support of the peasant communes such as those of Gattinara and Serravalle where initially they had been favourably received.

One of the most important reasons for firm organization and survival against considerable odds must have been the systems of belief which inspired them. These have come down to us through the writings of inquisitors rather than from authentic statements of the Apostles themselves; but by this time the inquisitors had a quite considerable experience in unravelling the threads of various heresies, and many of them seem to have reported with reasonable accuracy. After all, they did not need at all to distort the views of the heretics in order to justify their condemnation. The beliefs of Dolcino and his Apostles are therefore fairly well known to us. They consist of a simplified, in some ways rationalized, restatement of the main millenarian themes of the Joachites.

The rational element lies in the recognition by Dolcino of the positive and necessary elements in preceding and superseded ages of human history. According to him, the first age, that of the Old Testament, contained not only the virtues associated with the patriarchs and the prophets, but also the seeds of its decline in the institutions of marriage and private property. For this reason the second age had to be initiated by the Redemption of the world by Jesus Christ. But the purity of this age had ended with Pope Sylvester and the Emperor Constantine when, in order to win converts from paganism, it had been necessary to dilute the principles and the spirit of the primitive church. The third age saw succeeding attempts, through monasticism, to renovate the church and the world. But both Benedict and Francis failed. It was to be the task of the Apostles to initiate the fourth age. Antichrist would follow, be overthrown, and then the church would return to its apostolic origins. The details of the initiation of the fourth age were directly related to the current political situation. There would be a good pope and two bad popes. The good pope was Celestine V, the hermit who had already been elected as pope and who had been deposed in 1294 as a consequence of political manoeuvres in Rome. The first bad pope was Boniface VIII, who was not only bad enough in terms of the critique made of the state of the church by contemporary heretics, but also died in suitably degraded circumstances in 1303, in time, that is, to give point to the remainder of the prophecy. This was that after the death of another bad pope, a good, last emperor would arise, namely, Frederick of the Aragonese House of Sicily, who would kill the cardinals, the secular clergy and most of the religious orders. He would then establish an Angelic Pope chosen by God. Dolcino and all spiritual men would reign over a society in which private wealth was to be eschewed, but (a significant departure from Franciscan doctrine) in which there would be no mendicancy.

Dolcino brought millenarian prophecy into an immediate relationship with the contemporary political situation, but in a posture of complete opposition to existing social and ecclesiastical hierarchies. In the only way possible for a leader of that period—in other words, in religious terms—he was a revolutionary. But even the tortured world of northern Italy was not ready for that sort of revolution. So Dolcino and his army were overcome by armed force, and in 1307 Dolcino, together with his wife, Margarita, and other leaders of the movement, were handed over by the Inquisition to the secular authorities, subjected to prolonged torture in the streets of Vercelli, and burnt, without recanting.

The Pastoureaux and the Apostles link the mass movements of the twelfth and thirteenth centuries in which political and social aims were not openly expressed or even perhaps consciously felt, with the mass movements of the late middle ages whose declared aims were often explicitly social and political.

Of these movements, we are here concerned only with those of the countryside, arising from the discontent of peasants. This does not mean that we can ignore the involvement of other social groups, including the artisans. We can, however, leave on one side struggles whose theatre of action was purely urban, except in so far as they became involved with peasant movements.

Nor must we assume that small-scale rebellions on a village scale against local oppression ceased. These continued, in England, for example, until and for several decades after the revolt of 1381.[21] In the largely feudal agrarian kingdom of Naples during the reign of Robert I (1309–43) there were very many cases of village riots and rebellions against unjust tax assessment, increased demands for services and the sheer oppression arising from a breakdown not merely in law enforcement but in the whole social order. These were brought to light by the historian Romolo Caggese in his work on the life and times of Robert of Anjou, written in 1921 on the basis of a detailed analysis of the registers of the kingdom which have since been destroyed.[22] Had Caggese not been as interested in these aspects of the social life of southern Italy as he was in the king's career, this whole phase of peasant rebellion would have been lost to us. This illustrates how our knowledge of peasant movements depends on the awareness of the historian that such movements were worth tracking down, as well as on the survival of documentary evidence.

In the Neapolitan kingdom we find such frequent clashes that one almost suspects something of a continuous Jacquerie, rather than a maintenance of traditional relationships punctuated by occasional rebellions, as was probably the case in England. Each clash was precipitated by a particular issue, such as the exclusion by the nobles of peasant communities from the local pastures. The predominantly violent turn of life, in which we find even the Bishop of Vico organizing bandit attacks on pilgrims and merchants, inevitably affected the lord–peasant relationships. Hence, in 1310, we find armed

[21] R. H. Hilton, 'Peasant Movements in England before 1381' in E. Carus-Wilson, ed., *Essays in Economic History*, II, 1962.

[22] R. Caggese, *Roberto d'Angio e suoi tempi*, I, 1921. The following cases were extracted by Caggese from the registers of the Neapolitan kingdom for chap. 3, 'Classi e conflitti sociali'.

men uprooting the Abbot of Montevergine's boundary mark and occupying his land in Mercogliano, and the occupation in 1313 by peasants near Barletta of the pastures of the religious of S. Maria dei Teutonici. Then there is the occupation by armed peasants of the lands of nobles in Monticello, Abruzzo, during the course of which four nobles were killed.

Particularly interesting is the rising in 1318 of the people of the *borgo* of Castroprignano against their lord, because of its similarity to the localized conflicts found in northern Europe, including England. The Baron of Castroprignano complained to the king that his tenants refused to pay their due services and tribute, that they had attacked him, his family and his retainers in person, and had killed his bailiff. The tenants collected funds to finance a legal action against him in the royal courts. Fortunately, another complaint, presenting the situation from the point of view of the peasant community (*università*), is also recorded. According to the peasants, the lord for ten years had been exacting an annual monetary tribute of eleven to thirteen ounces of gold. He had forced his tenants to carry lime, stone and water for the repair of his castle and his mills. He had appropriated hay and straw and other materials from them without payment. The baron had controlled the sales of the peasants' produce, demanding first refusal for himself (presumably at lower than the market rate). Not only serfs, but all the tenants of the baron, were forbidden to enter holy orders without permission and the payment of a fine. Rights of hospitality for the baron and his retainers including the provision of bed-clothes and beds had been claimed. He appropriated the best land for his own demesne, even if it was state property. In short, the peasants complained that conditions were so bad that many of them were obliged to flee their native village.

There is no record of the outcome of the Castroprignano suit, and no means by which the accusations of the two sides could be tested, but the issues involved are familiar. The same conditions occurred in other parts of the Neapolitan kingdom and in other parts of Europe. One suspects that research both in local archives and the judicial records of the late medieval states would bring to light many more issues of this sort, continuing as long as the seigneurial regime was to last.

Now we must continue to consider the mass movements for which these local actions were a necessary and continuing preparation. Here perhaps there is not the same problem of evidence. Mass movements by their nature impinged on the consciousness of contemporary writers—most of them clerical or monastic chroniclers. Even those historians whose interests lie in high-level political and constitutional developments cannot ignore them as they have tended to ignore the village movements. The European peasant risings of the late middle ages, and especially of the fourteenth century, therefore, have become part of the staple diet of the student of history— a 'subject' in its own right, like the development of representative institutions, or the elaboration of governmental machinery. Unfortunately, the historians' natural tendency has been to consider the risings as a succession of unique episodes, or more recently, as particular manifestations of problems specific to late medieval society.[23] These are legitimate approaches, but it is also possible to consider them, together with the early medieval (and many modern) movements, in terms of the common problems which they present to the analyst of peasant societies.

The best known of the late medieval peasant rebellions are: the revolt in maritime Flanders 1323–7; the Jacquerie in the Paris region in 1358; the Tuchin movement in central France, from the 1360s to the end of the fourteenth century; the English rising of 1381; and the wars of the *remensas* in Catalonia during the 1460s and the 1480s. This is not an exhaustive list. Other specifically peasant movements on a smaller scale included the strike of the vineyard workers of the Auxerrois in the 1390s;[24] and, more difficult to evaluate, movements involving peasants, in which the peasants might have formed the majority of participants, but which aimed at goals other than theirs or theirs specifically. The peasants might be full participants, or they might be being used by others for their own purposes.

The Taborite movement in Bohemia (the militant wing of the national Hussite movement against German and papal domination) was clearly to a considerable degree a peasant

[23] See above, p 12.
[24] M. Mollat and P. Wolff, *Ongles bleus, Jacques et Ciompi*, 1970, pp 244–7.

one in its composition and there were millenarian elements in its religious outlook, but it was led by gentry and clerics and there was a considerable artisan element. It hardly aimed, then, to fulfil specifically peasant demands. Peasants also participated in the risings in various parts of England in 1450, of which the most important was that in Kent led by Jack Cade, but their motivation was to such a degree political, and even dynastic, that there is some doubt as to whether they can be designated as peasant movements. In some ways they more resemble the provincial risings in parts of England in the 1530s which were directed against real or imagined oppression by the government, and to a considerable extent led by the local gentry.

What then are the problems posed by peasant movements, and particularly by the large-scale movements of the later middle ages? We should remember the basic tensions in a society where peasants were the majority of the basic producers, but the course of each movement must be investigated separately. And although a mere narrative history of events will not in itself throw much light on the fundamentals of the movements, such a narrative history must be established in order to discover the existence (or otherwise) of a common pattern in the sequence of events. Emerging, too, from an examination of the sequence of events must come some notion of the organization of the movements, and of the degree to which they either arose spontaneously, or were carefully planned by groups or individual organizers. This brings us to the vital question of the social and intellectual origins of the leaders of the movements—a problem which once answered necessarily involves the allied problems of the social composition of the participating masses. These considerations will lead us to the problem of the ideas guiding the various elements involved; this is by no means the same problem as that of the immediate or long-term goals, which also need scrutiny.

Finally some assessment of the historical consequences must be undertaken, not simply in terms of success or failure in the realization of explicitly stated goals, but also in terms of such changes of direction in the history of society which peasant movements may effect. An examination of the major

European movements in terms of the problems thus classified could in turn be used to look afresh at the history of the English rising of 1381—one of the most interesting and significant as well as the best documented of all medieval peasant rebellions.[25]

It is, of course, insufficient to prove that peasants and landowners had incompatible interests in the division of the social product, and that peasants therefore had a propensity to withhold rents and services and come into juridical or even political conflict with their lords. The fact is that the traditional social relationships between peasant and lord in varying forms persisted in different parts of Europe, probably from the bronze age until the eighteenth or nineteenth century. Something more than the natural antagonism between an exploiting and exploited class must therefore have precipitated movements which often seemed to the participants on both sides a break in the 'natural order' of things; this phrase gives us a clue to the outbreak of many of the more serious movements.

Peasants, even more than their lords, tended to cling to custom, even when, without knowing it, they were constantly seeking to mould custom to suit their own interests. Günther Franz, in his history of the peasants' war in Germany at the beginning of the sixteenth century, noticed that (at any rate to begin with) rebellious peasants saw themselves as defending 'the old law'.[26] And so it was innovation by the lords which (in peasant eyes) seemed to justify their own renunciation of their humble role in the social hierarchy. It was the imposition of the indemnity tax by the king of France to be collected by the officials of the Count of Flanders (who should have been their protector) which pushed the self-assertive, un-

---

[25] The principal general works on which the following comparative analysis is based are as follows: H. Pirenne, *Histoire de Belgique*, II, 1908; id., *Le soulèvement de la Flandre maritime, 1323–8*, 1900; S. Luce, *Histoire de la Jacquerie*, 1894; J. Flammermont, 'La Jacquerie en Beauvaisis', *Revue Historique*, 1879; G. Fourquin, *Les campagnes de la région parisienne à la fin du moyen-âge*, 1964; J. d'Avout, *Le meurtre d'Etienne Marcel*, 1960; M. Boudet, *La Jacquerie des Tuchins, 1363–84*, 1895; J. Vicens Vives, *Historia de los Remensas*, 1945; P. Vilar, 'Le déclin catalan au bas moyen-âge', *Estudios de Historia Moderna*, 1956–9; J. Vicens Vives, ed., *Historia social y económica de España y America*, II, 1957.

[26] G. Franz, *Der deutsche Bauernkrieg*, 1933 and 1968.

servile peasants and artisans in the maritime districts of Flanders into rebellion; it was the requisitions for the victualling of the castles of the nobility in the region of Paris, done at the expense of the peasants in the surrounding villages, which provoked the Jacquerie in 1358; it was the insolent taxation imposed by the king's lieutenant, the Duke of Berry, on his subjects in central France, when he was unable to protect them from the English and their hired *routiers*, which began the equally serious, though less well-known, Jacquerie of the Tuchins; and it was the extra demands by the lords of Catalonia for the so-called *malos usos*, or 'evil customs', which precipitated the long war of the *remensas*, the servile peasants.

In none of these cases can it be supposed that the breach of customary expectations was the only cause of the outbreak. There were important, indeed essential, predisposing factors. The resistance to the collection of the indemnity tax in Flanders in 1323 was not a sudden decision on the part of a normally passive population. This population was composed for the most part of descendants of free settlers in the coastal districts. Many of them were quite poor, although their leaders were among the richest of the peasants of the district, as is shown in the enumeration of the lands and goods of the dead after the defeat of the rising in 1327 at the battle of Cassel. Many of the peasants were involved in the textile trade, which was already spreading from town to country. Their obligations to their lords were mainly acquitted in money rent, and they were of free status, and made up a strong quasi-communal element in the organization of local government. Although presided over by the Count of Flanders' bailiff (usually a noble), the local courts were composed of jurors, *keuriers* or *échevins*, many of whom were peasants. And when the revolt reached fever pitch at the beginning of 1325, the peasants took over the existing organization and put their own captains in place of the count's bailiffs. Above all, there had existed since the beginning of the century a strong sentiment of hostility to the French-speaking nobility and their patrician allies among the great merchants of the towns. They had, for these reasons, supported the Count of Flanders so long as he resisted his suzerain, the King of France. No doubt they remembered the battle of Courtrai in 1302, when peasants and weavers defeated the mounted knights of France, but in spite of which they had had imposed upon them by the count's capitulation at Athis (1304) the first heavy indemnity payment to the French crown.

The general conditions in the area to the north, north-east and south of Paris, in the spring of 1358, were even more likely than those in maritime Flanders to enable any extra oppression to spark off a rebellion. For a year, the hired soldiers of the French and English, now under truce, had been living off the countryside, and the peasants could no longer distinguish between their 'own' and the enemy's supporters. The situation was further complicated by the entry into the game of Charles, King of Navarre, a possible pretender to the French throne, whose troops were as likely to be fighting for the English or for themselves, as for the Regent of France, the king being in prison in England. Furthermore, from March 1358, there had been civil war between the regent and his supporters, on the one hand, and a reforming party, on the other, led by Etienne Marcel, provost of the merchants of Paris.

The nobility was discredited, and unable to perform its traditional function of defending the other orders. Its landed income was insufficient, for rents were low; and the price of grain was low, while wages and other costs were high. Many of the male members of the nobility had to be ransomed. Hence, the nobles and their men-at-arms in the castles of the Île de France, were as likely to pillage and slay the local peasants as were the bands led by such foreign captains as the Englishman James Pipe, lieutenant of the King of Navarre, who was operating south of Paris. While the traditional explanation of the Jacquerie as a revolt against misery contains an element of truth, it is insufficient. Included in the rebellious area were prosperous villages, especially north of Paris, where exasperation at taxation and requisition, and disillusion with the collapse of the traditional social order, were combined with the economic grievances of the normally well-to-do cereal farmers who were unable to get a good price for their product. At the same time, the impoverished and badly harassed area to the south-west of the city—precisely where one would expect an explosion of pure misery—was virtually untouched by the rebellion.

A combination of pillaging by bands of soldiers, and heavy, even illegal, taxation was also responsible for the further and very different Jacquerie in the France of the Hundred Years' War—the counter-brigandage of the Tuchins. If the Jacquerie of 1358 in Paris gives the appearance (even if illusory) of being a short, sharp and elemental protest against miserable conditions, the Tuchins are the prototype of a very different form of poor people's protest, one which we have come to recognize as 'social banditry'. We find here no rising *en masse* of an outraged peasant population, but a cunning adoption by the mountain population of Auvergne, both the suburban artisans of towns like St Flour and the peasants of the district, of the pillaging habits of their erstwhile oppressors. From the early 1360s until the middle of the 1380s, the Tuchins troubled the authorities, while the Jacques around Paris were crushed after only two weeks by the noble companies under the command of the King of Navarre. All the same, the immediate causes were the same for both Jacqueries—the pillage of the military companies, and government taxation.

One of the most sustained of peasant wars was that of the Catalan *remensas*, or servile peasants, in the fifteenth century. Catalonia, compared with most other parts of Spain, was heavily seigneurialized, and the majority of peasants were unfree. Apart from the various rents and services which they owed to their lords, they were particularly restricted in their freedom of movement, and these restrictions had been strengthened from the thirteenth century—the lords' response to emigration southwards to colonize the newly conquered lands and to the growing cities. After the Black Death, there was a further seigneurial reaction, prompted by the fall in landed revenues, when extra rents in kind were demanded, and boon services were made compulsory.

All those peasants who were already forbidden to leave their holdings except on payment of a heavy redemption, the *remensas*, were now reckoned automatically liable to what had become known as the 'five evil customs' (*malos usos*). These were: *intestia*, a death duty of one-third of movables payable in case of intestacy; *exorquia*, another death duty; *cuguicia*, one-third or one-half of movables payable in case of a wife's adultery; *arsina*, a fine paid if the farm caught fire accidentally; and *firma d'espoli violenta*, a fine aimed at restricting the raising of a mortgage. These obligations were not new in the fifteenth century, but they had not been universally applicable. It was their generalization and imposition on all peasants liable to *remensas* and the fear of free tenants that they would spread to them which united the Catalan rural population against their lords. This resentment arose as much because these obligations were obvious earmarks of personal servility as because they were economically burdensome. But the search for freedom was, it seems, also exacerbated by a conflict with the lords over abandoned holdings (*casos ronecs*). The question was whether these should be shared among surviving tenants at low rents, or absorbed into demesne or let on lease on short terms at high rents.

Small-scale local revolts against the seigneurial reaction had already begun by the late 1380s, and continued into the early part of the fifteenth century. The *remensas* attempted to have the *malos usos* abolished by the crown, and offered enormous sums for their redemption. Their abolition was accepted by Alphonso V in 1455, under peasant pressure, and it was the refusal of the nobles, led by the Bishop of Gerona and the patricians of Barcelona, which precipitated the war of 1462. In this war the reactionary nobility and the urban patricians found themselves fighting not only the peasants but the king. A renewal of the war in 1483 was due entirely to an attempt by the nobility and the patricians to put the clock back to the pre-1455 situation, but social tensions became critical as a result also of the prolonged crisis of Catalonia's declining economy.

It will be seen that the immediate causes for some of the most serious of the mass movements were actions by landowners or governments, or both together, which altered the customary relationships or disappointed normal expectations, to the detriment of the peasant class as a whole, rich and poor. Although a heavy tax, or a requisition order, or the reversal of a concession might not in itself precipitate a rising, it might do so in the context of the strained social relationships which we find in each of the areas we have considered. This strain is normally seen by the peasants from an apparently conservative standpoint. They cannot accept the abandonment of traditional roles by any one of the orders of the society—whose basic structure they do not, to begin with, challenge. This seems always to be the most important factor, and the significance of precipitating causes (taxes, for example) is that, as they affect all, they unify all—and focus existing resentments.

If we can see common features in the causation of these movements, contrasts rather than similarities appear when we look at the pattern of events and the form of the struggle. The most obvious contrast is the duration of the rebellions. The rising which has bequeathed to history that most familiar name, the Jacquerie, and the supposedly typical characteristics of peasant rebellion—namely, extreme violence and a hatred of the nobility—was in fact the shortest and worst-organized. The first of the recorded conflicts between peasants and the plundering brigands, the nobles, was at St Leu d'Esserent, near Senlis, on 28 May 1358, though there were probably almost simultaneous outbreaks further west. The destruction of the main peasant army under Guillaume Cale by the King of Navarre near Mello occurred on 10 June, and the peasants who were helping the Parisians in their siege of the royalist nobles in the fortress at Meaux were defeated and slaughtered on the following day. The Jacquerie began and was militarily defeated in a fortnight.

On the other hand, the armed revolt of the peasants of maritime Flanders which began in 1323 did not end until June 1328, when the King of France and the Flemish nobility defeated the peasants and artisans at Cassel. The Tuchins began their independent operations as groups of 'social bandits' in the mountains of Auvergne in 1363 and were not destroyed as a social force until the summer of 1384. Even after their defeat at Mentières, sporadic bands were operating until the general amnesty of 1381, and there was a brief revival in the early fifteenth century. The struggle of the *remensas* was even longer lived, if we count the earliest sporadic outbreaks as occurring from 1388. The mass campaigns lasted from 1462 until 1471, and from 1484 until 1486—

though there is some difficulty here in separating the peasant war for the abolition of the *malos usos* from the civil war which involved the crown, the nobility and the bourgeoisie.

It must be due partly to a failure in organization when a mass peasant movement is as quickly suppressed as the Jacquerie: a failure to organize according to the needs of the situation, the known strength of the enemy and the reliability of the allies. The Jacques gathered in village groups and operated separately. Owing to the surprise experienced by the nobles at this sudden insubordination, the rebels, with some assistance from the Parisians, managed to destroy a considerable number of castles, along with the records which the owners kept of the peasants' obligations to them. In common with other rural risings, the example of rebellion rapidly spread by word of mouth from village to village, without the separate bands concerting a common policy. Eventually, their most experienced captain, Guillaume Cale, managed to get together a force of several thousands; but this numerical strength gave an illusion of power which Cale tried to dispel. Militarily inexperienced, the fact that they had come together to present a single target for the knights and men-at-arms under Charles of Navarre led to their downfall. Special methods of fighting were needed for peasants to defeat armed horsemen in pitched battle, as the Taborites with their battle-wagons made from farm carts were to show after 1420 in Bohemia.[27] Even the successors of the victors of Courtrai were defeated in the end by an army of French chivalry at Cassel, although they had, it seems, succeeded for a time in organizing themselves on the basis of the existing administrative framework of the *ambachten* or castleries.

The most successful peasant military organization (if we put on one side the Hussite armies as not being the product of a specifically peasant movement) was undoubtedly that of the *remensas*. They had already begun to meet in assemblies in the 1440s, in order to discuss the redemption of the *malos usos*, and when the peasant army was eventually organized in the 1460s, their leader Francisco Verntallat did so by recruiting one man from every three households. The removal at the end of the first *remensa* war of peasant garrisons

[27] F. J. Heyman, *Jan Žižka and the Hussite Revolution*, 1955, p 98.

from castles shows that they had learnt the importance of
fortification, and a later royal veto, on the eve of the second
war, on peasants or artisans having riding horses, shows that
they must have learnt, too, this other aspect of medieval
armed combat. Above all, the peasant army rested on the
basis of sworn association, the *sacramental*, created in the
peasant assemblies.

This, then, was one way of organizing: the creation of a
military force based on a form of political and social institution, the village or district assembly. It was more successful
in Catalonia than in maritime Flanders; but the Tuchins show
that it was not the only way in which peasants and plebeians
could organize to harass the authorities. Here we return to
the more elemental form of organization in small bands, but
in the case of the Tuchins there was no attempt to engage in
head-on conflict with the military forces of the nobility or the
crown. Continuing with their ordinary agricultural or artisan
occupations in village or suburb, these bands of twenty or
thirty men, or occasionally more—associates, bound together
by terrible oaths—organized themselves for the pillage of livestock, valuables or cash, and for the capture of churchmen,
gentry or merchants for the purposes of ransom. In Auvergne,
between the 1360s and the 1380s, the habitual prey of the
Tuchins were the English or Gascon *routiers*, who were des-
poilers of the countryside but whose booty was then looted by
the Tuchins like wolves drawn to the sheepfold.

The Tuchins were able to play an intricate political game.
Local authorities, such as the consuls of St Flour, made truces
·with the English in order to be left at peace, while the Tuchins
robbed the English, and so embroiled the local notables whom
the English suspected of breaking the truce. In the eyes of the
royal government, however, such truces were illegal, and the
peasant and artisan brigands came almost to appear—quite
unintentionally as far as they were concerned—as patriots.
The Tuchins kept going as long as conditions favoured them,
that is, while disorder created by the operations of the *routiers*
and general hostility among peasants and town artisans to the
nobles and to the authorities, resulting from the failure to
defend them from the Anglo-Gascons and from the excessive
taxation of the king's lieutenant, lasted. When relative peace

and stability returned, the Tuchins' bands could only prey on the mass of the peasantry, so losing their support.

The Tuchins were not all peasants. Artisans from the suburbs of St Flour and elsewhere were also involved. Furthermore, the leaders of the bands were often members of the nobility. Even so, it is by no means the case that we should not examine the Tuchinat as a peasant movement. For there were, in fact, very few 'pure' peasant movements, at any rate on a mass scale, in the sense that the participants and leaders were exclusively of peasant origin. The number of nobles in the leadership of the Tuchins is not difficult to explain. In the first place, they were often outcasts from their own class, sometimes using the Tuchins only for their own purposes, but used by the Tuchins in turn, who found it convenient to employ the military skills of the class which still regarded itself, by profession as well as status, primarily as a warrior class.

Thus, Mignot de Cardaillac, a Tuchin leader in the Paulhac region in the 1360s, was a bastard of a prominent noble family involved in disputes with other nobles over succession to property. Pierre de Brugère (or de Brès), a Tuchin leader during the 1380s, was connected by family ties with many leading families of Auvergne and Languedoc, and probably joined the Tuchins after robbing his relative, the Bishop of Albi, and perhaps because of domestic troubles when his squire became his wife's lover. After Pierre was killed, other gentry leaders appeared, such as the Lord of Pertus and Jean de Dienne. At the fag-end of the Tuchin movement, Jean de Chalus, returning to Auvergne from Agincourt in 1415, was captured by a band of Tuchins and forced to join them, to take part in their assemblies and to bind himself to them by swearing an oath.

The leadership of peasant bands by members of the nobility, even for quite specifically peasant objectives, was not as rare as one might imagine. Even in a movement as frankly hostile to the nobility as a class as the Jacquerie of 1358, some nobles, as well as bourgeois, were engaged on the side of the peasants. The three or four whose names we know from letters of pardon issued afterwards by the king, naturally sought to excuse themselves, alleging that they had been forced to become leaders of the peasants' bands. This may, indeed, have been true, though we can never know what private or political rancours might have determined an individual to abandon his apparent class interest. The interest of the peasants in securing the leadership of locally prominent individuals is more explicable. In the case of the Montmorency district, we even find them asking Simon de Bernes, provost and captain of the county of Beaumont, for permission to choose a leader, a choice which fell on Jacques de Chennevières, who afterwards pretended to have accepted against his wishes and to have attempted to moderate the peasants' violence. As we have already suggested, some peasants may have been conscious of their lack of military expertise. The question also arises as to what extent the concept of the gentry as the natural leaders of the peasants still persisted, even when the conflict of interest between the two classes seemed absolute.

It will not do to overemphasize the part played by gentry in the leadership of peasants' movements. There is the abundant evidence from the earlier period of peasant leadership of small-scale movements which we have already examined, and this source of leaders by no means dried up. Lack of contrary indication would suggest that Guillaume Cale of Mello must have been a well-to-do peasant, and Clais Zannekin, who began to play a leading role in the rising of maritime Flanders from 1324, appears as one of the better-off peasants with a holding of between thirty-five and forty acres of arable land, although it has been suggested that he had property in Bruges. In addition, was not Francisco Verntallat really a peasant, in spite of his poor *hidalgo* ancestors on one side of the family, and his promotion and enrichment by the king after the end of the first war of the *remensas?*[28] And the more radical Père Jean Sala likewise? The same kind of background was probably true of most of the minor leaders in all of the movements. Their names tend not to be recorded. Fewer but more exceptional individuals are mentioned by chroniclers or appear in the records precisely because their participation was unexpected.

[28] Joaquim de Camps i Arboix, *Verntallat, cabdill dels Remences*, 1955, p 20.

A frequently noticed source of outside leaders of peasant and other plebeian movements of the middle ages is the clergy, particularly the lesser clergy. Various explanations are given, such as that which states that the participating clerics may have been of peasant origin, and that their lowly position at the bottom of the ecclesiastical hierarchy made them resentful of the existing social order, and that, further, they were influenced by the radical, egalitarian element in the Christian tradition. The lesser clergy, as we have seen, often occupied an important position of leadership in the people's crusades and in heretical movements with peasant and artisan followings. On the whole, the clerics' presence is most frequent where movements have aims going well beyond the satisfaction of immediate social and political demands or the expression of immediate resentment of social oppression. Thus, even if the fight of the Apostles in northern Italy at the beginning of the fourteenth century had any of the characteristics of a peasant movement, by reason of its class composition, its aims were apocalyptic and were inevitably articulated by a man with a clerical background. Similarly, the extreme Taborites or Pikarts around the year 1420 in Bohemia—whatever the temporary practice of a sort of 'war communism' might have implied about their social views— were also apocalyptic visionaries, and their leaders tended to be priests, like the Moravian, Martin Huska. Similarly the views of the Taborite centre, of Waldensian inspiration, were articulated by priests such as Jan Zelivsky.[29]

Those movements, however, which we have taken to be typical, where not only was the mass of participants drawn from the peasantry, but where they were reacting against social pressures on them as peasants, and were seeking a peasant solution, had a remarkably weak priestly participation. The one important exception to this is to be found in England in 1381, and will be considered later in detail. Not only were there no priests in the leadership of the rebellion in maritime Flanders, but there is evidence of strong anti-clericalism. The refusal to pay tithes, for example, in the area of Ghent, shows a clear anti-clerical disposition, though this could have been compatible with a certain type of radical

[29] H. Kaminsky, *A History of the Hussite Revolution*, 1967.

clerical inspiration. But under the later leadership of Jacques Peyt, anti-clericalism sharpened. In November 1325 an interdict had been placed on Flanders, and Peyt and his successors had forced priests either to perform their office or to emigrate. Peyt was said to have wished to do away with all priests. Some evidence of a minor participation by a few clerics in the Jacquerie of 1358 can be shown, but there is no leadership. The Tuchins not only had no leaders from the clerical order, but at times shows signs of anti-clericalism. In the 1380s, for instance, clerics in Tuchin-dominated areas thought it prudent to disguise themselves as laymen (in areas of military operations it was usually the other way round); a Trinitarian friar so disguised was killed when he was captured.

Nor does the *remensas* movement reveal any clerical participation or direction. It is true that one of the earliest rebellious actions of some of the *remensas* was participation in the anti-Jewish pogroms of 1391, in which there was clerical direction and which assumed a social character unexpected by some of these clerical agitators.[30] *Remensas* were also involved in a jointly anti-semitic and anti-landowner action in Gerona in 1415. But the essential movement against the *malos usos* had no clerical or even religious inspiration. Indeed the historian of the movement, J. V. Vives, particularly noticed how little religion there was in its ideology. This, he discovered, was mainly of juridical inspiration, namely the idea that by natural law all men are free and have the right to be protected by the king against the nobles. It was the jurisconsult Thomas Mieres, not a cleric, who voiced these views.

We have emphasized that no mass peasant movement of the later middle ages was 'pure' in the sense of its being composed only of rebels drawn from the peasant class. A peasant community did not in any case consist only of agriculturalists, but also contained artisans, small traders and the like who were essential to its functioning. No rebels have been so well recorded as those of maritime Flanders, so far as their numbers, names and property are concerned. It is worth looking fairly closely, therefore, at the document which lists those who were

[30] P. Wolff, 'The 1391 pogrom in Spain: social crisis or not?' *P & P*, 1971.

killed at Cassel and those who escaped.[31] The lists were drawn up for the King of France by local investigators, since the king regarded himself as entitled to confiscate the belongings of those involved in *lèse-majesté* against him. The lists are not complete, because some victims were not counted and even complete areas seem to have been omitted—although it is known from other sources that they were involved. The movable goods of the victims are not normally counted, and this constitutes a serious loss for the historian since an enumeration of these would clearly indicate whether the person followed an occupation other than, or as well as, agriculture. Landed property of the slain is listed, but the list only includes hereditary holdings, omitting land held on lease. This probably underestimates, then, the landed holdings of a good many peasants. Finally, those who escaped death are listed by name only, and their property is not counted.

The information, even so, is considerable. The persons in the list came from 113 parishes or other places (including the towns of Furnes and Nieuport). There were 3,185 dead and 675 who escaped. The majority of the dead (who alone had their lands inventoried) possessed at least some land, but there was a significant number, namely, 891, who owned no land, though there are reasons for supposing that this number is exaggerated. In spite of this, it implies a substantial number of men who were not cultivating the land for their living, unless as agricultural labourers; and since the small scale of peasant farming in maritime Flanders does not allow us to assume much of an agricultural wage-labour force, these landless men must have included many artisans. But in addition to landless artisans there are clear indications that many artisans, as was common throughout medieval Europe outside the towns, had some agricultural land to work in addition to the practice of their industrial craft. Thus: a smith of Ysenberghe in the castlery of Furnes had a house and sixteen measures of land (rather more than sixteen acres); a carpenter from Lenseles in the same district had a house and seven measures; a fuller from Stavele in the same district had seventeen measures; a weaver from Ser-Wellems Chapel in the same district had three measures; a tiler of Nieuport had a

[31] H. Pirenne prints the lists in *Le soulèvement* . . .

house and thirteen measures outside the town; a weaver from Houtkerke in the castelry of Bergues had a house and three measures; a draper of Hondschoote in the same district had five quarters of land; a fuller from Hondschoote had one quarter; and a fuller from Bambeke in the same district had a house, a barn and six measures.

On the whole there are rather few occupational designations; but many persons whose occupation is not given may well have been craftsmen, for we know that Furnes, Hondschoote, Bergues, Nieuport and other parts of the maritime district were already considerably involved in the manufacture of textiles. Such manufacture was not of high-priced cloths, in which the now declining towns had specialized, but a rural industry producing cheap or moderately priced goods. So the peasants of maritime Flanders, in addition to having as allies the artisans of Bruges and Ypres—who also hated the Leliaerts (Francophile) urban patricians and landowning nobles—were probably mingled inextricably with rural artisans, side by side with whom they lived, suffered and plotted.

There is no similar information to the list of the dead at Cassel which would give us any clue about the social composition of the Jacques in 1358. Most of the chronicles refer to peasants alone, though that is not conclusive. For Froissart, for example, the 'villeins, small dark and very poorly armed' must have seemed simply an undifferentiated lower-class mass. Another chronicler, Jean de Venette, who was not unsympathetic to the peasant plight, writes only of peasants,[32] though the more official *Grandes Chroniques* refer to the presence of some rich men, including the bourgeois, in their assemblies. As we have seen, the letters of pardon mention the names of some members of gentry who had assumed by force or otherwise a position of leadership. Some craftsmen and clergy also appear in these *lettres de rémission*. Such documents must however always be regarded with some suspicion, since pardons in the middle ages were frequently obtained as an

[32] The important *Chronicle of Jean de Venette* has been translated into English by J. Birdsall and R. A. Newhall, 1953. Most English translations of Jean Froissart's *Chroniques* have the complete description of the events of the Jacquerie. See G. Brereton's edition in Penguin Classics, 1968.

insurance against accusations which might or might not be false. The rural rising, therefore, seems to have included, as one would expect, representatives of most elements of agrarian society, whether agricultural producers or not.

There were other allies, too, from outside the ranks of rural society, though these were at the best ambivalent in their attitude to the Jacques. Paris was in the hands of Etienne Marcel and his supporters. They were great merchants for the most part who were entirely without social sympathies for the peasants, and who were playing a game of high politics in which nobles such as Charles, King of Navarre, were their allies. But the mass of traders and artisans in Paris, caught up in Marcel's action against the Regent of France and his supporters, were hostile to nobles as such. Jean de Venette tells us that they suspected Charles of Navarre, precisely because he was a noble. He also tells that the burgesses of the small town of Meaux 'hated the nobles because of exactions and would gladly make war on them'. The contingent of Jacques was present at Meaux when the nobles in the fortress defeated their besiegers and in effect brought Marcel's whole movement to an end. The burgesses of Compiègne, however, would have nothing to do with the peasants and rejected an offer of negotiations by Guillaume Cale. They were excluded, too, from Senlis, though some of the inhabitants of Senlis came from behind their walls to help the peasants sack the castles of the nobles in the district around the town.

Marcel, who in spite of accusations by his enemies, certainly did not initiate or encourage the Jacquerie, was prepared to use them in his campaign to intimidate the members of the nobility in the region around Paris—just as he tried to mobilize on his side the still-powerful support of the Flemish towns. At least two companies of men-at-arms from Paris were sent to join the peasants in response to an appeal from Guillaume Cale, one to the north-east towards Senlis, another to the south. But having used peasants to destroy the castles of the Regent's supporters, the Parisian contingents gave them no further aid, and were careful not to become involved in the general peasant assault on the nobility as a class. Indeed, Etienne Marcel boasted that Paris provided a refuge for over one thousand noblemen and noblewomen who were in flight from peasant vengeance. The relationship between the Parisian bourgeoisie and the peasants was not even an uneasy class alliance based on a genuine if temporary coincidence of social and political interests, but was rather a situation in which the peasants were manipulated by the Parisians and then abandoned.

Political manipulation of this sort seems to have been absent in central France during the Tuchin period. The movement in any case was completely different in character from the other movements in which peasants were involved. Mass uprisings at moments of general political tension were susceptible of manipulation when the ruling class was politically divided and when the factions were looking for supporters. The Tuchinat as a form of social banditry had, to quote its principal historian, 'become acclimatized in the very habits of the people of the mountains'. Peasants and artisans who worked at their normal occupations by day, moved freely as members of brigand bands by night. They were almost powerful enough to become political manipulators themselves, though since they were in the nature of things uninterested in such manipulation, what they did was to bring to naught other people's manipulations, in particular local truces between urban authorities and the Anglo-Gascon *routiers*.

One among many examples of this kind of happening is the operation between December 1382 and February 1383 of a band of Tuchins from a place of ambush near Murat (Cantal). Led by a person originating from among the St Flour bourgeoisie known as La Borgha, the Tuchins specialized in pillaging the English to the embarrassment of the consuls of St Flour who had a truce with the English. But these consuls were also obliged to temporize with the Tuchins under La Borgha because they could rely not only on the support of other Tuchin bands but on the many covert supporters in the town itself. As far as class alliances are concerned, the special feature of the Tuchins is the way in which their form of social protest or better self-protection against feudal pillaging and fiscal oppression (which has been natural to peasants from medieval times until the twentieth century) was adopted by suburban craftsmen and petty traders. This aspect of the movement is not surprising. Even within the walled area of many towns in the south of France there were many agricultural workers; in the suburbs the line between peasants involved in some sort of by-occupation and artisans with small landed holdings would be difficult to draw.

From one aspect, the wars in which the Catalan *remensas* were involved in the fifteenth century might appear as a conflict between crown and nobility, such as was by no means uncommon in medieval states. But it was also a social struggle: the peasants to a considerable degree retained their separate identity in the organization of their own armed force, and in the pursuit of their own aims. They were a force sufficiently powerful to manipulate others as well as being manipulated themselves, and they achieved a certain success. It was almost entirely a rural movement. The element of class alliance in the countryside is found in the union between the unfree *remensas* and the poorer free tenants who feared the pressure of the great estate-owners; this is typified by the involvement of Verntallat, a descendant of free tenants on one side of the family and of lesser gentry on the other. The peasants had little or no urban support. The great bourgeois of Barcelona, as collective feudal lords of three baronial estates, were altogether solid politically with the landed nobility and the clergy. Even the *Busca*, the small trader and artisan opposition to the Barcelona patricians, was unexpectedly unsympathetic to the *remensas*. The peasants' only allies were the king and his officials who, whether or not their declared sympathy for the abolition of the *malos usos* was sincere, needed as much peasant support against the nobles as they could get, especially since some of the peasants of maritime areas were fighting for their lords.

In spite of the considerable differences between these late-medieval peasant movements, there was one prominent feature which they had in common: the emergence, among some of the participants, of a consciousness of class. It was, however, a negative class consciousness in that the definition of class which was involved was that of their enemies rather than of themselves: in other words, the nobility. Henri Pirenne, writing about the revolt of maritime Flanders in his introduction to the list of confiscations after Cassel, insisted on its social character. It was, he wrote, 'a class war between the peasants and the nobility'.[33] This anti-noble characteristic was to the fore already in 1323 in an attack on members of local courts, the *keuriers*, who were of noble or patrician origin. Under the leadership of Jacques Peyt, in 1326, after the re-imposition of an indemnity payable to the King of France at the so-called peace of Arques, this deep emotion developed into a terror directed against both the nobility and their supporters. The peasant rebels were said by the official chronicler of the counts of Flanders to have threatened the rich with death, saying to them: 'you love the nobles more than you do the commons from whom you live'.[34]

This conscious hostility towards the noble class was very prominent during the Jacquerie of 1358. Without any declaration of aims, its existence could be concluded from the fact that the objects of the peasants' attacks were exclusively knights, squires and ladies, along with the castles in which they lived. A recent historian, commenting on the fiscal and other pressures on the peasants which were particularly irksome after the battle of Poitiers, goes so far as to say that 'the quick irritation that Jacques Bonhomme experienced in the face of these exactions was nothing compared with his permanent rage against the nobles whom he blamed, as a whole, for not having fulfilled their duty of protection which tradition and mutual obligation demanded of them'.[35] Froissart, at the beginning of his account of the Jacquerie, reports a discussion among the peasants (no doubt imagined):

... one of them got up and said that the nobility of France, knights and squires, were disgracing and betraying the realm, and that it would be a good thing if they were all destroyed. At this they all shouted: 'He's right! He's right! Shame on any man who saves the gentry from being wiped out.'

And again Froissart says (somewhat illogically) that when the peasants were asked the reason for their violent actions, 'they replied that they did not know; it was because they saw others doing them that they copied them. They thought that by such means they could destroy all the nobles and gentry in the world, so that there would be no more of them.'[36]

---

[33] H. Pirenne, *Le Soulèvement* . . ., p xxxiii.   [34] *ibid.*, p xxvi, n. 2.
[35] J. d'Avout, *op. cit.*, p 191.
[36] J. Froissart, *Chronicles*, ed. Brereton, pp 151, 153.

Jean de Venette emphasizes the same element of class hatred:

> ... the peasants ... seeing that the nobles gave them no protection, but rather oppressed them as heavily as the enemy, rose and took arms against the nobles of France ... the number of peasants eager to extirpate the nobles and their wives and to destroy their manor houses grew until it was estimated at five thousand.[37]

The social bandit, as compared with the peasants engaged in mass risings, operated mostly with a less precise consciousness of his position of social antagonism to his opponents. Any bird was worth the plucking, and if he did not pluck his own kind it was because there was little or nothing to be had. All the same, awareness of social conflict was not altogether missing. The evidence for the greatest degree of class consciousness comes from the last major phase of Tuchin activity, that of the 1380s, when, according to the life of Charles VI in the St Denis chronicle, the terrible mutual oaths of the Tuchin bands included the promise never more to submit to taxation, but only to keep the ancient liberty of their country (*patrie antiquam servantes libertatem*).[38] The social bandit's chosen prey were men of the church, the nobles, and the merchants. One of their captains, the renegade noble, Pierre de Brugère, gave orders to his lieutenants that no-one with smooth uncalloused hands or who by gesture, clothing or speech showed courtliness or elegance should even be admitted to their company, but rather slain. Such remarks about the Tuchins come from a hostile writer, writing no doubt like Froissart from hearsay evidence. But even taking exaggeration into account, the element of conscious class antagonism which is suggested may well have been present.

The ferocity which, rightly or wrongly, was attributed to the French rebels by the aristocratic chroniclers does not appear in the Catalan wars unless we can glimpse it in the physical demonstrations by some of the *remensas* peasants at the turn of the fourteenth century, when in order to intimidate the landowners, and perhaps unwelcome lessees of the lapsed holdings, they dug ditches and put up crosses and other signs,

[37] *Chronicle*, ed. J. Birdsall and R. A. Newhall, p 76.
[38] M. Boudet, *op. cit.*, appendix III.

the *senyals mort*, threatening death. There may have been some diversion from possible class antagonism on the peasants' part by the attitude evinced by the monarchy from time to time, and expressed in its strongest terms perhaps by Queen Maria de Luna in letters to Pope Benedict XIII. In these letters she describes the peasants' servile obligations as 'evil, detestable, pestiferous, execrable, and abominable . . . against God and justice, perilous to the soul and leading to the infamy of the Catalan nation'.[39] Whether or not such strong words reached the peasants themselves and perhaps counteracted the impression of later more ambivalent royal attitudes to the conflict, the fact remains that the peasants from the beginning made a distinction between rents payable simply for the use of land, which many of them were prepared to pay, and dues which resulted from the special jurisdictional power of the nobles as feudal lords, which they rejected as being 'against the natural justice of the liberty of man'. In the last phase of the *remensas* war under the leadership of Sala, the most radical demanded the end of all rent and the establishment of absolute peasant property rights. All this implies a generally radical outlook with respect to the institutions which underpinned medieval society, but one without a specific commitment to the eradication of the nobility as a class.

The 'moderates' among the Catalan peasants negotiated a settlement by which not only the *malos usos* were to be abolished together with compensation to the lords, but serfdom and the lords' right to impose their will by force (*ius maletractandi*). Perhaps this settlement, like other half-way agreements, would never have been embodied in the *Sentencia Arbitral de Guadalupe* (1486), had it not been for the pressure of the extremists. The *remensas* became almost peasant-proprietors and for some time enjoyed a relative prosperity, compared with their contemporaries in Aragon and Castile. This success was unique and undoubtedly due to the social and economic crises of fifteenth-century Catalonia and to the need of the crown of Aragon for allies against the Catalan nobility and the patrician government of Barcelona. No other mass movement, with the possible exception of the English peasants after 1381,[40]

[39] J. Vicens Vives, ed., *Historia social* . . ., II, p 259.
[40] See below, p 231.

achieved a comparable success. We have seen that the Flemish peasants were bloodily defeated, and Flanders entered on a prolonged period of crisis. The peasants of northern France were also crushed in 1358, and were to continue to suffer the main brunt of the Anglo-French wars until the final defeat of the English in 1453. And although we have not found it possible to accept the struggles of the Taborites in Bohemia as other than a national and social movement with peasant support, it must be admitted that in Bohemia in the long run, the position of the peasants, in a society whose structure was not fundamentally changed, worsened rather than improved. The successors of the Taborites adopted a pacifist and quietist position in politics which enabled the lords to bring to Bohemia the deteriorating conditions suffered by peasants all over eastern Europe.[41]

[41] P. Brock, *Political and Social Doctrines of the Unity of the Czech Brethren*, 1957, esp. chap. 7; R. R. Betts, *Essays in Czech History*, 1969, pp 279–84.

PART II
The English Rising of 1381

4 The Events of the Rising

The experiences of the European peasant class during the middle ages were immensely complex. Strivings for simple social objectives took many different forms—according to the character of the economy (and especially the level of production for the market), according to the nature of the social and political order, and according to the prevailing social mentality of the epoch. In spite of this complexity it has been useful to put certain straightforward questions about the nature of each movement in order to determine which features were unique to each and which were common to all. We have attempted to relate precipitating causes to the general background of changes in the social balance of forces. We have analysed, where possible, the class composition of the movements' membership, as well as that of the participants' allies. We have sought evidence about the origins and motivation of the leaders, and about their overt aims and ideologies. We have also discussed the impact of peasant movements on the rest of society and attempted to estimate the extent to which peasant aims were achieved. It is now proposed to apply the same method of enquiry, but in much greater detail, to the English rising of 1381, in the hope that our understanding of this event will be enhanced by looking at it in its European context. We cannot expect that a simple transfer of generalizations from the movements already considered to the English experience can be a valid method of approach, but, nevertheless, the evidence can probably be best understood if it is marshalled under the heads of enquiry that we have already established. But first we must attempt a simple, outline narrative of the main events for purposes of reference.

Already towards the end of May 1381, villagers in Essex were resisting the attempts of tax-collectors to gather in the monies which had been assessed on every adult following a grant in   *May 1381*

the Northampton parliament of November–December 1380.
The government's response was to dispatch justices to try
those indicted of violence towards the tax-gatherers, which
simply precipitated further discontent and massive gatherings
of people. A similar sequence of events occurred in Kent,
possibly in part stimulated by messages from the Essex rebels.
Discontent in this county seems to have been exacerbated by
attempts by the agent of Sir Simon Burley, a close adviser
of the king, to claim a man from Gravesend as a serf. His
imprisonment in Rochester Castle was said to be one of the
causes of the general rising, but a visitation of the king's
justices was probably, as in Essex, a more important factor.

Beginning of June

During the first week of June, Essex men were mobilizing
their forces, but most of our information during this period
concerns events in Kent. Dartford and Maidstone were

10 June

occupied by the rebels who eventually (10 June) marched
on Canterbury, entering the city without resistance. It was
during this period that Wat Tyler emerged as leader. Mean-
while in Essex the rebels were attacking the property of the
Knights of the Hospital of St John, whose Grand Master in
England was Sir Robert Hales, the Treasurer. Because of his
position, Hales was blamed for the gathering of the poll tax,
but he was also an object of the general hatred felt by the
peasants and artisans for all the king's advisers. This hatred

11 June

was first openly expressed by the rebels on 11 June when the
king, who was at Windsor, sent messages to the peasants asking them to explain their actions. 'To save him from his

12 June

treacherous advisers' was the answer. The next day the rebels
from Kent assembled at Blackheath, joined immediately by
those from Essex. A planned meeting with the king to discuss
their grievances was aborted as a result of advice given to him
by his council, headed by the Chancellor, Simon Sudbury,
Archbishop of Canterbury. It was at Blackheath that the
other leading rebel, a priest named John Ball, made himself
known by his radical preaching.

The failure of the rebels to enter into discussions with the
king was followed by further action against the property of
the leading men of the government, including the Archbishop's
palace at Lambeth, the Treasurer's manor at Highbury, the
Marshalsea Prison and the property of the Mayor of London

in Southwark. On 13 June (the feast of Corpus Christi) the *13 June*
rebels crossed London Bridge, unopposed, and entered the city,
where they were welcomed by the London poor who had
already begun to destroy the Duke of Lancaster's Savoy
Palace on the Strand. The duke, the king's uncle, was the
most hated of those in high places, but luckily for him he was
on a diplomatic mission in Scotland. The morning of Corpus
Christi was spent by the rebels pursuing their London
enemies, of whom the most important were the lawyers and
others connected with the judicial system. Another attempt—
this time from the Tower—was made by the king to parley with
the rebels, but he was unable to make them disperse. The
peasants demanded the death of the traitors, and for themselves charters of freedom, rejecting the king's offers of
pardon and promise to consider their grievances. On the
following day, Friday, the king and those of his council *14 June*
who were not directly threatened met the rebels at Mile End
where a first set of demands was presented by Wat Tyler,
to which the king pretended to agree. This meeting was immediately followed by the occupation by the rebels of the
Tower and the beheading of Sudbury, Hales and a Franciscan
friar who was the king's physician. Some other prominent servants of the government together with many Flemings and
other aliens were attacked and killed. The clerks of the royal
chancery were set by the king's advisers to writing out charters
of freedom, and it was this ruse which may have caused a preliminary dispersal of some of the Essex rebels. On the following
day, Saturday, after a visit to Westminster Abbey for con- *15 June*
fession, the king with his advisers met the rebels at Smithfield.
Once again, refusing to return home unsatisfied, the rebels
through their spokesman Wat Tyler put forward their second
set of demands. Shortly afterwards Tyler was killed by the
Mayor of London. The king and his advisers at last obtained
the dispersal of the rebel army, prudently avoiding an armed
clash in the city.

The efforts of the Essex and Kentish rebels, in spite of such
preliminary actions as the march on Canterbury, were essentially directed on London in the hope of exerting pressure on
the king to obtain the satisfaction of their demands. Although
influenced by events in London, movements in other regions

of the south-east operated independently. The main focus of activity in Hertfordshire was the town of St Albans, where the townsmen, traditionally at loggerheads with their overlord, the Abbot of St Albans, took advantage of the weakness of the government to force the abbot to give them certain elementary rights, long enjoyed by other townsmen. But in addition there were village risings throughout north Surrey and Middlesex principally aimed at the destruction of the manorial rolls which contained the evidence of tenants' obligations to their lords. In Hertfordshire, the townsmen of St Albans were supported by the peasants from the abbey estates, and there were attacks on other landowners in the county. The

St Albans
14 June

stirrings at St Albans occurred at least as early as Friday, 14 June, when a delegation from the town was in contact with the rebels in London. Under the skilful leadership of William Grindecobbe, the St Albans townsmen combined the threat of a march by the London rebels on the town with royal instructions obtained when they were in London, which were addressed to the abbot himself. As a result, the men of St Albans and the abbey's tenants in the market-towns and villages on the abbey estate obtained a number of charters granting away a whole range of seigneurial rights. It was not

St Albans
12 July

until 12 July, a month after the dispersal of the rebels at Smithfield, that the abbot was restored to power at St Albans by the king and his justices. The following day, in the same place, John Ball who had been captured in Coventry was hanged, drawn and quartered, a fate shortly afterwards suffered by William Grindecobbe and other leading St Albans rebels.

Suffolk, Norfolk and Cambridgeshire were also engulfed by

Suffolk
12 June

rebellions. In Suffolk the first signs of movement were on 12 June on the borders of northern Essex under the leadership of John Wrawe, parson of Ringfield—about a fortnight, that

Norfolk
16 June

is, after the first riots in Essex. In Norfolk the first serious attacks were on 16 June. The most prominent leader here was Geoffrey Litster, a dyer, supported for what seem opportunist reasons by one or two gentlemen with local scores to pay. In Cambridgeshire discontent was making itself felt by the end of the first week of June, though general insurrection did not begin until the thirteenth. No leaders with the apparent authority, perhaps even charisma, of a Tyler, a Wrawe or a Litster emerged, but a landowner of moderate possessions, John Hanchache of Shudy Camps, was prominent. The activities of the rebels in the East Anglian counties seem to have been rather uncoordinated, partly because most of the evidence is from the judicial records of the period of the suppression when individual attacks on manors and unpopular individuals were stressed. A certain focus was given to the rising in Suffolk because there was an upheaval at the same time in the sizeable cloth-manufacturing town of Bury St Edmunds, when the townsmen tried, in a manner analogous to the actions of the St Albans townsmen, to obtain a measure of autonomy and self-government from their overlord, the abbot. This led to the execution on 15 June of the Prior of *Suffolk* Bury and another official of the monastery by the townsmen. *15 June* They were supported by the country rebels under Wrawe, who had already, on the previous day, executed a judge, Sir John Cavendish. Similarly, in Cambridgeshire, there was not so much a line-up as a coincidence between rebellious movements inside and outside the county town. In Cambridge *Cambridge* town in June, the chief target of resentment was the University *15–17 June* whose privileges and muniments were attacked and destroyed between the fifteenth and seventeenth. In Norfolk, on the other hand, although the country rebels entered Norwich *Norwich* on 17 June, there seems to have been no supporting urban *17 June* rebellion. It was the Bishop of Norwich, Henry Despenser, who rallied the ruling class of East Anglia, and between the eighteenth and twenty-sixth of June regained East Anglia for the crown. The bishop's forces met the rebels, under Litster, at North Walsham on 26 June and succeeded in breaching the *Norfolk* rebel stronghold, protected by ditch, palisade and farm carts. *26 June* Two days later, one of the king's uncles, Thomas of Woodstock, and Sir Henry Percy, stormed a similar fortified position at Billericay manned by the Essex rebels. This was the last mass stand of the rural rebellion.

The rising was essentially one of East Anglia and the Home Counties with support from the London poor. This does not mean that there was not discontent and even sporadic trouble elsewhere. One chronicler reports a quickly suppressed *Peterborough* attack on Peterborough Abbey on 17 June. There was an *17 June* attack by tenants on the Priory at Dunstable, Bedfordshire, village disturbances in Buckinghamshire and rumours of trouble in Leicestershire. All these events occurred in mid-June, probably stimulated by news from the main centres of revolt. The farther away from London, the more delayed were local reactions to the news of rebellion. The Prior of Worcester Cathedral reported rebellion on his estates in the first week of July; there were rumours of disturbances in Warwickshire at the same time; Wirral tenants of the Abbot of St Werburgh, Chester, were in revolt against their lord as late as 29 July. In addition, internal troubles broke out in a number of provincial towns, quite unconnected with the main rising other than that a solution to long-standing and varied grievances was sought because of the apparent breakdown of traditional law and order. Thus in the first half of June there were faction fights in York. On 19 June there was trouble in Bridgwater, Somerset. In late June and early July there were riots at Scarborough and Beverley in Yorkshire, and at Winchester in Hampshire and at Northampton. Such urban disturbances had happened before and they would happen again. They were not part of the peasants' revolt.

Worcester early July

Chester 29 July

Various towns June–July

The discussion of the English rising which follows is divided into six chapters. The treatment is topical, rather than chronological. The first chapter (Chapter 5) is devoted to the general economic, social and political background to the revolt, indicating those features of fourteenth-century society through which the social tensions were built up which eventually exploded in the 1381 rising. In Chapter 6 an attempt is made to discover what particular features in the areas of revolt—Essex, Kent and East Anglia—caused the conflict to break out there rather than in other parts of the country. Chapter 7 deals with the social composition of the rebel bands, for there is a general problem here as to what extent the rising was a *peasants'* revolt, or whether it was as much an artisan rising. Indeed, the question has even been put as to whether it was not a rising of the whole people of the affected districts, including the gentry, against an unpopular government. This chapter also includes a consideration of an allied problem: from where did the movement get its leaders? From its own ranks or from outside? Chapter 8 describes the allies of the rebels, that is to say, those social groups which did not merely take advantage of the upheaval caused by the rebellion, but deliberately and consciously assisted the rebels. Chapter 9 brings together the scanty evidence about the way in which the rebellion was organized, or perhaps, not organized, and also deals with the very important but difficult problem of the rebels' aims and the general outlook which lay behind the specific demands of the moment. The book concludes with a brief assessment of the consequences of the rising and discusses the frequently made assertion that, in fact, it made no difference to the future development of English society.

5 The General Background

Our discussion of some of the main mass risings of peasants in late-medieval Europe, not to speak of some of the sidelong glances we have cast at more all-embracing movements such as that of the Taborites in Bohemia, has shown that we cannot assimilate them to a single pattern. Nevertheless, even if movements showed considerable variation in the overall pattern of evolution, from the predisposing and precipitating causes to the final outcome, there are frequent resemblances between the component features of these movements. The English rising of 1381 was not quite like any of the other movements. Then again the social and political history of fourteenth-century England and the structure of English society on the eve of the rebellion were unique in the arrangements of their particular elements, even if resemblances between some aspects of English and continental life were striking and significant. As with the examination of all historical problems, we insist on the fruitfulness of comparisons at the same time as we recognize the unique features of particular sequences of historical events.

The historian of the 1381 rising is well placed compared with historians of the other movements we have described. In the first place, perhaps most importantly, the survival of English manorial records has made it possible for him to gain a much more detailed and continuous knowledge of the facts of village life over the century and a half preceding the outbreak of the rising than has been possible in the case of other countries. Similarly, the survival of government records, including tax lists, but especially the records of the royal courts of justice, enables us to see, as if on a public platform, the conflicting issues between government and subject and lord and peasant. Even the deliberate destruction of manorial records as an act of policy by the peasants themselves in 1381 has not unduly reduced the evidence on which we can arrive at a fairly reliable picture of social discontent. Further, while the chroniclers of Flanders, France and Spain may have recorded important information about events in their countries, few measure up in detail or interest to such English chroniclers as Thomas Walsingham, or the author of the Anonimalle chronicle, to mention only two out of a half-dozen more or less independent sources. Finally, though we lack a source comparable with the list of the dead at the Battle of Cassel, surviving indictments of rebels presented in the royal tribunals after the defeat of the rising supplement the narrative of the chroniclers as to the scale of local actions, as well as containing information about the wealth and occupations of the rebels.

As we have seen in previous chapters, English peasant communities were as tenacious, even as pugnacious, as their continental counterparts in organizing resistance to the pressure of their manorial lords. Clearly, they were not so successful as those communities in France and Italy which managed to make genuine but small encroachments on seigneurial power. Even a preliminary search for peasant self-assertiveness in the thirteenth and early fourteenth centuries shows that the willingness of the peasant communities to go as far as litigation and even direct action was remarkably widespread. However, if known cases are plotted on the map it will immediately be seen that the main concentration is to be found in the central and east midlands, with the exception of East Anglia, and the Home Counties, with the exception of Kent. These are the areas of densest population,[1] of most complete manorialization and of production for the market. The significance of Kent lies in the fact that, from the early thirteenth century, the prosperity and bargaining power of customary tenants was so great that they were able to prevent their tenure from being transformed into villeinage (as happened elsewhere) and retained their freedoms, which were embodied in the customs of gavelkind.[2] It is important not to be too definite about the geographical distribution of conflicts between lords and peasants. Not all the evidence

[1] J. C. Russell, *British Medieval Population*, 1948; H. C. Darby, ed., *Historical Geography of England before 1800*, 1936.
[2] F. R. H. Du Boulay, *The Lordship of Canterbury*, 1966, p 138.

has been unearthed, and what has come to light has often still to be collated. What is certain is that disputes over rents, services and villeinage—sometimes followed by settlement, sometimes not—continued in traditional form up to the 1381 rising and after.

Other tensions and other pressures complicated the situation in the fourteenth century. These were diverse in character, but all tended to broaden the field of action and the horizons of the actors beyond the village and beyond the estate. In conflicts with the local lord over local customs, village communities gained experience of common action. To act on a wider front required the experience of wider problems. These were posed as a result of the monarchy's growing demands in fiscal and judicial matters. But owing to the fact that peasants, in the nature of things, were hardly ever able to convey their feelings about problems such as these, the effect of the new pressures on them is very difficult to document.

There is no doubt about the increasing fiscal pressure on the country as a whole.[3] First, there were the various feudal aids and scutages, which were levied on the knight's fees into which the estates of military tenants, from earls down to men who were practically peasants, were notionally subdivided. These were difficult to collect, and not very profitable to the crown—in Henry III's reign, scutages brought in only £2,000 at most. Much more lucrative were the subsidies which were taken from the clergy and laity, sometimes jointly, more often separately. These brought in varying amounts, but, like the feudal aids and scutages, could only be levied after negotiations between the crown, the baronage, the clergy and the burgesses, negotiations which were an important element in the emergence of Parliament. Therefore, from time to time, though not very often, the king would impose a tallage on the crown lands, including the royal boroughs, not subject to parliamentary negotiations.

The problem about estimating the incidence of the burden of taxation is to what extent it was passed down the line by lords to peasants. Feudal aids and scutages should have been

[3] S. K. Mitchell, *Studies in Taxation under John and Henry III*, 1914; J. F. Willard, *Parliamentary Taxes on Personal Property, 1290–1334*, 1934.

paid by tenants of knight's fees or fractions thereof, from their own income. But since their incomes consisted of variable exactions, such as profits of courts and above all of tallage, in addition to the more or less fixed rents and services from tenants, there were ample opportunities to shift the burden of taxation. The same, of course, could be true of any other fiscal burden, such as the lord's share of a lay subsidy. Ecclesiastics could also shift the burden of clerical subsidies, which settled down in the fourteenth century at one-tenth of the estimated revenue from 'spiritual' (tithes and the like) and 'temporal' (usually ordinary manorial) sources.[4] The cellarer's account of Worcester Cathedral Priory for 1294–5 shows that after the assembled clergy had promised the king one half of their annual revenue, the monks of Worcester, who paid to the king £150 levied on the basis of their (vastly under-assessed) temporal and spiritual income, got £133 towards this sum from their unfree tenants. This was additional to the £27 aid or tallage already taken from the unfree tenants at Michaelmas.[5]

The subsidies paid by the laity were however the main taxes which affected peasants. They paid them direct to the royal tax-gatherer rather than their lords, this direct relationship between the crown and taxpayer being a very ancient tradition. There had been only five subsidies levied during Henry III's reign (1216–72), besides a 'carucage', or land tax, in 1220. In Edward I's reign (1272–1307), nine were levied, as well as a tallage on the royal demesne and boroughs, not to speak of feudal dues, wool seizures, export duties and five clerical subsidies. In Edward II's reign (1307–27) there were seven lay subsidies and five from the clergy. In the first seven years of Edward III's reign (1327–77) there were three lay and two clerical subsidies. From 1334 onwards taxes were collected with increasing regularity, twenty-four regular subsidies and one heavy parish tax being levied in the remainder of the reign.[6]

[4] W. E. Lunt, in *The Taxation of Norwich*, 1926, deals in great detail with the way in which the clergy were assessed for taxation in the thirteenth century.

[5] *Early Compotus Rolls of the Priory of Worcester*, eds C. M. Wilson and C. Gordon, Worcester Historical Society, 1908, pp 24–32.

[6] The history of Parliamentary taxation is dealt with in most political histories of medieval England because of the major preoccupation with the

Until 1334, the lay subsidy was paid by individuals according to a locally made assessment of the value of their movable goods. As far as peasants were concerned, this assessment was made on their livestock, grain, hay, honey and other agricultural produce, but not on their tools and equipment, or the goods in their larder. Each taxpayer paid a fraction (such as one-tenth or one-twentieth) of the value of the assessment. A minimum assessment of something like ten shillings (it varied) exempted the poorest members of the community, but there was a good deal of evasion and corruption, of which the government must have been aware. For example, one-tenth of movables payable by rural and one-sixth by urban taxpayers in 1294 brought in £81,840, whereas in 1297 one-ninth from all taxpayers brought in only £34,420. The government must also have noticed that the number of taxpayers varied inexplicably from year to year. Within each village the richest should have paid most, but since the rich tended to control the assessment process, they could well be underassessed. This would mean that the poor and powerless would be overassessed or otherwise exploited by corrupt officials. In 1334 a new method of levying the subsidy was devised. Instead of reassessing individuals, commissioners were nominated by the government to negotiate a collective agreement within each village community, based on the 1332 returns, but with some correction for evasion and anomalies. A total of £27,430 was arrived at, some £3,000 more than in 1332. But whereas in 1332 the assessment for each individual taxpayer was returned to the exchequer as on previous occasions, in 1334 only a lump sum from each village was recorded. Henceforth the exchequer would not have a list of the names of the taxpayers in each town and village, but would simply keep a record of whether each town had produced its allotted share of tax.[7] The government was guaranteed a fixed return, which remained the same for about a century in spite of the drastic population fall after 1349. And within each town and village the way was open to the powerful to distribute the burden to their own advantage.

history of Parliament. Hence, W. Stubbs, *Constitutional History of England*, 3 vols, 1891, contains references to all known occasions on which taxes were proposed and/or levied.   [7] J. F. Willard, *op. cit.*, and *EHR*, 1913–15.

It is not easy to say how heavily the lay subsidies bore on the peasant population. If we look at the surviving details from the last of the subsidies levied directly on individuals, in 1332, we discover that there was an exemption limit of ten shillings' value on movables, only those with more than that assessed amount contributing one-fifteenth of their value. The lowest payment of tax therefore was eightpence or roughly the equivalent of four days' wages. The distribution of the tax can be illustrated from the Warwickshire subsidy of this year.[8] The village of Bishops Tachbrook, according to a detailed royal survey of 1280,[9] contained sixty-seven households: the heads of six of these were free tenants, one of whom had a substantial holding of some hundred and thirty acres; there were twenty-one customary tenants, sixteen of whom held 'yardlands', or twenty-four-acre holdings; five had half that amount; three were holding half a yardland on lease; and there were thirty-eight cottagers. It is unlikely that the population drastically changed in social composition over the next fifty years, though individual families might have died out and others come in. There may have been some reduction of population in the famine years of 1315–17, but any losses may have been replaced by 1332. In this year twenty-nine persons were taxed, a figure which could imply, if population structure was similar to that of 1280, that the smallholding population was below the exemption limit. Tax paid ranged from one shilling to six-and-eightpence; twenty-one people paid between one shilling and two shillings (inclusive). One taxpayer's entry is blank. Of the remaining seven, three paid over six shillings, the others between three shillings and five shillings. These might be regarded as well-to-do taxpayers, because their chattels were assessed at up to £5 in value, but it must also be remembered that all farmed on a small scale and would be liable for the payment of the equivalent of six to forty days' wages, in cash.

Payments of this magnitude, even if occurring only occasionally, could seriously deplete the cash reserves of even relatively prosperous tenants whose assets were more likely

[8] *The Lay Subsidy for Warwickshire of 6 Edward III* (1332), ed. W. F. Carter, Dugdale Society, 1926.
[9] Warwickshire Hundred rolls for 1279–80, PRO, E. 164, Vol. 15, f. lxvii.

to be in grain, livestock and equipment than in money; and indeed the pressure of the tax did not increase without complaint. A poem of the early fourteenth century, included in a manuscript anthology, probably of west-midland origin,[10] seems to voice the grievances of husbandmen. The noticeable feature of the poem is the lumping together of private as well as public exactions, and of the demands of manorial officials, including the bailiff, hayward and woodward, as well as of the king's tax-collectors. This official tells the husbandman he is 'writen y my writ' and must get ready 'selver to the grene wax' (a reference to the colour of the sealing-wax used by the exchequer), a payment which the peasant complains he has already had to pay ten times before. In order to pay he has to sell produce, implements and seed: 'thus the grene wax us greveth . . . he us hontethe as hound hare doth on hulle.' The tale of ruin is sharply depicted, and the fact that manorial officials as well as tax-collectors are criticized suggests that the poet has in mind the villein rather than the free taxpayer. The poem is in the difficult and sophisticated alliterative style popular in the west midlands and is obviously written by an educated person, probably a cleric, perhaps of peasant origin or at least with peasant sympathies—a possibility in itself significant.

The levying of tax was not only an act which added to manorial and other burdens, such as 'purveyance' (or compulsory sale of goods) to royal officials. It was also an act of the central government which affected all areas uniformly without respect to local exemptions or franchises.[11] While it was not an equalizing measure, it nevertheless made men conscious of their wider connexions. This uniform pressure of government did not apply only to fiscal measures, but also to jurisdiction. One must be wary of exaggeration here. Historians have tended to overemphasize the effectiveness of royal centralization under the Norman and Angevin kings, particularly with regard to the undermining of local, feudal

[10] In R. H. Robbins, ed., *Historical Poems of the 14th and 15th Centuries*, 1959; N. R. Ker, introduction to *Facsimile of British Museum MS. Harley 2253*, 1965.

[11] For a useful survey of the governmental and judicial machinery, see J. F. Willard, W. A. Morris, *et al.*, eds, *The English Government at Work 1327–36*, 3 vols., 1940–1950.

jurisdictions. The country people, however, continued for centuries to be under the domination of the local landowner, whether abbot, earl, baron or squire. Edward I's enquiry into local franchises, whether aimed at their abolition or simply their integration into the royal judicial system, was not so successful as he had hoped.[12] All the same, the central judicial system, with the constant extension under various types of commission of the powers of the king's justices, was recognized as a national institution and a national grievance pressing down on all.

In the fourteenth century, the dreaded 'general eyre', the visitation with all-embracing powers of the king's justices to all counties, was abandoned. But the king's justices continued to circulate under specific commissions from the crown. These included: 'gaol delivery', that is, the trial of all accused persons held in prison; 'oyer and terminer', or the hearing and completion of cases against accused felons; and 'trail-baston', the specific pursuit of those accused of local violence and disorder. Furthermore, increasing judicial and administrative powers were conferred, during the course of the four-teenth century, on the local nobility and gentry who received commissions of the peace. At the time of the 1381 rising these Justices of the Peace were not only supplementing the work of the professional judges in trying felons and other offenders, but were also enforcing the government's attempted wage-freeze under the Statute of Labourers, 1351.[13]

The enforcement of law and order has never been a purely neutral act of government, especially when the power to do so is held exclusively in the hands of one social class. The oppor-tunities for local chicanery by persons of influence caused men to regard the visitations of the justices with considerable hostility. It was a visit to Essex of the Chief Justice of the Common Bench, Sir Robert Bealknap, in May 1381, under a commission of trailbaston which was sent to put down the anti-tax riots, which escalated the rebellion in that county. It was another judicial visitation, sent to Kent under the same commission at the beginning of June, which had a similar

[12] D. Sutherland, *Quo Warranto Proceedings in the Reign of Edward I*, 1963.
[13] B. H. Putnam, *The Enforcement of the Statute of Labourers During the First Decade after the Black Death*, 1908, has not been superseded on this subject.

effect in that county. Even the Commons, representing the interests of the gentry, complained in 1339 that the commissions of trailbaston did more harm to the innocent than to the guilty.[14] A poem in Norman-French, dating from the earliest days of the trailbaston commission, probably written some time between 1305 and 1307, illustrates the fears that were prompted by the operation of the judicial system. The author of the poem complains that he was framed by a false indictment.[15] Certain that he would get no justice, he became an outlaw and fled to the woods. Here he would find no deceit, no false laws. The complaint in the poem is echoed again in 1381, for it was false indictments at the sessions held by Bealknap which were feared, and the jurors presenting these false indictments were the first people to be killed by the rebels.

By the middle of the fourteenth century, then, the fiscal, administrative and judicial pressures of the king's government were being applied by royal officials (who were usually drawn from the country gentry) or by the officials of the private franchises of great lords. The growing uniformity of these pressures, in England as on the continent, was one of the factors which widened and generalized the responses of the ruled, the peasants in particular. But before any situation approaching general revolt could develop, additional grievances had to be experienced. After the first severe visitation of the bubonic plague in 1349, made worse by subsequent plagues in the 1360s and 1370s, further grievances were experienced by the mass of the people. These arose first as a result of fairly general seigneurial reaction against inevitable attempts by tenants to take advantage of the changed land–labour ratio. At the same time, those very lords who were resisting through the manor courts, their tenants' attempts at self-improvement were, in their alternative roles as justices of labourers and J.P.s, administering through the public courts the statutory wage-freeze of 1351. Deteriorating relationships between the rulers and the mass of the ruled were exacerbated in the 1370s by political scandals, news of unsuccessful mili-

[14] M. McKisack, *The Fourteenth Century 1307–99*, 1959, p 206.
[15] 'The outlaw's song of trailbaston', in I. S. T. Asplin, ed., *Anglo-Norman Political Songs*, 1953.

tary action in France and, from 1377 to 1380, the sharpest fiscal pressure of the century, which bore directly and unequally on the poorest sections of the population.

It is an apparent paradox that the rising should have occurred when the general trend in the distribution of incomes between landowner and peasant was in favour of peasants, whether in their capacity as tenants or in their capacity as labourers.[16] The fall in rents was almost universal. Rents per acre in northern Norfolk fell from elevenpence in the 1370s to sixpence in the mid fifteenth century. On the Leicester Abbey estates in the central midlands, rent income fell by about one-third between 1341 and 1477. Valuations of demesne land (which would reflect rental value) on the estates of Glastonbury Abbey in the south-west fell between two-thirds and three-quarters between the early fourteenth and the early sixteenth centuries. From Ramsey Abbey estate in the east to the estates of the Bishop of Worcester in the west midlands, the problem of increasing and uncollectable rent arrears mounted from the 1380s on. Admittedly, not all estates were as badly hit. The Duchy of Cornwall estates seemed to prosper, but this was due to a combination of special circumstances; the Archbishop of Canterbury's estate revenues remained fairly stable, perhaps because of the proximity of the London markets. These are exceptional cases. Furthermore, estate-owners were conscious of these trends working against them. A canon of Leicester Abbey, looking back over the long period 1335–1493, made a note in a collection of charter evidences he was compiling concerning the decreasing returns from both spiritual and temporal sources during the period. More significant for the time was a realization of financial crisis by the auditors of the estate of the man so hated by the rebels, the Duke of Lancaster. These auditors were obliged, in 1388, to detail various aspects of revenue deterioration, such as the failure of sales from demesnes to cover costs, the falling rents from mills and fisheries and faltering profits of manorial jurisdiction.

The failure of the Duke of Lancaster's bailiffs to cover the costs of demesne cultivation could not have been unconnected

[16] The following summarizes the material in my *Decline of Serfdom in Medieval England*, 1969, in which references will be found.

with rising wage costs. Looking again over the long term we
find that whereas between the beginning of the fourteenth
century and the middle of the fifteenth century agricultural
prices had fallen by ten per cent, real wages had multiplied
nearly two-and-a-half times and cash wages had nearly
doubled. In the shorter term, the immediate impact of the
Black Death had been that both agricultural and other
workers demanded, according to the strength of their local
bargaining power, up to twice or even three times their previous wages. These demands led first to the Ordinance
(1349), then to the Statute of Labourers (1351).

This legislation was an inevitable reaction by a Parliament
of landowning employers whose demesnes by now were
cultivated much more by wage labour than by the customary
services of servile tenants. Rich peasant employers of wage
labour seem to have reacted rather differently. For them,
harvest labourers and other employees were a supplement to
family labour rather than the only available labour force.
Consequently, in a tight labour situation, when they were
competing for workers with lords of manors, they must have
been prepared to offer higher wages. At any rate, there is no
indication that the rise in wages caused social conflicts between
peasant employers and their employees—as it certainly
seems to have done between lords of manors on the one hand
and the plebeian mass on the other. The reason for this is not
hard to find. From one point of view many of the peasants or
manufacturing artisans were employers of labour, and from
another they were heads of families, some of whose members
would be bringing in wages from outside. The family income
of the peasant or artisan employer would therefore be just
as likely to benefit as to suffer from the rise in wages.

The keepers, or justices, who were empowered to apply the
Statute of Labourers received a commission to do so from the
crown, which until 1359 was separate from the commission
to keep the peace, although the same persons had usually
sat on both commissions. After that the two commissions
were combined. There was always a great lord (who would
not often attend) among the commissioners, the rest being
members of the gentry, some with legal training, and all
identifiable with the interests of lords of manors. For example,

the J.P.s in Suffolk between 1361 and 1364 were headed by Robert of Ufford, Earl of Suffolk, and included two lawyers and eight members of the gentry, six of them knights and four at one time or another Members of Parliament. One of the lawyers was none other than Sir John Cavendish, who was killed by the rebels in 1381.[17]

The result of this social identity between the justices enforcing the statute and the lords of manors who were the principal interested employers, was that the statute, which in any case gave the lords the right to the first call on the villeins' labour, simply strengthened the existing seigneurial rights of lords of manors. These previously had been effective only locally, but now they were guaranteed by a national system of enforcement. The most important aspect of the legislation was, of course, that it made it illegal to demand or offer higher wages than had been the case in 1346. Reinforcing clauses aimed to prevent the mobility of labour, put employers in a bad bargaining position. In addition: labourers had to contract to stay with the employer for a year or other customary period; there was to be no daily hiring; labourers had to swear an oath to abide by the provisions of the statute, or be placed in the stocks; and only those with enough of their own land to keep them occupied were exempt from the obligation to work for wages. This meant that all smallholders were liable. Those breaking the clauses about compulsory service or forms of contract were liable to imprisonment. Those demanding excess wages had to pay a fine, usually double the amount of excess. The justices' wages were paid from the fines, and the rest went to relieve the local tax burden—considerable incentives for the act to be operated efficiently. In some districts during the first decade of the statute's enforcement, labourers, through their fines, were paying as much as one-third or one-half of the tax burden, which the better-off normally had to pay.

The conflict over wages was one of the issues that must have further tightened social tensions in the thirty years before the rising, especially in the south-east where wage earners constituted an important element in the plebeian population.

[17] B. H. Putnam's *Proceedings before the Justices of the Peace in the 14th and 15th Centuries*, 1938, includes the record of these proceedings.

Nevertheless, judging both by their actions and their demands, it was serfdom and those things which flowed from the rights of lords over tenants which bulked largest in their grievances. This was what lay behind the widespread destruction of manorial records, since it was in the manorial surveys and especially the records of the manorial courts that tenants' obligations were recorded. Manorial lords and their stewards were even then in the habit of collecting and enrolling precedents about terms of tenure from court records, to be used to bolster up the lords' rights. Tenants, conversely, wanted to destroy these precedents and set up a completely new tenurial system.

There are good reasons for supposing that what lay behind such drastic action by men who were normally very respectful of customary practice, was a feeling that lords had already taken the first step in the repudiation of custom. It was not, as was once thought, that the lords were reimposing labour services which had long since been commuted. This did not constitute much of an issue, since most regular work on those demesnes which were not leased out continued to be done by wage labour. There was still, however, friction over the performance of some services, especially harvest boon works. It should be remembered, too, that the labour-service system was not one which survived only in backward, non-commercialized areas. Labour services were likely to be demanded in certain circumstances, precisely where landowners were trying to keep up production for the market. They were being fully used on the Canterbury Cathedral estate until the 1390s. The archbishops of Canterbury had had several tussles with their tenants over the performance of boon services. There is evidence of similar conflicts and attempts to intensify labour-service demands as far afield as Durham, the West Riding, Berkshire, Surrey and Somerset during these years between plague and rebellion.

There were other ways in which lords tried to compensate for the inevitable effect on their revenues of a drastic decline in the number of tenants. Attempts to push up money rents are found in Durham, Oxfordshire, Worcestershire, Suffolk and Hertfordshire. As we have indicated, in the long term rents fell. In the short term, the attempts to counteract prevailing trends could only worsen social relations. Alternative ways of keeping up cash revenues were tried, including large fines imposed on various pretexts by virtue of lords' jurisdictional powers over servile tenants, such as the huge collective fine of £20 imposed in 1356 by the Earl of Warwick on his tenants at Elmley Castle, Worcestershire. The villagers had declared that a fugitive from the manor was a freeman, whereas they had previously recognized that he was a villein. In 1369 the Abbot of Evesham is found charging a villein tenant 20s 8d for permission to employ his own brother. Although in general many holdings made vacant during the plague were fairly quickly reoccupied, there were, in fact, places where villein tenants were either compelled to take holdings they did not want, or to pay money (as at Forncett, Norfolk, in the 1370s) in order to avoid the obligation.

– These, then, were the most important of the elements of social tension in the years after the Black Death. In themselves they were not enough to provoke a general rebellion, but without them the rebellion could not have been precipitated by other causes. Other factors arising from the general background of English social life before 1381 may be added. Of these the most important were a new phase in the war with France and the political crisis of the 1370s. Our difficulty here is that while we know from records that lord–peasant relations at local level were inflamed by the seigneurial reaction, and that the operation of the Statute of Labourers bore down precisely on those social groups which rebelled in 1381, we can only guess to what extent the changing fortunes of war and scandals at Westminster entered into the consciousness of peasants and artisans.

Countrymen were, of course, well aware of the wars with France and Scotland, as they had been long before the outbreak of the so-called Hundred Years War in 1337. In addition to volunteers attracted by the prospect of loot and adventure, men were recruited from towns and villages by commissioners of array.[18] Whether the government got the soldiers it wanted or whether communities got rid of local misfits or of those too poor to bribe for their exemption, is difficult to say. The process must have been disruptive as well as expensive, for

[18] M. R. Powicke, *Military Obligation in Medieval England*, 1962.

the communities had to pay for the equipment of those who went. In addition to these recruits, local men of middling status would go and return in a more voluntary fashion in the retinues of the local nobility and gentry. Many of those returning made their mark in a particular way. Pardons for acts of murder and robbery, issued as a reward for military service abroad, are recorded in assize rolls from Edward I's time onwards.[19] One does not know how much disturbance was caused by the departing or returning soldiers. But local communities must have been well aware of the foreign campaigns, their conduct—and their cost.

However, after the Treaty of Bretigny (1360) and the recovery of French military and naval power, the English themselves may have felt, as well as caused, the devastation and pillage of war. The 1360s and 1370s saw a number of successful raids by French and Castilian warships on the Channel Islands and the southern coast of England. These raids clearly did have an impact, for the Anonimalle chronicler tells us that the commons of Kent when mobilizing their forces at the beginning of June 1381, instructed those persons living within twelve leagues of the sea to stay at home and keep the coasts free from enemies. On the other hand, Kent was very little affected by the French raids compared with Hampshire and Sussex, and Essex and East Anglia hardly at all. Attempts to attribute to the English lower classes a revolutionary rage at the military aristocracy's failure to fulfil its traditional protective role are not, therefore, convincing.[20] There is no adequate analogy between the French Jacques in the Beauvais and the Paris regions in 1359, and that of the rebels who formed the bands that marched on London in 1381.

There does seem to have been a sense of betrayal, however, which focused on John of Gaunt, Duke of Lancaster.[21] This great lord, brother of the king, owed only some of his importance to that relationship, for he was in his own right the leading aristocratic landowner in the kingdom. By marrying

[19] R. H. Hilton, *A Medieval Society*, 1967, pp 250–51.

[20] The case is interestingly argued by E. Searle and R. Burghart in 'The defence of England and the Peasants' Revolt', *Viator*, 1972.

[21] To the now out-of-date biography by S. A. Smith, *John of Gaunt*, 1904, should be added R. Somerville, *History of the Duchy of Lancaster*, I, 1953, and G. Holmes, *The Estates of the Higher Nobility in 14th Century England*, 1957.

the daughter of Duke Henry of Lancaster (himself second cousin to Edward III), John acquired not merely the Earldom of Lancaster, but some of the land as well as the titles of the defunct earldoms of Derby, Leicester, Lincoln and Salisbury. His estates were to be found all over England, especially in the north and midlands, and he was a great landowner in Gascony. His immediate retinue of up to two hundred men, indentured to serve him for life, included barons as well as knights and squires. Because of the widespread scope of his influence, few people could be unaware of his existence or his importance.

Scandals seem to have been inseparable from medieval government, and especially government which involved widespread military expenditure. Gaunt was the dominant government personality on the royal council in the mid-1370s, and thus was presiding over the liquidation of the English grip on France. Gaunt himself had led an unsuccessful expedition in 1373. In the Good Parliament of 1376 his aristocratic political rivals, in alliance with the knights of the shire in the Commons, impeached those who were regarded as Gaunt's creatures: Richard Lyons, Adam of Bury and John Pecche, merchants of London, William, Lord Latimer, and the old king's mistress, Alice Perrers. The accusations of corruption were standard form, and may well have had some truth in them. They reflected also the normal behaviour of those in a position to take advantage of government employment. Gaunt got his revenge in the following year in a Parliament packed with his supporters. His chief critic, the Speaker of the Commons in 1376, was imprisoned, but Gaunt's dominance was not maintained and there was a balance of power between the court factions after Edward III's death in 1377. The dangers of 'a king called John' in 1381 were non-existent.

Nevertheless, Gaunt remained a bogey-man because he could be held to typify failure abroad and corruption at home. If we are right in assuming that by 1381 William Langland's great poem *Piers the Ploughman* had become familiar to a popular audience, we may also assume that it must have had some effect as political propaganda. There were apparent references to the Good Parliament in the Prologue. Gaunt is not named, but he could be thought to be referred to when Langland

describes 'a cat from a certain court' who preyed on the rats
and the mice (the Members of Parliament) who futilely discussed how to 'bell' him. The second book is a scathing attack
on corruption, and it could be that contemporary men, as well
as modern literary critics, saw Alice Perrers in the allegorical
figure, Lady Meed.[22] Langland had, of course, more profound
objectives than political denunciation, but his pungent satire,
in popular language, coming at the very beginning and therefore the best known part of the poem, may have been a factor
in keeping Gaunt and his supposed associates in the popular
eye.

It could of course be argued that in 1376 or 1381 the mass
of the population would be profoundly uninterested in the
aristocratic factions in Parliament and at the king's court.
There was a good deal of popular preaching, orthodox as well
as unlicensed, and much of it involved the denunciation of
corruption in high places which,[23] though generalized, could
be given particular applications. Furthermore, rural communities, particularly those in the commercialized Home
Counties and East Anglia, were by no means sealed from the
outside world. They were much influenced by London, where
Gaunt was universally hated. People had to travel perhaps
more than we realize to obtain things in local markets which
would not be brought to them in their villages. Markets and
fairs were always good places for rumours. Political divisions
and hatreds among the great, who lived their lives in public
to a much greater extent than their modern descendants,
could soon become common knowledge, adding to the general
sense of unease. It was in such an atmosphere that the additional fiscal pressures which eventually precipitated the rising were introduced.

There was fairly general unanimity among contemporary
observers that the poll tax was perhaps the most important
of the immediate, precipitating causes of the rebellion. At
this point, it should be emphasized that the chroniclers who
stress the existence of resentment at fiscal demands make no

[22] J. F. Goodridge's translation into modern English of Langland's
Piers the Ploughman, Penguin Classics, 1959, contains references to the recent
critical literature on these matters.

[23] G. R. Owst, *Literature and Pulpit in Medieval England*, 1961.

comment about living conditions at the time—to be more specific, to the abundance or shortage of grain. In fact, judging by what evidence of grain prices is available, harvests had been good between 1376 and 1378, and about average in 1379 and 1380.[24] The rebellion was no grain riot; it was human agencies rather than natural phenomena which were thwarting rising expectations. The agency which most of the chroniclers chose to blame was the government.[25] The Evesham chronicler says bluntly: 'This exaction was the cause of the unheard-of evil which followed.' The Anonimalle chronicler refers to corruption in the spending of the one-tenth and the one-fifteenth and other subsidies, and to the pressures for the collection of the poll tax. Henry Knighton (the Leicester Abbey chronicler), the Dunstable annalist, the Bury St Edmunds chronicler, and the author of the English-language chronicle, the *Brut*, all give first place to the tax. The author of the *Eulogium Historiarum*, possibly a monk from Canterbury, gives the same view, and although the Westminster chronicler does not mention the tax at the beginning of his narrative, he tells us that the men of Essex in their last stand after the debacle in London swore that they would die rather than 'bend their necks to the servitude of the greedy tax'. Walsingham, it is true, philosophizes more widely, ranging in his explanations from the shortcomings of the nobility to the faults of the common people. His only reference to the tax is to

[24] Grain prices in J. E. Thorold Rogers, *History of Agriculture and Prices*, I, 1866, p 234, and II, 1866, pp 152–5. The detailed tables in Vol. II enable one to examine separately the grain prices in the south-eastern counties. The harvests after 1378 certainly worsened but were by no means catastrophic.

[25] From this point onwards there will be frequent references to the principal contemporary chroniclers who wrote about the rising. The relevant parts of most of the important chronicles have been translated by R. B. Dobson in his useful collection of documents, *The Peasants' Revolt of 1381*, 1970. To these must be added: Annals of Dunstable (*Annales Monastici*, III, RS, 1864–9); *Memorials of St Edmunds Abbey*, III (RS, 1896); *The English Brut*, II (Early English Text Society, 1908); *The Kirkstall Abbey Chronicle* (Thoresby Society, 1952); *Chronicle of Dieulacres Abbey 1381–1403* (in 'The Deposition of Richard II' by M. V. Clarke and V. H. Galbraith, *Bulletin of John Rylands Library*, 1930). Froissart's observations and attitudes are, of course, important to the historian, but his version of the sequence of events is of relatively little importance since he wrote many years after the rising.

say that the men of Kent wanted no tax except for the familiar subsidy of one-fifteenth. Chancellor Pole, addressing the 1383 Parliament, put the blame for the 'treacherous insurrection' on the disobedience shown by the people to the lesser ministers of the crown, such as sheriffs, escheators and tax-collectors. This (he said) escalated into rebellion against the great officers of the realm and eventually the king himself. The more remote chroniclers from Kirkstall, Yorkshire, and Dieulacres, Staffordshire, also ignore the tax, since they are more concerned with the later generalized demands such as the abolition of serfdom.

The third poll tax was the culminating tax at the end of a decade of extraordinary fiscal exactions, beginning with the parish tax of 1371.[26] This decade of oppression was all the worse in that it had succeeded a dozen tax-free years. The reintroduction of heavy taxation was linked with the military failures in France, so that it was failure in war, rather than war itself, which could be blamed for the government's demands. The parish tax was an attempt to improve the yield of the fixed subsidy, and involved a considerable increase, particularly in the assessments in Norfolk, Suffolk and Essex. It was so unpopular, especially in the poorer parishes whose richer neighbours had refused to help them, that the next levy (1372–3) was a normal subsidy, followed by a double subsidy collected in 1374–5. In 1377 the first poll tax of fourpence per head on all lay adults over 14 years and (separately) on the clergy was levied. Although this was not as heavy as the subsidy, it was even more regressive, because only genuine beggars were exempt. In 1379 another double subsidy was collected, and in the same year a second poll tax covering both clergy and lay folk was levied (this time graded so that the rich paid more than the poor). In 1380 a subsidy-and-a-half was collected, and Parliament granted the third poll tax, the collection of which in 1381 provoked the rising.[27]

This third poll tax was levied at the rate of one shilling per head on all adults over 15 years, except for genuine beggars.

[26] See E. B. Fryde's introduction to his new edition of Charles Oman's *The Great Revolt of 1381*, 1969.

[27] M. W. Beresford, 'The Poll Tax returns of 1377, 1379 and 1381', *Amateur Historian*, 1958.

Within each village the wealthier were expected to help the poor, provided that the former did not have to pay more than one pound and the poor less than fourpence. This, however, was a matter for local benevolence, and a study of the returns suggests that there was considerable variation from county to county in the extent to which the burden was spread. A shilling was the equivalent of three days' wages, so that a family consisting of four adults would have to pay out the equivalent in cash of twelve days' wages. Of course, there was mass evasion, the government having to expend a considerable amount of administrative effort in order to get the money in. Some of the chroniclers noticed this and, with their nose for corruption in government circles, produced a variety of stories which were no doubt in circulation at the time. The Anonimalle chronicler and Knighton refer to attempts to check up on the shortcomings of the collectors, and Knighton adds the story that impudent commissioners were examining girls to see whether they were virgins, and if not, to tax them as adults. The author of the *Eulogium* has the piquant story of two squires sitting in a London tavern discussing the shortfall in the collection of the tax. They go to Chancery, suggest that the matter should be subjected to a judicial enquiry in Kent and Essex and offer the king some gold for permission to collect the balance. The Evesham writer has a similar story to the effect that certain greedy ministers of the crown, pointing out that the collectors had failed to collect the tax properly, paid for the right to collect the balance. Armed with royal writs they went and sat at various collecting-places in Kent and Essex.

These stories reflect, in a garbled way, an elaborate checking-up procedure which involved the appointment of two commissions of enquiry in January and March 1381, whose job was to check up on the actions of the normal collectors.[28] So, in addition to the initial assessment in December 1380, when people's names, rank, and occupation were noted down, towns and villages would be harassed again by special commissioners, as well as by the collectors with the commissioners at their heels, come to levy the undoubted arrears. In effect,

[28] This procedure is well described by T. F. Tout in *Chapters in the Administrative History of Medieval England*, III, 1928, pp 359–66.

quite apart from the collection of money, the exchequer officials were making a census of all adults three times in less than six months—a procedure which even sophisticated modern populations find objectionable once every ten years. The collectors and controllers from London and Middlesex refused, in fact, to make the third census, and in April told the Barons of the Exchequer that although they could get the numbers of the taxpayers it was considered too dangerous to collect their names, ranks and conditions.

6 The Areas of Revolt

Fiscal and judicial pressures, added to the basic tensions between lord and peasant, operated on a by no means homogeneous community. It is one of the surprising aspects of the rebellion of 1381 that, like many of the other mass movements, there were swept into action persons of varying social status whose interests might often seem contradictory, but all of whom in one way or another were so affected by the action of the government and of all its representatives that they were prepared to make common cause.

The principal focus of the rising was in East Anglia and the Home Counties, though echoes of discontent were to be found farther away. For example, the Prior of Worcester Cathedral excused himself in a letter of 5 July 1381 from attendance at the Benedictine Chapter (the meeting of representatives of all the English Benedictine monasteries), due to be held in Northampton three days later. The reason given was that his free and unfree tenants with their supporters, on the pretext of certain manumissions (no doubt a reference to the king's promises at Mile End on 14 June), were refusing the rent and services which constituted 'the greater part of his and his monastery's sustenance'. The prior might have expected this, for sporadic refusals of rents and services had been occurring since 1378, leading to the prior's seizure in 1380 of the goods and chattels of all the serfs on the estate. Similar conspiratorial movements were reported from the estate and the monastery of St Werburgh at Chester, also in July, again a belated echo of the south-eastern rising. And, as is well known, the heated social and political atmosphere, the demonstrable weaknesses of the rulers of the country, triggered off local conflict in various towns well away from the centre of the rising, such as York, Winchester, Beverley, Scarborough and Bridgwater.[1]

[1] Dobson, Part V: see chap. 5, n. 25. The evidence for the previous refusals of rents and services at Worcester is in the unpublished court

The risings in the west and the north were, then, secondary to the great rebellion in the south-east. Insofar as the explanation for the movement is to be found in the nature of local social and political relations, it is this area which we must examine. Apart from London itself, the main focus was in Essex, Kent, Middlesex, Hertfordshire, Cambridgeshire, Norfolk and Suffolk with some spillover to the north and west. These counties were, of course, densely populated compared with other parts of the country. In 1377, the population density of most of the area south-east of a line from Gloucester to Scarborough was twice as great as that of the counties to the north-west of that line. Norfolk and Suffolk were particularly densely settled, and only Epping Forest and the Weald brought the overall population density of Essex and Kent below that of East Anglian counties. The area was also much affected by having at its heart the great city of London, by far the biggest urban centre in the country, comparable, with an intra-mural population of 35,000 to 40,000, to some of the bigger cities of the continent. But what strikes one most is not the population density or the political and social importance of London, but the contradictory features of south-eastern society, the coexistence of contrasting social structures, the persistence of the archaic side by side with the foreshadowings of modern social forms.

One of the best known features of the rural population in the area of the revolt was a high proportion of persons of free status, who, insofar as they were tenants of land, held it in free tenure. In Kent, the customary tenure of the county (tenure by gavelkind) was reckoned to be free, even though it was not the same as common-law free tenure. The custom of gavelkind covered a high proportion of the tenanted land of the county.[2] But free tenure was also very prominent north

rolls of the Cathedral Priory estate in the archives of the Dean and Chapter at Worcester. C. Oman, *The Great Revolt of 1381*, 1969, also deals with risings away from the main centre as does C. Petit-Dutaillis in his long introduction to what is still one of the most useful works on the rising, by A. Réville, *Le soulèvement des travailleurs d'Angleterre en 1381*, 1898.

[2] F. R. H. Du Boulay, *The Lordship of Canterbury*, 1966, p 138. Also J. E. A. Joliffe, *Pre-feudal England: the Jutes*, 1933, a work full of interesting information, but emphasizing remote origins as being responsible for this form of tenure rather than recent conditions.

of the Thames. It was not evenly distributed, but from Buckinghamshire and Bedfordshire eastwards there were many areas where well over half the peasant population was free from the incidents of serfdom; in the Hinckford Hundred of Essex, ninety per cent of the peasants were free tenants in 1381.[3] The reasons for this relative freedom are to be found much earlier than the fourteenth century, and are complex rather than simple. It was not simply the privileged position of early ethnic groups such as the Jutes in Kent or the Danes in East Anglia, though this factor may have had some importance. It was also due to the early development of production for market by the peasants themselves, which strengthened the sinews of peasant war against such lords as might try to depress their status.

At the same time, as far as the legal freedom and independence of the peasants were concerned, there were balancing factors which were not in the peasants' favour. There were, in all of the south-eastern counties, very large and influential landed estates, especially ecclesiastical, which tended to preserve servile aspects of peasant status even when the forces making for free status were very powerful, within as well as outside these estates. Some of the best endowed Benedictine abbeys in the country were in the south-east, though in many cases their landed property included many manors in the midlands and the west.[4] The Archbishop of Canterbury and the Cathedral Priory at Canterbury had considerable estates in Kent, as well as in the other counties of the Thames valley and East Anglia. St Augustine's Abbey in Canterbury was one of the richest estate-owners in the country. The Bishop and the Cathedral Chapter of London had numerous possessions in Essex, where the immensely rich nunnery of Barking was also situated, not to mention institutions of more moderate

---

[3] For pre-fourteenth-century free tenure see D. C. Douglas, *Social Structure of Medieval East Anglia*, 1927; E. Miller, *The Abbey and Bishopric of Ely*, 1951; E. A. Kosminsky, *Studies in the Agrarian History of England in the 13th Century*, 1956; the free tenants of the Hinckford Hundred of Essex figure in the appendix to Oman, *op. cit.*, where the 1380–81 poll tax returns are printed.

[4] Westminster Abbey, England's wealthiest monastery, possessed a lot of property in the west midlands since much of its endowment by Edward the Confessor was taken from the estates of the old Worcestershire Abbey at Pershore.

wealth such as the Abbey of St John in Colchester and the abbey of Waltham Holy Cross. Hertfordshire was much influenced by the presence of the royal Abbey of St Albans, whose chronicler, Thomas Walsingham, wrote so eloquently about the rising, and with such hostility to the peasants. In Suffolk, old-style monastic-landed domination was represented by the Abbey of Bury St Edmunds, while its counterparts in Cambridgeshire were the estates of the Bishop and the Cathedral Priory of Ely. The Cathedral Priory of Norwich and not least the bishop were great landowners in Norfolk, a county with many other influential religious houses, such as St Benets Holme and Walsingham. There were, however, no individual church estates in Norfolk comparable to Bury St Edmunds or St Albans.[5]

Emphasis has been placed on the rich, powerful, old-established church estates in the south-east, because they tended to be one of the most conservative influences in social life. Great lay landowning families also added to this weight of conservatism, because it was on the big estates that old-style social relations between lord and serf were most likely to be longest preserved. The most important of these big lay estates were located in Essex and the East Anglian counties. It is true that they were not able to survive intact as did the ecclesiastical estates, owing to the uncertain fortunes of families whose heirs might fail entirely or whose estates might be sub-divided among female heiresses, or who might suffer the consequences of political misfortune, namely, confiscation. Thus, by the mid fourteenth century, the enormous inheritances of the Clare Earls of Gloucester and the Bigod Earls of Norfolk no longer survived intact. But the Clares' land in East Anglia still existed as a working unit in the possession of the Earls of March, and the bulk of the Bigods' estates was kept together by being acquired by Edward II and passed to his half-brother, Thomas of Brotherton, whose long-lived daughter inherited them to pass them to the Mowbray family. The very old aristocratic family, the Vere Earls of Oxford,

[5] Some of the above-mentioned religious houses have been the subject of study, e.g. R. A. L. Smith, *Canterbury Cathedral Priory*, 1943; A. E. Levett, *Studies in Manorial History*, 1938 (for St Albans); E. Miller, *op. cit.*; H. W. Saunders, *An Introduction to the Rolls of Norwich Cathedral Priory*, 1930.

also had an important estate in Essex, East Anglia and adjoining counties. Thomas of Woodstock, the king's youngest uncle, later to become Duke of Gloucester, also had important property in Essex, focused on his castle at Pleshey. He had acquired these lands by marriage to one of the heiresses of the Bohun family, the Earls of Hereford. The Duke of Lancaster, in addition to his enormous property in the midlands and the north, had manors in Norfolk.[6] But we must not overstress the ability of the estate-owners to hold up social and economic change. To quote only one striking example, a pioneer study in medieval economic history, written in 1906, showed how on the Countess of Norfolk's manor of Forncett, about twelve miles south-west of Norwich, the old social structure was transformed in the second half of the fourteenth century.[7] A peasant society governed by customs in which serfdom and labour services played an important part was shattered by uncontrollable peasant mobility and the commercialization of all transactions in land. In 1378 on the very eve of the rebellion about a quarter of the freeholdings and three-quarters of villein holdings on this estate had been abandoned. The remaining tenants, most of them in theory unfree, were dealing briskly and commercially in the available land, taking parcels of, on an average, three to four acres on lease for short terms.

It would be misleading to examine the social structure in the south-east solely from the evidence of manorial records, but these records, insofar as they have been examined, do show that what was happening in Forncett was fairly general. In Essex, the market in peasant land was developing a social differentiation among the inhabitants of villages, dividing the landless and the cottagers from the few well-to-do. In Suffolk, as well as in Norfolk, traditional holdings were disintegrating, and short leases were replacing customary terms of tenure. In Hertfordshire, even on the estate of St Albans Abbey, where the administration tried hard to maintain old customs,

[6] Apart from G. Holmes, *The Estates of the Higher Nobility in 14th Century England*, 1957, the basic work of reference to the fluctuations of the noble families is G.E.C., *The Complete Peerage*, 1910–40. For Thomas of Woodstock, see also A. Goodman, *The Loyal Conspiracy*, 1971, p 89.

[7] F. G. Davenport, *The Economic Development of a Norfolk Manor 1086–1565*, 1906.

the tenurial situation became complicated as people from London moved in to take up holdings. Most of the big estates like that of Canterbury Cathedral Priory were being obliged to abandon the direct cultivation of their demesne, a trend that was gathering speed in the 1370s. Yet in spite of these symptoms of disintegration in the old social system, everywhere one finds that estate administrators tried to exact some labour services, restrict the mobility of agricultural tenants, and demand the traditional servile dues. These features, which can be seen in the estate accounts and the records of the manorial courts were however not peculiar to the counties affected by the revolt. They can be found in the midlands and the north, well away from the areas of turbulence. The special features of the south-east are revealed only faintly in the manorial documents, which necessarily deal with land tenure and issues arising from it. These special features are shown in the very manuscripts that record the final act of government which precipitated the rising.

These manuscripts are the unfortunately fragmentary returns of the poll tax which was granted to the king in the Parliament held in Northampton in November 1380. The peculiar feature of these returns, compared with those of the poll taxes of 1377 and 1379, is that each taxpayer's name and occupation are listed. In the 1379 return, some occupations or status designations are given, but these describe only a small minority of the total number of taxpayers. In 1377 only the total sum (at fourpence per head of the adult population) paid from each village is mentioned. Hence, although there were clearly many evasions during 1380–1381, these must have been mainly of female members of households, of adolescents near the lower age limit and certainly of some male servants. Therefore, although the evasions make the tax returns useless for demographic purposes, they remain most useful for making an overall survey of the main means of livelihood of the bulk of the population, a range of information which would never appear in estate or manorial documents with their preoccupations with tenurial obligations.

Such returns as survive give us pretty clear indications of the very special features of the East Anglian and Essex population on the eve of the rising. They show that those earning their living as tenants of landed holdings were in a minority, sometimes quite a small minority. The majority of the villagers were either self-employed craftsmen, whose occupation is given us, or were servants and labourers, possibly in husbandry, but equally likely in the service of some master craftsman. Let us look at some of these returns—a mere selection, unfortunately, of surviving fragments—from districts in Essex, Sussex and Norfolk. (None have survived for Kent, apart from a return from Canterbury itself and some fragments of the 1379 tax return, and none from Hertfordshire or Cambridgeshire.) The main Essex returns are for thirteen villages in Hinckford Hundred in the north of the county, between the Cam and the Stour.[8] Those from Suffolk are of the twenty-nine villages in Thingo, Lackford and Stow Hundred, mostly in the Bury St Edmunds and Stowmarket areas, together with a fragmentary return from Flixton and St Margaret, near Bungay.[9] The only adequate Norfolk returns (from the point of view of occupational analysis) are rather fragmentary, but include details of North Walsham and of four villages between it and the sea, an area of intense activity in 1381.[10]

In all, the names of some 3,700 taxpayers are legible in the three counties, the vast majority of whose occupations are stated. In Essex, a rough calculation gives the following broad proportions: 14 per cent were peasants; 31 per cent were craftsmen or tradesmen; and 55 per cent were labourers or servants. In north-west Suffolk there were: 15 per cent peasants; 21 per cent craftsmen and tradesmen; and 63 per cent servants and labourers. In Flixton and St Margaret, east Suffolk, the proportions were rather different, partly owing to the presence of two gentry households and a small priory: the peasants constituted rather more than 27 per cent

[8] See n. 3 above. An unpublished fragment records the taxpayers from some coastal villages. The details are complete for only two of these. At Tilbury there were seven free tenants and twenty-eight labourers. Only one free tenant is shown to be married and twelve of the labourers. The return for Middleton shows a sharp contrast—thirteen tenants and the wives of eight of them are the only taxed inhabitants. PRO, E.179. 123/44.

[9] The Thingo, Lackford and Stow returns are printed by Powell as an appendix. The Flixton and St Margaret returns are PRO, E. 179. 189/33.

[10] PRO, E.179. 149/59.

of the taxpaying population; craftsmen and traders 23 per cent; the remainder (apart from the gentry and the clerics) being servants and labourers. In Norfolk, about 25 per cent were peasants; 55 per cent craftsmen and traders; and 18 per cent servants and labourers.

These figures give only general indications, rather than precise designations, of the occupational structure. The descriptions vary in detail from county to county, so that in Essex it is not possible to distinguish servants and labourers employed in husbandry from those employed by craftsmen and traders. Sons and daughters are sometimes described as servants in the households of their parents. And there is, of course, considerable matter for doubt as to whether one should classify certain occupations closely connected with agriculture, such as carters or thatchers among the crafts, rather than with the peasants. Again, of course, many country people brewed ale, frequently as a by-occupation to agriculture, but sometimes in such quantities that it became a principal source of income. It is possible in such circumstances that these would be described in the tax returns as 'brewers' rather than 'cultivators'. In some returns (as in Essex), all the persons of one occupation are listed together. Elsewhere, as in Norfolk (and other counties which do not concern us, Gloucestershire, for example), the servants who apparently lived in their employers' households were listed together with the employer. But there is no mistaking the contrast between the occupational structure of many of these south-eastern villages and those, for instance, of even such a well-populated midland agricultural county as Leicestershire. The Leicestershire returns show quite a high proportion of wage workers (about 30 per cent according to the extant poll-tax return), but they are clearly for the most part servants in husbandry; and the substantial element in most villages is composed of peasant farmers.[11]

Some actual examples will demonstrate our point, and for illustration we choose that fragment of the poll-tax return which describes, either completely or in part, four villages near North Walsham and which includes a long list of names

[11] R. H. Hilton, *The Economic Development of some Leicestershire Estates in the 14th and 15th centuries*, 1947, app. V.

which can hardly be other than from North Walsham itself. This is the area which has been described as the 'cradle . . . the supreme fortress and the tomb of the Norfolk rebels'.[12] The villages for which the information is complete are Ridlington and Crostwight; the list of names for Witton and Smallburgh are possibly substantially complete, but it is also possible they run on to a missing membrane of parchment whose existence can be guessed at by stitch marks at the end of the surviving membrane. There are forty-four and twenty-eight names respectively on the complete list, thirty-five and thirty-two names on the incomplete list, so if the villages were of similar size, few names are likely to be missing. On the other side of the membrane are 211 names which we take to be from North Walsham itself. The names are normally those of male heads of households, the occupation and the words 'and wife' (*et uxor*) being added.

At Ridlington there were thirteen peasants, that is *cultores*, tillers of the soil, who are not likely to have been of gentry or franklin status, otherwise we would have been informed. Two of these peasants employed a full-time ploughman, but these are the only hired men attached to the households of individual peasants. There were also two threshers, not attached to any peasant household. The normal village crafts connected with husbandry were represented by a smith, a carpenter and a rope maker. There was a baker and, as one would expect near the coast, three sailors (*nautae*) and a fisherman. There were also a pedlar and a skinner. But the significant group for this area was concerned with textiles, five spinsters and six weavers. The other villages show a similar industrial element. The Witton list reveals seven cultivators with five others in agricultural occupations; three carpenters and a shoemaker; two pedlars and three sailors; and a textile group consisting of seven weavers and two spinsters. The overlap of occupations is illustrated by the fact that one of the sailor's sons was a weaver. In Crostwight and Smallburgh, the textile group was slightly smaller, including: three weavers, two spinsters, a dyer and a fuller in Crostwight; and three weavers, a spinster and two fullers in Smallburgh. While there were nine

[12] Réville, p 137.

cultivators in Crostwight, only three are found in the (incomplete) Smallburgh list.

North Walsham was a larger and more diversified place—between a village and a town. From the incomplete list we can reckon that the agricultural element was probably very much a minority. There were twenty cultivators, one of whom had two and two of whom had one servant each. Other agricultural occupations were (possibly) five labourers, four threshers and a miller. There was a normal supply of service occupations, such as shoemakers, victuallers of various types, merchants and pedlars and workers in the building trade. The textile industry provided the biggest single group of occupations: forty-six weavers, eight fullers, three dyers, two spinsters and a slay-maker. Ten weavers had between them sixteen servants, some of whom were probably apprentices or journeymen, though they could have been ordinary household servants. There was also a not inconsiderable clothing trade consisting of eight tailors.

The focus of the rising was London, the administrative and political capital of the country. The rebels' efforts came nearest to success in London and suffered conclusive defeat there in their confrontation with the king and his advisers. But it was not the political aspect of the rebellion which explains why it occurred in the south-east. This was the most industrialized and commercialized part of the country and this therefore was the area where lord–peasant relationships (or if one likes to use the expression, the feudal relationships which had been born of a natural economy) were pushed to the limit. This tension between the developing market economy of the peasants and the system of social relations between themselves and those who not only owned land but jurisdictions, is one which we have seen to be responsible in different ways for peasant movements all over Europe at least as early as the eleventh century. Whether it was resolved in a deal which, as in Italy or France, gave the peasant community the privileges analogous to those of the urban communes, or in an outburst of violent and elemental fury, the fact remains that it was normally in the most developed regions economically that discontent reached the point where fundamental social change seemed the only way out. One has only to consider the economic characteristics of the Paris basin, the county of Barcelona, maritime Flanders, Lombardy or the Rhine valley, scenes of major European movements, to appreciate that the English peasants' revolt could only begin in market-oriented southeast England.

7 Social Composition

One would expect that the occupational diversity of the main regions of the rising would be reflected in the leadership and the membership of the rebel bands. To what extent were contemporary observers able to appreciate the social diversity of the movement? The poet John Gower describes the rising in the first book of his *Vox Clamantis*, using the familiar image of a dream, or rather, a nightmare. He presents the rebels exclusively as peasants *serviles rustici, servile genus, rusticitas*.[1] Walsingham, whose elaborate history has so much influenced subsequent interpretations, strongly emphasizes the peasant component, as one would expect of a monk from a land-owning monastery whose rural tenants were as much involved in the rebellion as were the townsmen of St Albans itself. The initial rising in Essex, according to him, was of 'peasants, whom we call serfs or bondmen, together with their rural neighbours' (*rustici namque quos nativos vel bondis vocamus simul cum ruralibus accolis*). He refers to the rebels at the Tower of London as 'not merely peasants (*rusticos*) but the most abject of peasants'. A demonstration for charters of freedom at St Albans was attended by 'peasants and serfs of the abbot and convent, together with the common people of the district and certain of the townspeople' (*rustici et nativi abbatis et conventus simul cum communibus patriae et quibusdam de villanis*). Gower occasionally refers to the 'commons' as distinct from peasants as, for example, when describing the composition of the Kentish contingent. Otherwise, he uses terms of abuse, such as 'ribald', 'debauchees', or 'idle rascals' (*ribaldi, ganeo, nebulo*). There is no emphasis on the artisan element, which could have been subsumed under the term 'commons' or 'rural neighbours'.[2]

---

[1] *The Works of John Gower*, IV, *Latin Works*, ed. G. C. Macaulay, 1902, pp 20–81; English translation in E. W. Stockton, ed., *The Major Latin Works of John Gower*, 1962, pp 49–90.

[2] T. Walsingham, *Historia Anglicana* I, RS, 1863, pp 454, 459, 477.

The other writers who stressed the peasant element are the chroniclers from the big Benedictine landed monasteries of Westminster, Bury St Edmunds and Evesham: 'a great crowd of rustics' (Westminster); 'a cursed band of country men and peasants' (Bury St Edmunds); 'Common people from the country as well as others' (Evesham). Others, however, stressed the general lower-class composition of the rising rather than either the peasant or the artisan element. Knighton, the Augustinian canon from Leicester, refers to the 'commons' and to the 'plebs', but adding that at Blackheath were apprentices who had left their masters. A short official account in the City of London Letter Book refers to 'commoners and persons of the lowest rank'. The chronicler of Dunstable Abbey says that the rebels consisted of the 'communities' (*communitates*) of Kent and Essex, of the St Albans estate, of Barnet and of Berkhampstead. The chronicler of the Yorkshire Cistercian monastery of Kirkstall calls the rebels' peasants and others working in the mechanical trades' (*in mechanicis artibus*). The chronicler from Dieulacres in Staffordshire refers to the 'plebeians' of Kent and Essex, the Bermondsey annalist to a 'community of the people', while a spokesman from the House of Commons after the revolt, Sir Richard Waldegrave, describes them as the 'lesser commons' (*menues communes*).[3]

The names and occupations of some of the leading figures were well known to the chroniclers nearest in time and place to the revolt, Walsingham and the Anonimalle chronicler being the best informed. These leaders were, of course, Wat Tyler, whose surname may well have been a correct occupational description, John Ball and John Wrawe (priests) and Geoffrey Litster (dyer). But even at this date, surnames were not entirely fixed and hereditary and many names may have been pseudonyms or nicknames, rather than names which would have been entered on a rent roll or tax list. Jack Straw, about whom nothing is known, sounds like a nickname. Knighton thought it was an alias for Wat Tyler. The Dieulacres chronicle also attributed the role usually played by

[3] R. Higden, *Polychronicon* IX (*continuation*), RS, 1866, p 1; *Memorials of St Edmunds*, III, p 125; *Vita Regis Ricardi* II, ed. T. Hearne, 1729, p 24; H. Knighton, *Chronicon*, II, RS, 1895, p 131; Dobson, p 209; *Dunstable Annals*, pp 415–17; *Kirkstall Chron.*, p 110; *Dieulacres Chron.*, p 164; *Rotuli Parliamentarum*, III, 1783, p 100, no. 17.

Tyler to Jack Straw and suggested that this was the pseudonym of a black sheep from the Kentish gentry family of Culpeper. This chronicler even thought one leader was Piers Plowman, and clearly such names as Jakke Mylnere, Jakke Carter and Jakke Trewman, supplied by Knighton, come into the nickname category. Who provided the nicknames? The Evesham chronicler evidently thought that all the names were pseudonyms, given by the rebels to those whom they chose as leaders (*sibi judices et praenuncios vel capitaneos eis praefecerunt huiusmodi nomina imponentes. . . .*),[4] such as Jak Sherp, John Wraw, Thomas Meller, Watte Taylor (*sic*), Hobbe Carter and Jak Straw. If the letters supposed to be dispatched by John Ball and others, and recorded by Walsingham and Knighton, are authentic, these would confirm that the pseudonyms were chosen by the rebels rather than attached in a derisory way by the chroniclers. If anything, they tend to stress the rural origins of the leadership with their emphasis on agricultural associations. The fact that there seem to be positive echoes in them from William Langland's *Piers the Ploughman* does not contradict the suggestions, though it does pose interesting problems about lower-class culture at this time.

The peasant element in the local leadership and membership of rebel bands appears rather less prominent when we look at the indictments and the escheators' records of confiscations after the defeat of the rising.[5] The indictments were based on presentments by local juries and are very risky to use if quantitative evidence is sought. Sometimes the occupation of the accused person is stated, sometimes not. It may be that a name without an occupation would, normally speaking, indicate a peasant, since occupational designations are almost invariably descriptive of non-agricultural occupations. The status terminology for agriculturalists which came into legal

[4] *Vita Regis Ricardi II*, p 24.

[5] Many of the indictments and escheators' inquisitions and accounts have been printed. W. E. Flaherty, *Archeologia Cantiana*, III, IV, 1860–1; J. A. Sparvel-Bayly, *Transactions of the Essex Archeological Society*, N.S., I, 1878; E. Powell and G. M. Trevelyan, *The Peasants' Rising and the Lollards*, 1899; Powell, app. II; Réville, app. II; W. M. Palmer and H. W. Saunders, *Documents Relating to Cambridgeshire Villages*, 1926. Some unprinted escheators' inquisitions for Norfolk and Suffolk are in PRO, E.153/1167, 1168. No. 1167 includes T. Sampson's inquisition which was printed by Powell. See below, p. 180.

records as a matter of course after the statute of 1413—
gentleman, yeoman, husbandman and so on—is not found,
other than the designation of knightly status.[6] Furthermore,
in so far as one wishes to investigate the occupations of the
rank and file of the rebel bands, the jury's habit of giving two
or three names and adding such phrases as 'with a multitude
of other unknown persons', makes any precision impossible.
We can only say, therefore, on the basis of the indictments,
that among the many names of the accused, there is a fair
scattering—perhaps almost a substantial minority—of persons
with other than agricultural occupations. Apart from the
clergy, who are worth considering separately, these are men
who for the most part ply essential trades in any peasant
society. Carpenters, sawyers, masons, cobblers, tailors, weavers, fullers, glovers, hosiers, skinners, bakers, butchers, inn-
keepers, cooks and a lime-burner are found in the Kentish
indictments. Much the same is true in Essex, with the addition
of a couple of glaziers; and similarly Suffolk, though here the
occupational descriptions attached to names are fewer.

The indictments were necessarily indiscriminate. Some
presentments were for offences which implied no commitment to the purposes of the rising. Juries of presentment
display as much social prejudice as monastic chroniclers,
so that accusations can by no means be accepted as being more
impartial than the observations of writers such as Thomas
Walsingham of St Albans. We are told, in fact, by the author
of the Anonimalle chronicle that, together with tax-collectors
and lawyers, jurors were among the earliest targets of rebel
hostility. Jurors were those persons of local standing who had
become identified with the judicial apparatus of courts leet,
J.P.s' quarter-sessions and sessions of assize justices. If they
had earned the resentment of the local population before the
rising, they might well have been all the more inclined afterwards to make vindictive presentments.

Not all indictments were accepted, and it may have been
that some of the more untenable accusations fell down, or
that for political reasons it was felt best to press home accusations more stringently against those regarded as ringleaders
than against those considered to have been misled. For these

[6] *Statutes of the Realm*, II, 1816, p 171.

reasons the lists of confiscations of the property of those judged guilty may well be more reliable evidence of participants in the rising than the initial indictments. They also have the advantage of being more precise. No question here of two names and a vague reference to 'other ribalds and traitors'. The lists drawn up by the escheators are not of course complete, nor are the surviving manuscripts all in a legible condition. But they have the advantage that, in addition to giving occasional indications of occupation, they also indicate the degree of wealth or poverty in the description of the convicted persons, chattels or land.

The best known of these escheators' inquisitions, published many years ago by Edgar Powell, concerns the property of the Suffolk rebel, Thomas Sampson, one of those who assembled, supported and linked up the rebel bands (*congregatores sustentores et interligatores hominum*) in five of the Suffolk hundreds. Sampson was a well-to-do yeoman, with 137 acres under crop in the three villages of Kersey, Harksted and Freston, implying with allowance for fallowed land an estate of at least 200 acres. He had some 300 sheep and nearly 100 head of stock additionally and an eighth share in a ship at Harwich. The corn, whether still growing or in the barns, the hay, the livestock and the deadstock were valued at some £65, without taking into account the price of the land. It is worthwhile bearing in mind this valuation of chattels to compare with the valuation of goods of other condemned men.

We must, of course, be as critical of the escheators' inquisitions as a source as of any other piece of evidence. The local informants of the escheators could be unreliable. Some of the goods may have been removed by friends or enemies of the convicted persons. Lands held in villein tenure or as unregistered sublettings from other peasants might not be valued. The escheators themselves had by no means a spotless reputation when it came to reporting to the exchequer all the property in their purview which was to be taken over by the crown. Unfortunately, while recognizing these possible defects in the evidence, there is little that we can do to check it. We have to do the best that we can with it.

There were other convicted rebels as rich as Sampson. The

leading Cambridgeshire rebel, John Hanchache of Shudy
Camps, was a landowner whose holding was described as
comprising one-fifth of manorial property in Barham and
six other villages. It was not valued, and many Cambridgeshire manors were quite small, but clearly, Hanchache was at
least a rich yeoman moving up perhaps into the lesser gentry.
Property described in manorial terms implies tenants as well
as land directly cultivated by the owner. Another Cambridgeshire rebel had land in six villages. This was Geoffrey Cobbe
of Wimpole, whose holdings are not described in manorial
terms, but must have contained several hundred acres, for they
were valued at about £24 a year. William Gildeborne, one
of eight rebels from the original storm centre at Fobbing,
Essex, who was hanged, had goods (including 72 sheep)
worth £49, and land which judging by its rental value could
have been about 100 acres in area. Farther down the scale of
wealth we find other convicted rebels, still comparatively
well-to-do. The beheaded rebel John Coveshurst, from
Lamberhurst in Kent had land in three parishes (Lamberhurst, Brenchley and Hadlow) valued at 18s 11d a year and
containing 37 acres of arable, 50 acres of pasture, 5 acres of
meadow and 20 acres of woodland; his goods were not valued.
John Cook of Barton, Cambridgeshire, convicted as a local
leader, had 50 acres of land in addition to his house and goods
to the value of £6 7s 6d. John Brux of Caxton, Cambridgeshire, who was beheaded, had two ploughlands (perhaps
200 acres), a rent income of 15s 8d and £9 8s 10d worth of
goods. William Bokenham of Hinxton, Cambridgshire, convicted as a traitor rebel, held as a tenant at will 61 acres of
arable and 2 acres of meadow; his goods were not valued.
Landed holdings such as these were possessed by only a
minority of convicted rebels, but it should be emphasized
that only a minority of tenants at the apex of village society
were farming on this scale. The yeomen may have contributed
to the rebellion proportionately to their numerical strength
in the population.

A noticeable feature of the lists of rebels who appear in the
escheators' inquisitions is the apparent landlessness of the
majority of those convicted. This does not necessarily reflect
the real situation. Lands held in villein or customary tenure

would lapse into the hands of the lord of the manor on a tenant's conviction as a felon. With few exceptions (such as the land held at will by William Bokenham of Hinxton), the lands valued by the escheators must have been held in free tenure, which the crown was entitled to confiscate from felons convicted of treason. Even if the immediate lord had a claim on the land of convicted felons, by the end of the fourteenth century the lordship of small free tenures, especially in eastern England, had long been rendered meaningless as a result of complexities produced by the buying and selling of land. We are therefore dependent on an analysis of the valuation of rebels' chattels to gain an indication of their economic status, rather than on an attempt to estimate the value of their landed holdings. This is not a simple matter, for the value of a person's goods at a particular point of time does not give an infallible indication of his prosperity. Let us remember, however, that in 1332 those who had less than 10s-worth of goods were exempt, being regarded as too poor to tax. Now the Norfolk and Suffolk escheators in 1381 seem to have been working on the following valuation: 13s 4d per horse; 10s per ox; 5s–7s per cow; 5s per stot (working horse); 3s per bullock; 8d or 9d per sheep; 2s 6d per acre, or 5s a quarter of wheat or barley; 2s per acre of rye; 1s 6d per acre of drage; and 1s 4d per acre of peas and oats. These were the most important and essential of the peasants' movables—tools and furniture in poor households constituting a relatively low proportion of the total value of goods.

Out of about 180 examples from the escheators' inquisitions in most of the counties affected by the rising, only 65 had valuations of goods under 20s. These must have been very under equipped, as a list of the chattels of Richard of Narston, made on the day of his indictment, would indicate. This man, whose valuation at £6 was high, had nevertheless no more than the following: 4 horses (53s 4d); 4 cows (28s); wheat and barley (20s); and other goods valued at 18s 8d. There were 15 rebels out of 180 who had chattels valued at more than £5. In other words, a majority were probably equipped with at least the minimum of necessary stock, a sizeable minority rather inadequately provided and a small minority either reasonably well-to-do or even affluent.

This leads us, of course, to consider the evidence of the escheators' inquisitions concerning the participation of persons not directly engaged in agricultural production. We are again obliged to do a certain amount of guesswork, particularly as regards occupational surnames. By the time of the rising many people were using the surnames of their father and mother. A century earlier a man's surname more often than not described his current occupation or place of origin. In 1381, it was rather less often than not. And yet surnames in some official documents, particularly in tax returns, were simply occupational descriptions. An appropriate example is Geoffrey Litster of Felmingham, described in the escheator's inquisition as 'traitor and principal insurgent'. His chattels were valued at 33*s* 9*d*.[7] 'Litster' means 'dyer', and this was indeed Geoffrey's trade. Another example which illustrates the uncertainty is the entry concerning Thomas Flecchere of Bergholt, who had been beheaded and who was stated as having held a cottage, an acre-and-a-half of land, with 29*s*-worth of chattels.[8] Was this man, then, a 'fletcher', or arrow-maker, with his own smallholding, like so many village craftsmen? If we add the number of persons without agricultural–occupational surnames to the number of persons whose (non–agricultural) occupations are given in addition to their surnames, there are just under 50 possible non-agriculturalists out of 180 in the escheators' lists—including persons with 'craft names' from places like Dartford and Rochester. On the other hand, it might exclude persons with surnames of topographical origin who were in fact craftsmen without this being stated. William Gore, or Corre, of West Wickham in Cambridgeshire was a tailor before the rising, a fact not revealed by his surname but only by the official enquiry; this showed also that he did not return to his trade, but became a sort of social bandit at the head of a band of nine robbers operating around Royston, Walden, Buntingford and Clavering. These men remained uncaptured until October 1382.

Bearing in mind the incompleteness of the records which renders quantitative precision impossible, the surviving facts about the sort of people who were involved in the rising do

---

[7] PRO, E.153/1168.   [8] *ibid.*, E.153/1167.

make some generalizations possible. The names of the indicted, and of those whose property was confiscated, would naturally tend to include those men and women who took a prominent if not always leading part in the events. A full list of all participants might suggest a rather different balance between different occupations, but, with the exception of the clergy, this difference might not have been all that great. The proportion of the well-to-do against those of middling and lesser fortune, and of craftsmen against agriculturalists, suggests that the social composition of the rebellious bands reflected the stratification of contemporary society. In other words, the rising was one of the whole people below the ranks of those who exercised lordship in the countryside and established authority in the towns. Those few members of the gentry, like Sir Roger Bacon from Norfolk, who took part on the side of the rebels were not typical of their class or even of an important minority element. This emphasizes that even in the relatively industrialized and socially very differentiated southeast, those major social grievances acute enough to generate rebellious actions were not the ones that divided the poor from the middling and rich peasants, or the labourers from their employers, but rather those which divided the mass of the population from the lords, the lawyers and government officials.

This conclusion does not basically differentiate the English rising from uprisings on the continent, though (with the exception of the rebellion in Flanders) we are fortunate, in spite of its deficiencies, in having rather better evidence than elsewhere of rebel social origins. There are, of course, inevitable differences in emphasis between one revolt and another. The importance of the artisan element which we notice in the English rising is naturally most closely matched in the Flemish movement where the union of artisan industry and peasant agriculture was such an important feature. On the other hand, what little we know about the personnel of the Jacquerie of 1359 suggests that the rich peasant element, also found in England, was prominent. This may also be true of Catalonia in the fifteenth century, though the case of Verntallat should warn us that the narrowness of the social gulf between the poor *hidalgo* and the rich peasant may have meant a greater participation of the lesser nobility than in England. This general problem may merit further research, because, as we have seen in the Beauvaisis in 1359 and in the Massif Central during the period of the Tuchins, there were opportunities, even invitations, for discontented nobles to achieve positions of leadership. With these parallels in view, it may be thought that we have unnecessarily minimized the role of the occasional gentleman in England on the side of the rebels. But with the evidence which is at hand it would not be possible to give the gentry anything like a leading or formative role in the events of 1381. In any case, we must not fall into the common error of supposing that social and political leadership could not be expected from any lower class in medieval English society than this.

8 The Allies of the Rebels

When accounting for the presence in the ranks and in the leadership of the rebels of non agriculturalists, such as artisans from the villages and small towns, we are discussing the involvement of one of the elements of rural society. These were not so much allies of the peasantry as part of them. But there were elements of English society at this time who were involved in the rising with the peasants as their allies, without being part of them. These were the townsmen. Here we must make a distinction. There were disturbances in some towns which were simply the continuation, or revival, of struggles having a purely urban context, and which took place because of the generally disturbed condition of the country at large. On these occasions there was no sort of alliance or combination with the peasant rebels. In other towns, while the same factors of inner-urban conflict might have existed, a new situation emerged, constituting a conscious effort by rebels of town and country to take advantage (at the least) of a temporary coincidence of revolutionary interests. Thus, some urban conflicts, however fierce, did not link up with the rural rebellion, and these occurred over a wide area—York, Winchester, Bridgwater, Beverley, and Scarborough. But in London, St Albans, Bury St Edmunds, and possibly in Canterbury and Cambridge, a rebellious urban element became closely associated with the rural insurrection, and in consequence found itself in revolt not simply against a local lord or local oligarchs, but against the king's government.

Not much is known about those internal conflicts in the small towns which led to an alliance between the factions out of power and the country rebels. A good deal more is known about London, but here the interpretation of happenings is complicated by a large amount of deliberately misleading evidence, in the form of indictments. These were drawn up after the revolt with the aim by one of the city factions of pinning responsibility for complicity with the rebels upon its rivals.[1] Complicity certainly existed between part of London's population and the rebels from Kent and Essex, but as almost all of the contemporary chroniclers make clear, it was, as one might expect, the London poor who were the allies of the country rebels.

London's social and political structure much more resembled some of the big continental trading and manufacturing towns than it did that of other English towns. Its population, calculated from the poll-tax returns of 1377 was, as we have seen, something between 35,000 and 40,000. The next biggest English town, York, the capital of the north, had barely 11,000 inhabitants, while Bristol had about 9,500, Coventry about 7,200 and Norwich about 6,000, these being the biggest of the provincial towns.[2] The majority of the adult males in London were poor and were excluded from any participation in the running of the city or of its institutions. As in most big European towns the merchants and craftsmen who were organized in the various companies, misteries or gilds were quite a small minority. Although over 180 different trades have been counted from the records, only 51 misteries had political representation in 1377. It has been calculated that only one Londoner in four was a freeman of the city with political rights exercised either through his gild or through the machinery of the ward in which he lived. Quite a large number even of skilled workers from other parts of England or from abroad were unenfranchised. These industries also employed unskilled and semi-skilled journeymen who were excluded from the secrets of the trade in which they were employed. Finally, there was a large and indeterminate mass of casual labourers without any sort of industrial training. Naturally these shaded off into a 'Lumpenproletariat' of varying degrees of destitution and criminality.[3]

[1] B. Wilkinson, 'The Peasants' Revolt of 1381', *Speculum*, 1940.

[2] There is a useful list of the numbers of taxpayers in 1377 in the appendix to W. G. Hoskins, *Local History in England*, 1959. The conversion of these figures to total population depends on one's views about the age structure of the population at this period, and about the amount of tax evasion. The taxpayers were those over the age of 14.

[3] A. H. Thomas, *Calendar of Plea and Memoranda Rolls of the City of London*, II, 1929, pp lx–lxiv; E. M. Veale, 'Craftsmen and the economy of London in the 14th century' in *Studies in London History*, 1969, A. E. J. Hollaender and W. Kellaway, eds.

Much of the history of medieval London is written in terms of the political and industrial conflicts affecting the enfranchised and organized population of gildsmen.[4] These were, of course, the people who alone could provide the continuous political history of the city, for they were the only persons to have power—in varying quantities. For it is not to be imagined that the whole of the enfranchised quarter of the adult male population would equally share in the rule of the city. Political, social and economic power were narrowly concentrated in the hands of a small group of rich merchant capitalists. Although they might be in any one of a number of leading companies, such as fishmongers, grocers, vintners, mercers or goldsmiths, they traded in a wide range of commodities, provided the trade brought in a profit. They were usually aldermen, representing one of the city wards, and expected some time in their lives to fill such leading posts as mayor or sheriff. It was a custom in the city that its freemen had the right to trade wholesale in any commodity. The consequence of this limited form of *laissez-faire* was that we find men, ranging from the rich grocer and national politician Nicholas Brembre to such a lesser civic dignitary as the ironmonger Gilbert Maghfeld,[5] investing their money in a whole range of commodities of internal and international trades. Brembre was dealing with such imports as iron, wine and woad and was exporting raw wool. He lent money to individuals and to the government, and was a considerable landowner in London, Kent and Middlesex. Maghfeld dealt in iron, woad, fish, wine and grain, as well as cloth, spices and a range of miscellaneous commodities.

The fierce factional struggles which occurred in the upper reaches of the mercantile oligarchy of the city of London are sometimes rather too simply represented as a conflict between the victualling and the manufacturing interests. At the time of the rebellion the conflict was in full swing, a fishmonger, William Walworth, being mayor. But soon a rival party led

[4] G. Unwin, *Gilds and Companies of London*, 1908; S. L. Thrupp, *The Merchant Class of Medieval London*, 1948; R. Bird, *The Turbulent London of Richard II*, 1949. The last work is an important corrective to Unwin's book, which nevertheless is essential reading.

[5] M. K. James, *Studies in the Medieval Wine Trade*, 1971, chap. 7.

by John of Northampton, a moderately prosperous draper, backed by a substantial element from the middling manufacturing crafts, was to come to power. It was while John of Northampton was mayor, in October 1381, that the indictments were drawn up which accused aldermen Sibley, Horne, Fresshe, Carlile and Tong of being in league with the rebels to let them into the city. They were of course supporters of the party which was in control of the city government at the time of the revolt. The first two were fishmongers, while Fresshe was a mercer, Carlile a grocer and Tong a vintner. The most that they are likely to have done was to temporize in the hope of preventing a sack of the city. When their party, headed by Nicholas Brembre, returned to power they were acquitted. All the same, the ease of entry of the rebels has to be explained, and in fact the explanation is quite simple.

The contemporary chroniclers, none of them involved in London's factional politics, are unanimous about the entry of the rebels over London Bridge and through Aldgate on Corpus Christi Day, 13 June. The Anonimalle chronicler says that it was the commons of Southwark who obliged the keepers of the bridge to lower it and let the rebels enter. According to Walsingham, the city commons and especially the poor prevented the mayor from closing the gate. The monk of Evesham writes that on the eve of Corpus Christi the city commons held the Bridge Gate open for them. The author of the continuation to the *Eulogium Historiarum* has a slightly more elaborate story. He writes that both the mayor and burgesses (presumably aldermen) asked the citizens as a whole if they wanted to exclude the rebels, but the citizens refused, claiming the rebels as their neighbours and their friends. Messengers whom the aldermen sent to ward off the rebels in fact encouraged them to come in. The Dunstable annalist refers to the agreement between the rebels besieging the city and the commons within, while, although the Westminster monk does not refer to the role of the London poor in letting the rebels through the gates, he does refer to the divisions within the city population. The citizen body, he says, failed to stand up to the rustics because they feared that in resisting them the commons of the city would rise with the serfs against the rest of the citizens. This is a clear enough, though indirect, reference to the conflict between the enfranchised burgesses and the unen-franchised mass.[6] The London masses were no doubt excited by the political conflicts in the city between Northampton's party and the top oligarchs; and undoubtedly, too, they took a hostile attitude to John of Gaunt in his conflicts with the city as a whole, a struggle which was exacerbated by the attempts of the royal marshall to exercise his jurisdiction in the city to the contempt of the city courts. They were certainly aware of the scandals of 1376 which were exposed in the Good Parliament, and which revealed corruption in the aldermanic ranks of the city. This episode in the politics of the realm had its reflection the same year in the politics of London, when Northampton and his supporters succeeded for a time in obtaining the annual election of the aldermen by their wards and the election of members of the common council from the crafts instead of the wards.[7]

These were not, perhaps, issues of such fundamental importance as wages and the cost of food. Indeed, London differed somewhat from the smaller English towns where the main internal conflict was between the rank-and-file masters of the crafts and the mercantile oligarchs. It is not that this position did not exist in London. It was an important element in the conflict between John of Northampton and the narrow group of rich entrepreneurs, many with victualling interests, of whom Brembre was typical. The craft masters themselves did not constitute a homogeneous group. In addition to the fifty or so craft misteries which elected representatives to the common council in the 1370s and 1380s, there were as many again which were too insignificant or ephemeral to do so. Furthermore, even in established and prosperous crafts, small masters and journeymen tended to be interchangeable categories. Even the largest enterprises seldom had a staff of more than a dozen or so apprentices and journeymen; most of them only had one, two or three. There was no basis for the existence of a homogeneous proletariat. Nevertheless, the division between employer and employee was much clearer

---

[6] Dobson. For the Evesham version, *Vita Regis Ricardi II*, p 25; *Dunstable Annals*, p 416.
[7] These issues are dealt with in the works cited by Unwin and Bird.

than it was in smaller towns, and was expressed in various regulations, already half a century and more old, which aimed to prevent combinations of journeymen for the purpose of putting up wages.[8]

Journeymen's combinations took traditional forms, as in the well-known case of the journeymen saddlers in 1396.[9] These journeymen claimed simply to be a well-established fraternity of pious working men who met once a year at Stratford, to the east of London, on the feast of the Assumption of the Virgin Mary. This, they said, was for the purpose of walking in procession, clad in the livery of the fraternity, from Stratford to St Vedast's church, near the west end of West Cheap, so that they could hear the Mass. The religious aspect of the fraternity no doubt, was genuine enough. Most craft gilds, rich or poor, were religious fraternities as well as being organizations with economic purposes. The other aspect of this fraternity of saddlers' journeymen was that they discussed their wage problems and were suspected by the masters of being in agreement to increase their wages 'under a certain feigned colour of sanctity' to double or more what they had been thirteen years earlier. The mayor and aldermen suppressed the separate organization as they had done previously with similar journeymen's fraternities in this same and in other crafts. In addition to their civic authority by which such subversive organizations were disbanded, the mayor and aldermen had further powers derived from Parliamentary statute, for they were also Justices of the Peace with authority to apply the Statute of Labourers. The wage-earners themselves were not of course a homogeneous mass. Apprentices and serving men in the rich companies earned good wages from which they hoped to accumulate enough to set up as masters on their own account. It was the journeymen in the lesser crafts and above all the unskilled and casual labourers who would be most likely to support the rebels. The fact that the trend of London wages was upwards—as it was in the country as a whole—would do nothing to diminish their militancy. In town as well as

[8] S. L. Thrupp, *op. cit.*, pp 73–4.
[9] A translation of the official account of the dispute is published in A. E. Bland, P. A. Brown and R. H. Tawney, eds, *English Economic History: Select Documents*, 1933, pp 138–41.

country, when rising expectations came up against official
regulations, and when officialdom for other reasons was
discredited, a positive response to a revolutionary initiative
was inevitable.

It is by no means easy to separate the actions of the London
rebels from those of their allies from the counties. The difficulty is well illustrated by contradictory stories about the
burning of the Duke of Lancaster's home, the Savoy,[10] which
was between the Strand and the river. The Anonmialle
chronicler gives the most detail about London's events. He
suggests that the Savoy was burnt by the London commons
because of their hatred for the duke before the arrival of the
men of Kent. But he also tells us that the commons of Kent
passed through London from the Bridge to Fleet Street, presumably through Ludgate, without doing any damage. It was
not until they were outside the city walls again that they
picked various targets of political or social significance. The
chronicler, having told us already that the Londoners burnt
the Savoy, describes in detail an attack by the men from Kent
on the Savoy, but qualifies this by saying that some people,
all the same, blamed the Londoners. In this, the author of the
continuation of the *Eulogium Historiarum* agrees with him,
emphasizing that the Londoners attacked Gaunt's palace
before the arrival of the other rebels.

Walsingham, however, attributes the initial attack on the
Savoy to the invaders. The Westminster chronicler also
blames the countrymen (*agrestis illa societas*), as does the
Evesham author of the life of King Richard. Henry Knighton,
who as a canon of Leicester Abbey lived in a house having
close connexions with John of Gaunt, also implies that the
Savoy was burnt by the generality of the rebels. The first
London inquisitions, made during the Northampton regime
with the object of framing the aldermen of Brembre's party,
blamed the outsiders, though the second of these inquisitions
says that they were led by Thomas, a malcontent and illegiti-
mate member of the prominent London family of Farringdon.
The official account in the London Letter Book, which reflects
the views of the other party, blames the burning on an alliance

[10] See, in addition to sources quoted by Dobson, *Vita Regis Ricardi II*,
pp 25–6.

of the Kent and Essex commons with those from within the city: 'perfidious commons of their own condition'. The Middlesex indictments name several Londoners, but in particular men from the extra-mural suburbs, as implicated in the attack on the Savoy. A London leadership, in fact, does seem likely. Indeed, was the moral rigour involved in the refusal by the rebels to loot the burning palace, which several chroniclers noted, an urban characteristic? Walsingham and the author of the *Eulogium* thought so. The others who comment on this episode treat it as a policy of the whole rebel army.

The refusal to loot is characteristic of the behaviour of the rebels in London in the case of the political and social targets at which they aimed. The question is: were these the Londoners' targets or those of all the rebels? As in many popular rebellions, prisons were broken open and the victims of the law were released. Apart from the prisons at Canterbury, Rochester and other Kentish jails, the first prison closely associated with London which was opened was the Marshalsea prison in Southwark. As we have seen, Londoners particularly resented the jurisdiction of the Earl Marshal. After opening the Marshalsea prison, the rebels dragged Richard Imworth, its warden, from sanctuary in Westminster Abbey and beheaded him—not in Westminster, but in London, in Cheap. Newgate prison, which had been the city prison was also broken open. By this time it was used by the government for all particularly dangerous prisoners, Londoners or not. Another prison from which the prisoners were released was the Fleet prison, once also a London prison but by now in general use by such Westminster courts as Common Pleas and Exchequer, as well as by the King's Council and Chancery. The prison at Westminster Abbey gatehouse, which contained clerical and lay prisoners from the jurisdictional liberties of the abbot as well as from those of the Bishop of London, was also broken open by the rebels. The London prisons, then, were not obvious targets for the London rebels alone.[11]

The leading men of the government, in particular Simon Sudbury, Archbishop of Canterbury (who was Chancellor)

[11] For the status of the various London prisons in the late fourteenth century, see R. B. Pugh, *Imprisonment in Medieval England*, 1968.

and Sir Robert Hales, the Prior of the Hospital of St John of Jerusalem (who was Treasurer) were prime targets and lost their lives at rebel hands. The general attack on Hospitallers' property in London as well as in the country can be attributed to the Treasurer's unpopularity, for John of Gaunt was the only other leading personality whose property in London and elsewhere was systematically despoiled. Another government official whose property was selected for attack was the Keeper of the Privy Seal, John Fordham, Bishop-elect of Durham, who was lodging in the town house of the Bishop of Chester. Lesser government officials included John Butterwick, under-sheriff of Middlesex, whose house near Newgate was burnt down. John Legge, a royal serjeant-at-arms, was beheaded at the same time as Sudbury and Hale. He was popularly supposed to be involved in the final stages of the screwing out of the third poll tax as well as being on the commission of trailbaston for Kent. Londoners might have known more details about these official personalities than the rural rebels, but it would be unwise to suppose that the attacks on them were particularly London's contribution to the rising.

The same observations might be made concerning the assaults that were made on lawyers and others connected with the apparatus of justice. When the rebels in London attacked the Temple it was not simply because it belonged to the Hospitallers, but rather that it was already tenanted by lawyers, whose records they burnt. They attacked not only the lawyers themselves—attorneys, pleaders, clerks of the courts— but others closely associated with the judicial processes. These included 'questmongers' who made a profession of sitting on juries of inquisition. One of them, Roger Legett, was killed by the rebels and his house burnt. It has been suggested that this was an example of London revenge, for he had been accused of setting up man-traps in the area of the present Lincoln's Inn Fields.[12] But the houses of the jurors and questmongers of the Marshalsea had already been destroyed by the Kent rebels in Southwark and the houses of other quest-

[12] R. Bird, *op. cit.*, p 53. The various misdeeds of 'questmongers' are succinctly listed in a sermon on swearing in W. O. Ross, ed., *Middle English Sermons, Early English Text Society*, O.S. 209, p 101.

mongers near the Savoy were burnt. Legett, therefore, may have suffered as much because of his profession as because of his previous actions. This hostility to lawyers and jurors and to legal records was not of course peculiar to the Londoners. The widespread destruction of manorial court records is well known. The Essex rebels beheaded jurors acting on the inquests to the trailbaston commission headed by Sir Robert Bealknap, the Chief Justice of Common Pleas. For the author of the Anonimalle chronicle and especially for Thomas Walsingham, there was a general threat against all involved in the processes of the law 'not only apprentices [that is barristers below the rank of serjeant] but also old justices and all the kingdom's jurors'.

The conclusion that the London allies of the country rebels were largely confined to the poor, the unskilled, the semi-skilled and the unenfranchised might be subject to at least one exception, namely the organized weavers.[13] It is not that indictments offer any hard evidence that the weavers were heavily involved, but there were many attacks on the Flemings (among whom we should probably include Brabanters) who are assumed to have been weavers, rivals of the native craftsmen and organized separately from them. The native weavers had certainly been jealous of the privileges the Flemings enjoyed. By 1378 there was a lot of anti-alien feeling in the city, though the Flemish weavers agreed in March 1380 to submit to some of the search regulations and financial obligations of the English craftsmen.[14] It could also be that some of the attacks on the Flemings were mounted not by English weaving masters, but by English journeymen employed by Flemish masters, class antagonism being cloaked, consciously or unconsciously, by xenophobia. The existence of such an antagonism as early as 1362 is revealed in a petition by the Flemish and Brabantine weavers to the city authorities. In this petition reference is made to agreements or 'covins' between workmen, by which any alien master weaver in dispute with one of his workmen would be boycotted by all the journeymen weavers in the city. In setting up a gild organization (which was the object of the petition) the alien master weavers gained the right to have their elected wardens and

[13] *ibid.*, pp 55–6.   [14] G. Unwin, *op. cit.*, p 140.

to discipline their workers, with the ultimate sanction of an appeal to the mayor and aldermen.[15]

The murder of the Flemings is commented on by most chroniclers who deal with London events, and is the only episode of the 1381 rising mentioned by Geoffrey Chaucer, who was probably living in London at this time.[16] But the first reference by the Anonimalle chronicler is not to attacks on Flemish weavers but to attacks on Flemish prostitutes living in a brothel in Southwark which they were leasing from the Mayor of London. Walsingham, the Westminster chronicler, the continuator of the *Eulogium* and the monk of Evesham[17] all comment on the killing of the Flemings. None give details of the victims' occupations, and naturally (since they were in effect relying on eye-witness or second-hand accounts) differ as to numbers. The *Eulogium* mentions 400 Flemings and others, the Anonimalle chronicler refers to thirty-five Flemings taken from the Church of St Martin in the Vintry and Walsingham says that forty-seven were taken from the church of the Austin Friars, and from one of the parish churches. The Westminster chronicler, who gives no figures, tells us that the Flemings mostly lived by the banks of the Thames. This fits in with the location of St Martin's in the Vintry. We also know that the two parish churchyards which they and the Brabantines used for the hiring of labour were St Lawrence Pountney and St Mary Somerset, both near the river. But the Austin Friars' Church was near the north wall of the city by Bishopsgate. And in fact there are some names of payers to the Middlesex poll tax in St John's Street and Shoreditch (both on the north side of the city) which could be Flemish. St John's Street was near to Clerkenwell where seven Flemings had been killed on 13 June when St John's Hospital was attacked. However, most of the certainly Flemish names in this tax return are from Tower Hill, near the river.[18]

The London Flemings who were killed by the rebels may have been master weavers at daggers drawn with rival native master craftsmen. They could also have been at daggers

[15] A. E. Bland, P. A. Brown and R. H. Tawney, pp 195–7.
[16] 'The Nuns' Priest's Tale', see N. Coghill's English translation of *The Canterbury Tales*, Penguin Classics, 1960, p 245.
[17] *Vita Regis Ricardi II*, p 25.
[18] PRO, E.179. 141/35; Réville, p 203.

drawn with English employees. The taxpayers with Flemish names in the tax return mentioned above were all employers of labour, though there is no hard evidence about the occupations of these particular Flemings. They may even have been merchants.[19] But the attack on the Flemings was not peculiar to London. Once again Londoners shared an objective with the country rebels. A group of insurgents from Kings Lynn (or Bishops Lynn as it was then known), mostly craftsmen (but only one of whom was a weaver), killed a certain Haukyn Fleming on 18 June, and on the following day went to the coastal village of Snettisham, where they tried to induce the local inhabitants to attack any Fleming they could find. This led to an attack on one Simon Wylymot, who bore a Flemish name, but who does not appear to have been a weaver or indeed any sort of craftsman. The indictment against his attacker, one Roger Loksmyth, indicates pretty clearly that Simon was an inn-keeper and maltmonger (a frequent combination of occupations). Another attack on Flemings was at Yarmouth on 19 June. The followers of Litster and his knightly ally, Roger Bacon, broke open the jail and beheaded three Flemings while releasing an Englishman. The next day, at Litster's orders, another three Flemings were beheaded. There is no indication of the occupations of any of these six unfortunates. There is some evidence, too, that Manningtree on the estuary of the Stour, was another centre of anti-Flemish feeling. A Fleming was deliberately slain there by members of the Essex contingent on their return from Mile End on 14 June. This may not have been an isolated case, for several Flemings were reported to have been killed at nearby Colchester in an indictment against Adam Michel, a leading rebel in the town.[20]

It is of some interest that the attacks on the Flemings in Norfolk and Essex took place in ports or in other seaside places. These areas had always been closely linked with the continent, particularly the Low Countries, and the number of inhabitants or visitors of Low Country origin might have

---

[19] In 1362–5 there were 129 aliens exporting wool from London. Only 17 are identifiable, but 6 of them were Flemings. A. Beardwood, *Alien Merchants in England 1350–1377*, 1931, p 36.

[20] Powell, pp. 32, 135; Réville, pp. 96, 111, 216, 217.

been quite large. The antagonism in these places can hardly be attributed simply to rivalry among weaving craftsmen. The anti-Flemish xenophobia must have a more general explanation. Like other xenophobic movements which have been linked with popular rebellions, the solution probably lies as much in the understanding of the frustrations and sufferings of the aggressors as in the status or actions of the victims. This would merit further investigation. For the moment, however, the point must be repeated that this aspect of the rising is not one in which separate interests of urban and rural rebels appears.

Paradoxically, it may have been that the majority of the London allies of the rural rebels were nearer to them in sympathy than the political activists of such smaller towns as St Albans, Bury St Edmunds and Cambridge. The London sympathisers were for the most part, like the countrymen, part of a disenfranchised mass. The leading townsmen of St Albans and Bury also felt themselves to be disenfranchised, but they were the top men in their own communities with grievances against their ecclesiastical overlords. Their opposite numbers in Cambridge had similar grievances, but in this case against what they felt to be powerful ecclesiastical usurpers of their rights, the religious houses and the scholars of the university.

St Albans, Bury St Edmunds and Cambridge typify the conscious alliance of the townsmen with rural rebellion in pursuit of their own sectional aims. St Albans and Bury were political anachronisms, sizeable urban communities whose leading members were deprived by monastic overlords of the rights which their opposite numbers in smaller towns had enjoyed for one and a half centuries. A good deal is known about Bury. In 1377 it had a taxpaying population of 2,445 adults, which means that its total population (in view of the high proportion of children in medieval populations) was probably near to 4,000. After London it was the fourteenth most populous town in the kingdom.[21] Its prosperity was based on the production of woollen textiles, and on the goods and services which it supplied to a rural hinterland which was also significantly industrialized. Less can be said about St Albans. No poll tax returns survive to give us even the most

[21] W. G. Hoskins, *loc. cit.*

inaccurate insight into its numbers or occupational structure. The main evidence about the town comes from the hostile pen of the St Albans monastic chronicler, who always refers to its inhabitants as *villani*, a deliberately ambiguous word which could mean 'villein', that is unfree tenant, or 'townsman', that is inhabitant of a 'villa', which could mean anything from a village to an unenfranchised town. Walsingham was denying to the men of St Albans the coveted title of 'burgess' and using the term which emphasized their unenfranchised state. His implied assimilation of St Albans to the status of a mere village almost receives confirmation in the demands of the men of St Albans themselves in 1381. Apart from chartered independence, what they seemed most concerned about was their freedom to grind their own corn, full their own cloth and to enjoy pasture rights, just like other villages on the St Albans Abbey estate.[22]

Yet St Albans was not a village. In 1334 it was assessed at £17 4s. For though this was not particularly high, compared for instance with the Bury St Edmunds assessment of £24, it was the highest assessment in Hertfordshire. The tax relief which was granted after 1351, and paid from the fines of delinquent labourers punished under the Statute of Labourers, can be expected to be proportional to the importance of the place so favoured. St Albans obtained a £10 relief, the highest in the county, compared with £5, for instance, for the market centre of Ware. Furthermore, although the lack of a 1377 poll-tax return prevents us from seeing whether the position of St Albans was advancing or declining relative to other towns after 1334, the town's position in the subsidy returns of 1524 make us suspect that it was in fact thriving during the last two centuries of the middle ages. In 1524 it was assessed for tax at a higher sum than Winchester, Rochester and Nottingham, towns which had been assessed at twice or three times the St Albans rate in 1334. Unfortunately, there is very little known about its economy. One suspects that in some respects it suffered, as far as industrial development was concerned,

[22] T. Walsingham in his *Gesta Abbatum Monasterii Sancti Albani*, III, Rolls Series 1869, pp 318ff. reproduces charters forced from the monks by the men of the town and of the estate. For his summary of their demands in his *Historia*, see Dobson, p 270.

from the proximity of London, while at the same time benefiting as one of the market centres of an area whose prosperity must have been stimulated by the demand of the London food market.[23]

Some inkling of the type of economic development which St Albans might have enjoyed can be gained from a fourteenth-century undated tax return for the fifteenth in the Liberty of St Albans.[24] The return from St Albans town is missing, but returns for less important neighbouring townships such as Barnet and Watford suggest what might have been the economy on a rather larger scale of St Albans. This return of the fifteenth is quite unusual. It has already been explained that after 1334 the fifteenth of movables was a fixed sum imposed on all inhabited places other than boroughs and manors of the ancient demesne of the crown. These particular returns give the conventional money totals established as from 1334, but for the Liberty of St Albans and the Hertfordshire Hundred of Dacorum, give names of individuals— not all taxpayers in each vill, but simply the names and occupations of traders and craftsmen. The fact that the returns from Saddington and Flamsted are headed 'The market in the vill of Saddington etc. . . .' suggests that for some reason the list was compiled by some authority interested in tapping mercantile or industrial as against agricultural wealth.

Watford's traders were as follows: three keepers of hostelries (*hostillarii*); two tavern-keepers (*tavernarii*); three bakers; six butchers; one fishmonger; four tanners; five shoemakers; three chandlers; five glovers; one cloth-seller or tailor; six cornmongers; three wool merchants; two smiths; and twenty-six brewers (some of whom had other occupations). Barnet, a smaller place, had a similar occupational structure: eight hostelry-keepers; two tavern-keepers; nine bakers; one mercer; four butchers; three cooks or fishmongers; twelve maltmongers; three tanners; two shoemakers; two smiths; and fifteen brewers. Here there was rather more duplication of occupations than at Watford, all of the eight hostelry-keepers

    [23] For the subsidy figure payable in the late fourteenth century, see PRO, E.179. 120/47 (a half subsidy of 7 Richard II); *VCH, Herts*, IV, 1914, p 194; W. G. Hoskins, *loc. cit.*
    [24] PRO, E179. 242/17, 18.

for instance being entered as brewers as well and some of them having other allied occupations, such as taverner, baker and cornmonger. All told, one has the impression that here is the range of trades characteristic of agricultural market towns. One suspects that St Albans, on a somewhat larger scale, was similar. Yet there must have been a more important industrial element than at Watford or Barnet, for the landmarks of the St Albans fishing rights granted under pressure by the abbot to the town in 1381 included two fulling mills. We know that the St Albans men and women had been quarrelling with the abbots as far back as 1274 about their right to full their cloths at home rather than in the abbey mills.[25] One of the mills used as a landmark in the 1381 charter is described as 'the old fulling mill', but whether this means that it was just that, or also out of use, we cannot know.

The details of the participation by the townsmen of Bury St Edmunds and St Albans are well known, and the events have been described many times.[26] Our concern here is with the nature of the alliance between the urban population and the rebels from the open country. The pattern was not the same in the two towns, although in each case we must recognize that the initiative in both places was in the hands of the leading mercantile or industrial element rather than with the urban poor, as in London. The main difference seems to be that at St Albans the leading townsmen openly took advantage of the disturbances and threw in their lot with the rebellion, while at Bury, although secretly encouraging the rebels from outside under Wrawe, they pretended that the physical attack on the monastery and its inmates was none of their wish or doing. This difference may be attributed to the fact that the urban community in St Albans was genuinely

[25] E. Carus-Wilson, *Medieval Merchant Venturers*, 1967, pp 201–2.

[26] M. D. Lobel, *The Borough of Bury St Edmunds*, 1935, There is no comparable work on St Albans, but see Réville, Pt I; A. S. Green, *Town Life in the 15th Century*, I, ix, 1894, a still useful work: and (less to be recommended) N. M. Trenholme, *English Monastic Boroughs* (University of Missouri Studies, II, 3, 1927). The *Gesta Abbatum* III provides the basic narrative source for the St Albans events. Similarly the documents printed in the third volume of the *Memorials of St Edmunds* give the essentials (from the abbey's point of view) of the disputed election and its consequences. Walsingham's chronicle shows that he had detailed knowledge of the Bury monks' side of the story.

nearer socially to its rural neighbours than was the case at
Bury, indicated by the agrarian element in the 1381 St Albans
freedom charter.

The reason, as we have mentioned, for the leadership of the
rebellion by the urban upper strata in these two towns was
that in both cases the administrative and judicial control over
the town by the monastic overlord had been preserved intact.
The inhabitants, even the richest, could not claim to be free
burgesses and did not have the normal forms of self-government enjoyed by the majority of English urban communities.
This had been the ground for bitter conflict between the
townsmen and the monasteries for over a century, a conflict
which had already broken out into open rebellion in both
towns during the disturbances at the end of Edward II's reign
in 1326–7. And yet the urban and monastic communities
were not hermetically sealed off from each other; tensions
within one group could be communicated to the other. At
Bury there was even a faction among the monks that had close
ties with some of the leading townsmen. In 1379, when there
was an abbatial election, the pope had provided (nominated)
to the post of abbot the proctor-general of the English Benedictines at Rome, Edward Bromfield. The monks, by a majority
of forty-two to seventeen, elected as abbot their sub-prior,
John Tymworth. Bromfield was related to a rich inhabitant
of Bury, Thomas Halesworth, the alderman of the gild, and
there was evidently a town party which supported Bromfield.
In turn, Bromfield appears to have committed himself to the
support of the townsmen's claims for independence, for Halesworth at the height of the disturbance in 1381 pledged his
goods that when installed as abbot his relative would fulfil
the townsmen's wishes. But before then, the king had moved
in support of the majority party in the monastery, for in
accepting the abbey from the pope, without royal permission,
Bromfield had committed an offence against the Statute of
Provisors. Bromfield was imprisoned and five of his supporters
in the town were bound over in the sum of £2,160. So there
were long-standing grounds for conflict between town and
abbey, now magnified by the struggle over the abbacy in
which the government had become a party. It was this
tension which resulted in the killing of the Prior of Bury at

Mildenhall in 1381, by a crowd of townsmen and peasants from the abbey estate, with Halesworth, Robert Westbrom, a mercer and Geoffrey Denham, esquire, a lay official of the abbey in the lead.

Less can be said about the internal affairs of abbey and town at St Albans. The leader of the urban movement was William Grindecobbe, said to have been educated in the monastery. He had some relatives among the monastic body, and owned real property in the town. Before the rebellion he had been involved in a fracas with the monks over the confiscation of measures by the abbot's officials from some town houses. Even less is known of other leaders such as the baker, William Cadington, Richard of Wallingford or John Barbour, these gaps in our knowledge being possibly caused by the burning of some of the abbey's judicial records during the course of the rebellion. Whatever may be obscure, however, it should not be imagined that these men were drawn from the rank and file of the town's population. This was recognized at the time by the Westminster chronicler, who, in describing the repression of the rebellion, states that the king went to St Albans to punish those upper class townsmen (*nobiliores de villa*) who had wanted to destroy the abbey.[27] Though less rich than their opposite numbers in Bury, they belonged to the same social stratum. This fact is indirectly testified by the attempt of the St Albans jurors, drawn no doubt as local juries normally were from the richer inhabitants, during the initial enquiries by royal agents after the defeat of the revolt, to deflect the royal agents' attention from themselves. When ordered by Sir Walter atte Lee to restore to the abbey the extorted charters, these jurors, who did their best not to implicate Grindecobbe and others, excused themselves from finding the documents by saying that to search for them would rouse the fury of the masses.[28] This reminds one of similar attempts by the greater men of Bury to use the threat of riots by the populace in order to force the monks to surrender the abbey's charters and muniments.

The attempts by discontented urban oligarchs to push the blame for their opportunist alliance with the forces of rebellion on to the urban poor is also exemplified in Cambridge,

[27] R. Higden, *Polychronicon*, IX, pp 6–7.　　[28] Réville, p 143.

where the leader of the urban revolt was none other than the mayor.[29] This man, Edmund Redmeadow alias Lister was, as one of his surnames suggests, a dyer, who in the judicial enquiry after the suppression of the revolt declared that the common people of the borough threatened to cut off his head if he did not lead them in an attack on the property of Barnwell Priory, on the outskirts of the town. At this time Cambridge, though a county town, was a good deal smaller than Bury, having a population of something like 3,000 at the time of the rising. Its economic role was principally that of a market town for the agricultural produce of the region, that is, for the most part, grain. It was also connected by waterways with the Wash and in particular with Bishops Lynn, one of the important east-coast ports from which coastal as well as seagoing shipping plied. There was also an important annual fair, one of the most important in England, on the outskirts of Cambridge, that of Stourbridge. As befitted the market centre of an agricultural area, the occupations of the townspeople were for the most part in the service and victualling trades. In spite of Mayor Redmeadow's occupation there was no cloth industry of any significance, though it did exist.

This is naturally not all that is to be said about Cambridge. It was also the seat of the second of England's universities, an institution whose presence was the cause of much of the trouble in 1381. In the first place the vice-chancellor and the proctors of the university had enjoyed since 1270 a predominant role in the policing of the town. The vice-chancellor presided over the joint annual assembly (known as the 'Black Assembly') before which clerks and laymen were sworn to keep the peace. These two groups were not equal in the eyes of the law, for the scholars enjoyed benefit of clergy which for most offences took them away from the lay courts. Furthermore, from 1305 the vice-chancellor could cite laymen and burgesses before him to answer scholars in all sorts of personal actions, such as contracts concerning movable goods, leases of buildings, loans and so on. The university authorities had

[29] For the Cambridge revolt see W. M. Palmer and H. W. Saunders, *Documents Relating to Cambridgeshire Villages*, 1926, and H. M. Cam in *VCH Cambs.*, III, 1959. For Cambridge landowners, F. W. Maitland, *Township and Borough*, 1898.

long established power over the price of lodgings and in the exercise of jurisdiction over the price and quality of bread and ale. As a culmination of these already partially established claims, and as a punishment for the town's involvement in the 1381 rising, the university in 1382 obtained sole control over all matters connected with victualling in the borough and in the Stourbridge fair.

In addition to these legal privileges which were designed to protect individual scholars as consumers, the colleges in which many of the scholars lived had corporate privileges as land-owning institutions. They shared these with other ecclesiastical bodies of which the most important was Barnwell Priory. Corpus Christi College was the third biggest landowner in the open fields (because, ironically, it was founded by Cambridge gildsmen who endowed it with local property). These fields surrounded the town and over them the inhabitants, whether full burgesses or not, claimed rights of common. Other colleges had lands in these fields, as had Barnwell Priory. The townsmen thought that the Prior of Barnwell had enclosed part of the field, thus depriving them of common pasture and of an ancient droveway from one part of the field to another. It was this which led to the attack on the Priory on 17 June by a large crowd led by the mayor. Redmeadow may have been right in saying that he was forced into this action, for the encroachment on the commons was a grievance of the poor inhabitants rather than of the well-to-do burgesses. But the attacks on the university bedell, the breaking open of the university's chests in St Mary's Church and in the House of the Carmelites, the burning of the university and college charters of privilege, must have been the work of the leading burgesses, or at any rate of a substantial faction. This action was followed by the sealing by the university of charters renouncing its privileges which remained as evidence against the mayor until after the defeat of the rising.

The attack on the university began on the evening of 15 June, on the same day, that is, that two burgesses, John Giboun, Jr, and Richard Asshewell, led a party of horsemen from the town to join in an attack by country rebels on the property of the Duke of Lancaster's official, Thomas Hasledon, in the villages of Steeple and Gilden Morden. On the following day, the townsmen, in their turn, brought in a party of country rebels to help them against their local enemies. In at least one case, the country rebels and the townspeople had one enemy who united in his person a good deal of those functions that were widely detested at this time. This was Roger of Harleston, once a mayor of Cambridge, a Justice of the Peace enforcing wage regulations, a Member of Parliament, a commissioner for the poll tax, and, like so many of the richer burgesses, a country landowner as well. Hence, before the urban revolt got under way, his country house at Cottenham was sacked by rebels from the country. Not much is known about the factional tensions among the Cambridge burgesses, but Harleston was not alone among the burgesses to be attacked by rebels inside and outside the town. The houses of the former mayor and M.P., John Blankpayn, who had been a collector of the poll tax, were attacked, as was the town house of Roger of Harleston. These attackers of the houses of the local notables have in some cases names of occupational descriptions suggesting an artisan origin—hosier, furbisher, wright and lister. They may have been involved in those conventicles which were being denounced in December 1380 and February 1381 and which may represent the formation of some sort of party within the burgess ranks which took its chance at the time of the general rising.

St Albans, Bury St Edmunds and Cambridge provide the clearest and best documented examples, apart from London, of townsmen consciously seeking the alliance of the peasant rebels to forward their own ends and as such are clearly in a different category from urban factions which simply took advantage of the general upheaval to pursue ancient grievances. Further research may show that these cases are not isolated. Little is known, for instance, about the significance of those inhabitants of Canterbury who welcomed the Kentish rebels, though in a large town with a diversified occupational structure and a record of grievances against ecclesiastical corporations one would expect considerable elements of conflict.

The participation of a substantial number of townsmen, from the London poor to the wealthy burgesses of Bury St Edmunds, is peculiar to the English rising. Whatever may

have been their secret sympathies, the lower class in Paris
made no practical demonstration of solidarity with the
Jacques, and as we have seen the smaller towns on the whole
rejected them. If the Jacques fought at the side of the bourgeoisie at Meaux, it was no doubt because the latter could not
afford to reject any help they could get. Urban disdain for
country rebels certainly characterized the political climate
even of the radical bourgeois in Barcelona politics. The situation in St Flour was rather different, since it seems that suburban artisans mingled with peasants in the rather special type
of bandit operations which characterized the Tuchinat. But
the consuls of St Flour showed no sympathy with the Tuchins.
The situation was also ambiguous in Flanders, because outside the great cloth towns the difference between the agricultural and industrial aspects of the villages and small towns
was not marked, both involving economic interests which
clashed with those of such places as Ypres or Ghent. Nevertheless, the conflict between town and country seems to have
been sharper on the continent than it was in England, though
it was by no means absent here. Perhaps the apparently exceptional behaviour of the English urban population in the
rebellious areas is strongly coloured by the unusual subordination of the Bury and St Albans urban communities to their
well-connected Benedictine overlords and by the widespread
political antagonism to Gaunt and the other close advisers
of the crown which brought Londoners and countrymen
together. But we must now consider a group which exemplified
the church in a different light from that in which we have just
examined it.

In analysing the social composition of the leadership and
following of the rebels, a special place must be reserved for
the clergy. We have seen that this social group was not notice-
ably active in providing leaders in the continental peasant
movements, at any rate before the sixteenth-century peasant
wars in Germany.[30] In England things were different. Here
the lower clergy was conspicuous in the leadership of the
rising. Leaving on one side those who were involved in geographically peripheral movements (in Leicestershire, Somerset or Wiltshire), there seem to have been nearly a score of

[30] Above, p 124.

clerics in positions of sufficient prominence in the revolt of the south-eastern counties to merit mention in the chronicles and the official records. And behind the clerics named in the chronicles and the indictments, we have indications of a wider and anonymous grouping. At any rate, after the rising the government found it prudent to advise the officials of the exchequer not to press for contributions to the clerical subsidy from those chaplains and clerks in the archdeaconry of Essex who had gone into hiding for fear of proceedings against them for involvement in the rebellion.[31] The best known of the named clerical rebels are John Ball, who was with Tyler at the centre of things, and John Wrawe, the Suffolk leader who later turned king's evidence. Some, it is true, appear in the records only in connexion with episodes of local significance, such as the participation of the parsons of Stansfield and Ixworth, John Smith and a cleric named Walter, in the attack on the Abbey of Bury St Edmunds; or the vicar of Mildenhall's attack on the Cambridgeshire escheator in order to recover the victim of an alleged abduction.[32] But some seem to have become fully committed to the more general aims of the rising. For example, William, a chaplain officiating in St John's Church, Thanet (Kent), together with the parish clerk and the sacristan were presented as having attempted, with others, to prevent customary tenants from performing their labour services; with raising funds for the rebellion and mustering armed men by proclamation on the church itself 'by commission of John Rakestraw and Watte Tegheler'.[33] Geoffrey Parfey, vicar of All Saints, Sudbury, and his chaplain, Thomas, were fully committed helpers of Wrawe, who, in his confession,[34] accused them of playing a leading part in the exaction of tribute from the mayor and principal burgesses of Thetford. John Batisford, the Rector of Bucklesham, together with the rich yeoman Thomas Sampson, played a similarly conscious and leading role at Ipswich and in the surrounding countryside where they publicly proclaimed the rebellion and demanded the support of the population. John Michel, a chaplain from Ely, set out to join John Wrawe, an act presum-

[31] Réville, p 225.   [32] Powell, pp 14, 16.
[33] *Archeologia Cantiana*, III, p 76.
[34] Wrawe's confession is printed by Dobson, pp 249–54.

ably implying some wider interest than simply the satisfaction of some locally engendered resentment, although he did later return to take a leading part at Ely in the attack on the cathedral.[35]

The participation of the clergy in the revolt is usually explained as being the consequence of the exploited position of the greater number of their lower ranks, whether beneficed or unbeneficed. The unbeneficed, in particular, relied for a meagre living on getting temporary employment as parish priests during the frequent absence of the beneficed rectors and vicars or as chaplains saying masses for the dead in the numerous chantries throughout the country. They, like other wage-earners, were subject to the provisions of the Statute of Labourers. The rectors and vicars had their own grievances, such as the frequent clerical taxes (which fell on beneficed and unbeneficed alike), fees payable to the diocesan officials and very frequently a rather poor income. The vicars were particular sufferers, since in their parish the tithes and other income to which rectors would normally be entitled were largely appropriated by the monasteries, which frequently obtained for themselves the corporate rectorship of the parish with entitlement to the parish income. Only a small portion of this was left to the vicar. However, we must not forget that Wrawe was by all accounts the Rector of Ringfield, and originally, therefore, in receipt of a steady income, even if he was without property at the time of his execution. Batisford was also a rector, as were the two clerics already mentioned who attacked the Cambridgeshire escheator. Two clerics involved in the attacks on the university and Barnwell Priory at Cambridge were diocesan officials, Hugh Candlesby being the archdeacon's registrar, and John Tittleshall the rural dean of Wisbech (and therefore *ipso facto* a beneficed priest of the deanery).

In other words, there were, mainly at the parish level, well-to-do as well as poor clergy who rebelled, just as the social

---

[35] Powell, pp 22, 48–9, 127. The impact of the revolt at Ely is described by M. Aston, *Thomas Arundel*, 1967, pp 138–42. Her view that clerical participants in the rising were undisciplined and mutinous characters who specialized in trouble-making belongs to the ruling class folk-lore of all time and hardly helps us to understand the problem.

spectrum among the laity varied from the well-breeched yeoman to the landless labourer. The discontent, therefore, while
partly economic, cannot have been entirely so. The annual
income of the rectory of Ringsfield, of which Wrawe was once
incumbent, was assessed for ecclesiastical taxation (certainly
an underassessment) at £8. This was the assessment made in
1291 which continued to be used in the fourteenth century.
By the time of the pre-Dissolution survey of 1536 (known as
the *Valor Ecclesiasticus*) the rector's income was reckoned at
£12 a year. John Batisford's rectory of Bucklesham is not
valued in the 1291 return, but it was worth £9 19s in 1536.
Parfey's vicarage of All Saints, Sudbury, is also unvalued in
1291. The rectory was an appropriation of the Abbey of St
Albans and was valued at £10 13s 4d. The value of the vicarage in 1536 was £5; it may have been assessed at a lower figure
in the fourteenth century.[36] At any rate, the vicar would almost certainly be receiving less than half of the parish income.
Parfey would see the bulk of the value of the tithes going to
St Albans while he did the work of the parish. These were
average parish incomes, and if the lesser income of the vicar,
at say £3 or £4 a year, meant that he lived a difficult life
(for he had many parish expenses), rectors assessed at £8 to
£10 a year would be by no means poverty-stricken.

If the economic and social situation of many members of
the clergy would seem reason enough for some of them to identify themselves with peasant and artisan rebels, there is
evidently more to their attitude than this. Whatever the defects of their education, they were more literate and more
likely to be familiar with general concepts about the rights of
men and the duties of governments than the custom-domina-
ted laity. The better they knew the Bible and the writings of
the fathers of the church, the more explosive the mixture
of social and religious radicalism was likely to be. Here they
had to hand an enormous repertory of ideas, some of which
could be as profoundly critical of the social order as other
ideas from the same repertory could bolster up that same
order. The indictments which described their actions during
the rising cannot be expected to give any inkling of the

[36] *Taxatio Ecclesiastica circa A.D. 1291*, 1802, pp 118, 122; *Valor Ecclesiasticus*, III, 1817, pp 433, 450, 455.

motives which prompted them to abandon their appointed
priestly role as mediators between the accepted and established order of mankind and the God who, after all, was
considered to be the apex of that established order.

William Langland did not have a high opinion of the parish
clergy. He takes one of them to typify the vice of Sloth, a
man lazy, ignorant and entirely secular in his preoccupations.
This cleric's knowledge of the scriptures and the forms of
service is negligible; instead he is well versed in the popular
ballads of the day, those of Randolph, Earl of Chester, and
Robin Hood. The latter, at any rate, were socially subversive
enough, to judge by the earliest surviving examples, such as
'Robin and the Monk' or the 'Little Gest of Robin Hood'.[37]
However, John Ball was clearly not a man like Sloth. His
reported sayings are in the long tradition of Christian social
radicalism which goes back to St Ambrose of Milan, if not
before.[38] It is an ambiguous tradition. After all, St Ambrose
was one of the Fathers of the church. Sermons in denunciation
of the rich, as has frequently been pointed out, were not
exclusive to heretics or other conscious rebels against ecclesiastical or secular authority. They were a commonplace of
clerical moralists who selected the characteristic crimes of
every estate in the social order for castigation. The socially
rebellious clergy, familiar with such sermons as much through
reading sermon manuals as through listening at the pulpit,
only had to select from the rich store of invective and scrip-
tural citation such quotations as seemed to fit in with their
own observations of the social scene. Walsingham was no
doubt right in attributing to John Ball the sermon text 'Whan
Adam dalf and Eve span, wo was thanne a gentilman', but it
was already a commonplace in this or similar forms, as is
shown in an early fourteenth-century religious poem:

> When Adam delf and Eve span . . .
> Whare was than the pride of man?[39]

---

[37] *Piers the Ploughman*, ed. Goodridge, p 111; R. H. Hilton, 'The Origins
of Robin Hood', *P & P*, 1958.

[38] A. O. Lovejoy, 'The communism of St Ambrose', *Essays in the History
of Ideas*, 1948.

[39] G. R. Owst, *Literature and Pulpit in Medieval England*, 1961, p 291.

It must have been a commonplace throughout Europe, for we find it as far away as East Prussia in 1525:

> Do Adam rent und Eva span
> Wo war do der Edelman?
> Im Kustal war er. . . .[40]

(he was in the cowshed).

There is nothing new in the idea that social rebels of any class should seize on those elements in the literary and homiletic tradition which would legitimize their actions. What needs explaining is the comparatively prominent part played by the lower clergy in south-eastern England, an explanation which cannot be satisfactorily based simply on economic grievances, important though these were. Was there some more sympathetic relationship between the parish priest and his flock in England, as compared with other countries? It seems hardly likely that the social origins of the English clergy were nearer to the peasants and artisans than on the continent. Not many seem to have sprung from families lower in the social scale than the gentry. And indeed the canon law prohibition on servile recruits to the clerical order would have affected more aspirants in England than in France or Italy, though perhaps not in Germany. For villeinage in England which was still considered servile in the fourteenth century was more widespread than was serfdom across the Channel. The appropriation of tithes by monastic houses and by laymen was just as prevalent in Europe as it was in England,[41] so the parish clergy in all countries had this legitimate grievance. Nor was there anything less of a clerical proletariat on the continent.

A possible explanation for the clerical involvement in the events of 1381 may be found in the peculiarly retarded development in England of popular heresy. Between 1166 and the Lollard movement of the late fourteenth century, there is virtually no evidence of a heretical movement in England. The brief incursion of the Pastoureaux, already mentioned,

[40] H. Zins, 'Aspects of the peasant rising in East Prussia in 1525', *Slavonic and East European Review*, 1959–60.

[41] ' . . . by the end of the twelfth century, in spite of early theory and canon law, almost all monastic communities freely owned and accepted tithes.' G. Constable, *Monastic Tithes*, 1964, p 197.

and the occasional evidence for the punishment of sorcerers, do not add up to a movement. Yet England was hardly exempt from the social tensions or the critical attitudes to ecclesiastical abuses or the self-questioning of worried Christians about their faith and their church which lay behind the many continental movements. The apparently sudden outburst of Lollardy after the rebellion must have had more behind it than the theological writings of one man. The fact that contemporaries may have sometimes been mistaken to identify Lollardy with social and political subversion should not mislead us. Perhaps discontent, including that of the clergy, could flow into several channels. Perhaps the very absence of a heretical movement brought the critical elements among the clergy to express themselves in the social and political movements of 1381. Perhaps the now discarded idea of a close link between Lollardy and the rising of 1381 was not after all so mistaken, provided that we regard Lollardy as something wider simply than the following of Wycliffe. After all, Ball was first imprisoned for illicit preaching in the 1360s.[42]

[42] D. Wilkins, ed., *Concilia Magnae Brittaniae et Hiberniae*, III, 1737, pp 64–5, 172–3; H. C. Wood, ed., *Registrum Simonis de Langham*, Canterbury and York Society, 1956, p 149.

9 Organization and Aims

What sort of organization should we expect in a movement drawing its support from all strata of peasant society, including a sprinkling of the literate? It would be unlikely that, in a society based on family units of production in villages and small towns, the rising would have been centrally planned and put into motion by the issue of orders from a central leadership to committed supporters in the locality. And yet some historians have been led by the evidence to believe that this was so. G. M. Trevelyan thought that 'agitators now came bearing not general exhortations but a particular command from the Great Society as they called the union of the lower classes which they were attempting to form'; that the English rising was stimulated by messengers from Essex asking for support 'in accordance with the plan of cooperation framed by the Great Society' and that in Kent 'word was sent to the disturbed districts that no one in pain of death was to do custom or service to his lord without orders from the Great Society'. Edgar Powell took a similar, though less emphatically expressed view in his study of the rising in East Anglia. In considering the organization of the rising, it is necessary to deal first with this theory.[1]

The 'particular commands' were those cryptic letters reproduced by the chroniclers Walsingham and Knighton and attributed to John Ball[2] (a name which we have no reason to treat as a pseudonym), as well as to three others, Jack Mylner, Jack Carter and Jack Trewman, names which may (as we have seen) have been pseudonyms, possibly for Ball himself. There is no reason to suppose that the letters are not authentic messages passed at the time of the rebellion, but they are not particular commands. They are cryptic, loaded with allegori-

[1] G. M. Trevelyan, *England in the Age of Wycliffe*, 1899, pp 203, 209, 219; Powell, p 57.

[2] Dobson, pp 380–3; R. H. Robbins, ed. *Historical Poems of the 14th and 15th Centuries*, 1959, pp 54–5.

cal and symbolic meanings, couched in poetic language with internal rhyme and alliterations which are used with considerable skill. There are recognizable echoes from Langland's *Piers the Ploughman*[3]—unless both echo some unknown common substratum of popular moralizing. Insofar as they are not exhortations about the priority of morality over expediency, truth over deception, open dealing over corruption and against the deadly sins, they are warnings about the need for unity and preparedness. They could have been written at any time during the course of the rising.

The theory of the Great Society may be based on a misreading of the evidence, in Latin, in the indictments. George Dounesby, a Lincolnshire man, was accused of having come to Bury St Edmunds calling on the townsmen to rise and saying furthermore that he had been sent there as *nuntius magne societatis*. This Latin phrase can be translated 'messenger of the Great Society'. It could also be translated 'messenger of a large company' or 'big gang' or 'great band'.[4] Adam Clymme who was tried and hanged at Ely, was said to have instructed the local population to refuse to do their services *aliter quam eis informaret ex parte magne societatis*, which could mean 'unless he instructed them otherwise on behalf of the big gang'. Clearly there were several 'large companies, gangs or bands' moving around the countryside. The two men named Smith and Padinak in West Fleg Hundred were said to be on a journey in that district when they *obviaverunt cum magna societate et jurati fuerunt per societatem*, that is, 'met a large company and were sworn into that company'. John Hanchahe of Shudy Camps is reported as the leader-in-chief 'with his company and force made up of unknown men' (*cum societate sua et potestate congregata de hominibus ignotis*). Joan Smith of Rochester was one of the principals of a 'great band of rebellious evil doers from Kent' (*in magna societate malefactorum insurgentium de Kent tanquam principalis factor et ductor*).[5]

These bands, large and small, seem to have emerged as a secondary phase in the organization—if that is not too precise

---

[3] For other occurrences of the triad Dowell, Dobet, Dobest, see R. W. Frank, *Piers Plowman and the Scheme of Salvation*, 1957, p 42n.

[4] Réville, for example, translates it as 'une grande troupe', p. 68.

[5] The examples quoted are among the documents printed in Powell, pp 49, 127, 134, 137; and in Réville, p 199.

a term—of the rising. Combining what we learn from the indictments with other evidence, this organization of bands seems to have been preceded by spontaneous coming together of villagers. Henry Knighton's description of the way things developed in Essex seems to express succinctly enough this initial process. Knighton describes the first hesitation about what action should be taken in face of the 'new and almost unbearable burden which appeared to be endless and without remedy', an excellent description of the prolonged collection of the third poll tax. He then goes on to show how one man took the plunge . . . 'Thomas Baker of Fobbing (so called because of his trade) took courage and began to make speeches and to find supporters among some of the men of the village. Then others joined them, and then each of them sent messages to their friends and relatives, and so further, from village to village, district to district, seeking advice and asking them to bring prompt help with respect to those needs which they had in common and which bore so heavily on them. And so they began to gather together in companies with a great show of jubilation, as was their wont . . .'[6] According to the Essex indictment this all began on 30 May, the Thursday after Ascension Day; and with Fobbing in the lead, bands from seventeen other Essex villages joined the risings.[7]

Although a centralized organization like a modern revolutionary party is inconceivable in the peasant and artisan society of south-eastern England in 1381, one should not, at the other extreme, imagine that the rebels had no experience of organized actions. We have seen that for centuries villagers had been responsible for collecting the taxes; the village indentures for the poll tax of 1377 (which survive in great numbers in the Public Record Office) are made between the tax collectors on the one hand and the constable and two worthy men from each village on the other. The villagers were indispensable for the running of the business of the manor court. By this date they were in many places almost completely in control of the enforcement of the bylaws. All tenants of land were concerned in the operation of petty police jurisdiction through the courts leet, which were held either in the private manor court of the lord or the public court of the

[6] *Chronicon*, II, p 131.   [7] *Trans. Essex Arch. Soc.*, 1878, p 218.

hundred. These, of course, were official institutions of the
state and of the ruling class. But, in addition, and particularly in south-eastern England, there were innumerable gild
organizations run by their members for their own purposes.
These not only included craft gilds in the towns, but gilds in
the country parishes. According to an official enquiry of 1389
there were 160 in Norfolk alone.[8] A very ancient type of
organization, they were devoted to the worship of a patron
saint, to mutual help amongst members, to an annual feast,
and possibly to more mundane matters such as providing
money for emergency needs.

It was natural that even rebellious actions should be concerted within a traditional organizational framework, something that we have already seen in maritime Flanders at the
time of the rising in the 1320s. According to the Anonimalle
chronicle, the tax commissioner, John of Bampton, sitting in
Brentwood, summoned the representatives of the villages by
hundreds, and it was three adjacent coastal villages in Bar-
stable Hundred, Fobbing, Corringham and Stanford-le-Hope
which led the movement. It was around the Essex Hundred
of Chafford that William Roger of South Ockendon and John
Smith of Rainham rode in order to give the signal for the
rising. The rebels even used the official machinery of the
hundreds for the purpose of mobilization. Henry Bakere of
Manningtree, the bailiff of Tendring Hundred in Essex, gave
orders purporting to come from the king to various persons,
instructing them to join the Colchester rebels. James of
Bedingfield, a leading rebel, put pressure on the chief constable of Hoxne Hundred in Suffolk to muster ten archers
from the hundred to join the rebels, at the usual rate of pay,
sixpence a day. John Gerkyn, an official of the Hundred of
Wye, made a proclamation that all the men of the Hundred
should assemble in arms. The proclamation was made, wil-
lingly or unwillingly, under pressure from an esquire, Bertram
of Wilmington, who had already, with others, broken into a
house in order to burn the owner's muniments. A further indication that the hundred may have been the unit of mobilization is that one of the charges against Thomas Sampson, John
Batisford (the parson of Bucklesham) and Richard Talmache

[8] H. F. Westlake, *The Parish Gilds of Medieval England*, 1919, appendix

of Bentley, is that they were acting as liaison men (*interligatores*) between the men of the Suffolk Hundreds of Samford, Ipswich, Carlford, Wilford, and Loes.[9]

The hundreds were not the only existing topographical or organizational units which served as a basis for rebel organization. The Isle of Thanet, rather than either the lathe of St Augustine or the Hundred or Ringslow (within both of which subdivisions of Kent it was situated), was felt to be the natural focus for mobilization. The lead was taken by men in St John's parish, Margate, including the sacristan and the parish clerk. Claiming to have a commission from Wat Tyler and Jack Straw, they made a proclamation in the church, organized the mobilization of 200 men to burn the coroners' and tax collectors' records, forbade tenants to perform services or allow distraints to be taken should attempts at enforcement be made and made a financial levy for the maintenance of proceedings against all the lords of Thanet. Thanet was an ancient unit of settlement and as such could be expected to be the area of regional organization.[10] In Hertfordshire, it was the great estate of St Albans Abbey which provided the organizational basis. In this case the unit of lordship coincided with the Hundred of Cashio which to some extent was based on the abbey estate rather than vice versa. The heart of the rebellion was, of course, in the town itself, but the townsmen were able to boast that they had support from thirty-two confederate townships, most of them no doubt men from St Albans manors who owed suit to the abbot's court, under the St Albans ash tree. In fact, Walsingham tells us that the townsmen had ordered the villagers from the liberty of the abbey to assemble at the town in order to support the urban centre of rebellion.[11]

The successive phases in the organization of the rising, then, seem to have been somewhat as follows. The village risings in Essex and Kent were precipitated by the actions of the special commissioners who were attempting to track down those who had managed to evade the payment of the third

[9] Réville, pp 189, 216–17; Powell, pp 127, 130–1; *Arch. Cant.*, III, p 82.
[10] *Arch. Cant.*, III, pp 71–2, 76.
[11] A. E. Levett, *Studies in Manorial History*, 1938, p 130; *Gesta Abbatum . . .* III, pp 329–30; Dobson, p 273.

poll tax to the regular collectors. As we have seen, once they had taken the plunge those who resisted the commissioners tried to widen the basis of their support by appealing first to nearby villages and then to the inhabitants of such wider regions as the hundreds. Companies of the most active men from the townships and the hundreds were organized under the leadership of those who imposed themselves by force of personality or by virtue of traditionally accepted supremacy, as in the case of the occasional yeomen, clergy and gentry who appear in the indictments. Elements of common action and common direction, as when the St Albans men appealed to Tyler in London or when Tyler sent instructions to Thanet or when Wrawe established his supremacy in Suffolk, occurred when the revolt was well under way, not as part of a plan at the beginning. After the brief success in London, it was natural that local leaders should look to Tyler for help. Cohesion was not maintained from the centre, even in London, but by the oaths of mutual allegiance sworn by the members of each band and by the liaison work of the *interligatores*. The extreme localism was not simply the consequence of the greater trust the rebels felt in others from their own village, hundred or estate: it was a positive element in the rebels' outlook.

This is illustrated by the quite plausible statement, attributed to Jack Straw in his otherwise somewhat dubious confession, that they envisaged setting up a king in each county.[12] It is obvious, of course, that the movements were not confined within county boundaries. John Wrawe, on the eve of assuming the leadership of the rebels in eastern Suffolk, found that at Liston on the Essex–Suffolk border there was a gathering of people from Hertfordshire, Essex, Suffolk and Norfolk. Instances occur in the indictments of instructions sent across county boundaries, from Wrawe in Suffolk, for example, to northern Norfolk; and as has been mentioned, advice and help were sought from Tyler. But, on the whole, those who became established leaders operated within a county framework, as Wrawe and Sampson did in Suffolk and Geoffrey

---

[12] Jack Straw's supposed confession is reported both by Walsingham and the monk of Evesham (derivatively). The Walsingham version is translated in Dobson, pp 365–6. The problem of its authenticity has not been solved.

Litster and Roger Bacon in Norfolk. This local leadership did not have much time to consolidate itself before the government and its supporters recovered their nerve after the death of Tyler. But it was clearly developing in organizational strength in East Anglia rather in contrast with Essex and Kent. From those counties, the strength of the rèbels was poured into London, so that the local organization hardly had time to develop. Tyler, supported no doubt by Ball and Straw, assumed in London a position of leadership over rebels of whatever place of origin. In eastern Norfolk it was Geoffrey Litster who was the 'King of the Commons', 'the idol of Norfolk'. In Suffolk, Wrawe acted the same role, but because of his priesthood deputed his Bury lieutenant, Robert Westbrom, to be 'king' in his stead.

We have seen that some of the continental peasant movements were informed by a negative class consciousness, that is, bitter hatred of the land-owning nobility, sometimes even of all the rich or well-to-do. A positive consciousness of the mutual interests of peasants and other basic producers hardly made itself felt, still less the formulation of a long-term programme of political action. How far was this also true of the English rising of 1381?

There is a tendency in the recent historiography of late medieval popular movements in England to minimize the element of social conflict and to stress rather that these movements were violent reactions of traditional provincial societies against the pressures of the central government and of its agents. The reactions could be purely backward-looking in character, that is, in protest against the inevitable extension of the efficient central control of an increasingly unified state; or they could contain a 'progressive' element in that they reacted simply against the corruption of the individual agents of a government with which they were prepared to cooperate, provided their views were taken into account. But, whether reactionary or progressive, they were all-class movements of peasants, yeomen, artisans and merchants under their natural leaders, the local gentry. There is quite a strong case for interpreting in this sense the rising of 1450, usually associated with the name of Jack Cade, as well as the various provincial risings in the first half of the sixteenth century. Is it justifiable, however, to extend this interpretation to the events of 1381?[13]

There is more than one way of approaching this problem. We may again look at the social composition of the rebel bands. There is no question here of provincial society under the 'natural' leadership of the gentry, in spite of the occasional participation of discontented landowners in East Anglia such as Sir Roger Bacon, who in any case played second fiddle to the dyer, Geoffrey Litster. As we have seen, the composition of the rebel armies seems to have been a fair cross-section of rural society, but, apart from a few exceptions, below the ranks of the nobility, the gentry, the lawyers and the beneficed ecclesiastics. Insofar as we can use medieval social categories, it was a broadly-based popular uprising of the third estate (but excluding the London merchant capitalists) against the other two components of the tripartite society of the middle ages, not a movement of all social groups against a narrow governing clique. There is not the slightest sign of even the beginnings of an alliance between the rebels and any group which had a part to play in the accepted political game: in other words, no friends, no apologists even, either in Parliament or in the Convocations of clergy. Two years later, in fact, the Chancellor, Michael de la Pole, speaking in Parliament, referred to the obedience which the gentry manifested towards the crown during the rising.[14]

We may next attempt to discover whether the rebels or their leaders thought in terms of the traditional social categories or whether they held any general social and political outlook of a revolutionary or socially critical character. If there was in fact a pretty complete gulf between the rebels on the one hand and the nobility, gentry and clergy on the other, it would be surprising if this gulf was not reflected in rebel thinking. The main evidence here are the sermons and letters of John Ball. As we have already mentioned, the letters contain echoes of the forms and imagery in William Langland's *Piers the Ploughman*. Langland echoes orthodox preachers in criticizing

---

[13] M. E. James, 'Obedience and dissent in Henrician England: the Lincolnshire rebellion of 1536'. *P & P*, 1970, p 8; B. Wilkinson, *Constitutional History of England in the 15th Century*, 1964, p 37; Dobson, p 380.

[14] *Rotuli Parliamentorum*, III, p 150, 6.

the sins of the rich and powerful and in warning them of the
punishment which will be theirs on the Day of Judgement, but
there is also in both the preachers and the poet an acceptance
of the essentials of the existing social order. In addressing the
Knight in the sixth book, Piers defines this function in a
traditional sense: 'I'll sweat and toil for us both as long as I
live,' says Piers 'and gladly do any job you want. But you
must promise in return to guard over holy church and protect
me from the thieves and wasters who ruin the world.' The
relationship between lord and tenant is accepted, though
it must be observed in a spirit of justice, 'Never ill treat your
tenants and see that you punish them only when Truth com-
pels you to . . . and take care also that you never ill use your
serfs. It will be better for you in the long run, for though they
are your underlings here on earth they may be above you in
heaven. . . .'[15]

But Ball's utterances show that he rejected the concept of a
social balance between lords and serfs, and in this he echoes
many a previous Christian writer, orthodox and heretical
alike. According to Froissart he preached 'that matters goeth
not well to pass in England nor shall do till everything be
common and that there be no villeins nor gentlemen but that
we may be all united together and that the lords be no greater
masters than we be. . . .' He points to the basis of the lords'
existence . . . 'by that that cometh of our labour they keep and
maintain their estate. . . .' Walsingham also reports the gist
of Ball's sermon which he preached on the text 'whan Adam
dalf and Eve span, wo was thanne a gentilman. . . .' 'He tried
to prove . . . that from the beginning all men were created
equal by nature and that servitude had been introduced by
the unjust and evil oppression of men against the will of
God. . . .' This is an important twist to the old orthodox
doctrine that although men may have been equal in the state
of nature, serfdom had been introduced by God as a punishment when man fell into sin. Ball's practical advice on how to
achieve equality, reports Walsingham, was in 'killing the
great lords of the realm, then slaying the lawyers, justices and
jurors . . . so at last they would obtain peace and security,
if, when the great ones had been removed, they maintained

[15] *Piers the Ploughman*, ed. Goodridge, p 120.

among themselves equality of liberty and nobility, as well as of dignity and power.'[16]

We have seen that all over Europe and particularly after the thirteenth century, apocalyptic visions of the end of the world and the Last Judgement were adopted, not as visions of a more or less distant future to be awaited but as impending events in which man now living could take an active part. The complexities of some of the millenarian visions, with their calculations of the time of arrival, victory and defeat of Antichrist, with their confident identifications not only of Antichrist but of the Angelic Popes and Emperors, are hardly to be found in fourteenth-century England. Nevertheless millenarian hints have been detected in some of Ball's sayings. 'God has now appointed a time', said Ball, according to Walsingham. 'Now is the time' is a phrase repeated in four of the six reported letters from Ball's hand, and the even more menacing phrase

> 'Johan the Mullere hath ygrounde smal, smal, smal
> The kynges son of hevene schal pay for al,'

is found in two of them. If, as has been argued, there was a long-term apocalyptic vision in *Piers the Ploughman*, in Ball it was to be of immediate effect.[17]

Hints of apocalyptic expectations in 1381 are sometimes contrasted with the practical short-term demands of various groups of rebels at various moments of the rising. Such a contrast could be used to suggest that the mass of the participants in the rising were moderate men and women, firmly anchored in the existing situation and so separated from the mentally inflamed visionaries in the lead. Such an interpretation is not altogether satisfactory. There was, of course, all the difference in the world between the expectation that the old social order would be turned upside-down in some final catastrophe and such limited gains as those in the St Albans charters which redefined, in the interests of tenants, the scope of common rights of pasture, hunting and fishing. But there were other demands, also of a practical-seeming nature, which were in fact genuinely

---

[16] Froissart, *Chronicles*, ed. Brereton, p 212; Dobson, p 375.

[17] N. Cohn, *The Pursuit of the Millennium*, 1970, pp 198–204; M. W. Bloomfield, *Piers Plowman as a 14th Century Apocalypse*, 1962, esp. chap. 4.

revolutionary in the sense that at that time they could only be realized as an accompaniment to a radical reshaping of the social order.

Such was the demand for freedom from serfdom, which was the one most persistently presented when the rebels were directly negotiating with the king and his advisers. This was one of two demands made of the king in the initial parley on 13 June from the turret in the Tower overlooking St Catherine's, the other being for the surrender of the traitors; it was repeated as the first on the list of demands at the Mile End meeting on the following day and was the final, and, as it were, summing-up clause, of the programme presented at Smithfield on the 15th. It seemed to be the keynote of the rising to most of the chroniclers, including those observing from far afield—Evesham, Dieulacres and Kirkstall. Furthermore, it was an idea to which the Essex rebels clung, even when they knew that Tyler was dead. After the repression had started, they assembled together and swore to enjoy their new liberty or die fighting. They sent envoys to the king asking that they should have freedom equal to that of their lords, with no obligation to attend manorial courts. By now the king had the power to reply that they must remain in a harsher bondage than before.[18] It was easy for the king and his entourage to grant manumission charters on a county basis— and equally easy for them to be rescinded once the forces of 'law and order' got the upper hand and began the work of repression. In fact, had it been genuinely enforced, it would have involved an enormous social upheaval, particularly when linked to the demand for land to be let at fourpence an acre. It would have meant the end of manorial jurisdiction, for no homage or service of any kind was to be done. It would have involved the removal of all cases about land to the common law courts. Not least it would have set the seal on a transformation of rural mentality. At a stroke the material basis for deference and the respect for hierarchy which has dogged the English rural masses for centuries would have been removed. True, the future was to show that the main material disadvantages of serfdom would wither away during

---

[18] *Vita Regis Ricardi II*, p 28; *Dieulacres Chron.*, p 164; *Kirkstall Chron.*, p 110; *Chronicon Anglie*, p 315.

the course of the fifteenth century, as villein tenure was converted into copyhold. This was to happen without fundamentally altering the character of the English social structure.
But we must not allow the fact that this is what actually
did happen to blind us to the radical character of the demand
for freedom in 1381.

The demand for freedom was not simply a demand for the
advantages of common-law freehold, though that was contained in it, and had been an important element in individual
peasant litigation for over a century. More important, it was
part of a more general demand for an end to lordship. This,
already expressed at Mile End in the clause about the abolition
of homage and all service other than fourpence an acre, was
repeated more directly at Smithfield. Tyler asked, among other
things, that lordship should be enjoyed proportionately
by all men. This would mean the liquidation of lordship; but
it is an interesting indication of the power of the notion of
lordship that its equal partition rather than its abolition was
proposed. And of course not all lordship was to be shared out:
the king's was to remain intact. Was this illusion or a practical
recognition of the ultimate need for power in the state to reside
somewhere? Clearly, there was a considerable element of
illusion. The rebel watchword from the beginning was 'with
King Richard and the true commons'. The rumour was
strong during the whole course of the rising, and especially
in East Anglia, that the movement had the king's blessing.
The people did not understand the true nature of the monarchy, but this was a lack of understanding which they
shared with many learned men then and now. They thought
of the monarchy as an institution standing above individuals
and classes, capable of dispensing even-handed justice. They
recognized, of course, that the king's will could be determined
one way or the other by his advisers, so that the bad policy
could be blamed by them (as it was by the aristocratic opposition) on bad advice given by evil counsellors—hence the
demand for the execution of those whom they considered
to be traitors. There was nothing new in this, a commonplace
of medieval politics. But not only was there no proposal for
alternative advisers; some rebel thinking (as we have seen)
was on the lines of regional or county kings. In other words

they still clung to the idea of monarchy, one-man rule, but in their later utterances they seemed to have abandoned any conception of the legitimacy of the rule of the whole kingdom by the Plantagenet family.

The king's lordship, if preserved, would have had to be manifested through the application of law. The rebels' leaders were quite clear about the existing law. They rejected it entirely. The meaning of the famous Smithfield demand that there should be no law but that of Winchester has been variously interpreted. The American historian George Kriehn thought that it was a reference to the Statute of Winchester of 1285 which contained clauses which could be interpreted as giving the right to bear arms to all adult males with the attached responsibility of policing the countryside. V. H. Galbraith, in his edition of the Anonimalle chronicle, suggested that the rebels were asking for the general application of Winchester borough custom which provides for the mutilation instead of the death of felons. R. B. Dobson and others have considered that this was a reference to the privileges of ancient demesne, which were tested by reference to Domesday Book, sometimes known as the Book of Winchester because of its location there in the twelfth century. But ancient demesne privilege was a good deal less than the freedom which was being demanded; the Winchester borough custom seems a dubious privilege to put at the head of a list of otherwise far-reaching and radical demands; if anything the Statute of Winchester seems to fit the case best.[19]

This clause is not the main evidence for the rebels' rejection of existing law. It is to be seen more surely in other statements and in their actions. Ball, according to Walsingham, wanted to kill all lawyers, justices and jurors; the same chronicler says that Tyler, above all things, wanted the king's commission to execute lawyers and all concerned in the operation of the law, so that 'all things would henceforward be regulated by the decrees of the common people'. The supposed confession of Jack Straw, again according to Walsingham, contains the statement that having eliminated (among others) the

---

[19] G. Kriehn, 'The social revolt in 1381', *American Historical Review*, 1902; V. H. Galbraith, ed., *The Anonimalle Chronicle*, 1927, p 196; Dobson, p 164n.

learned, that is the lawyers, the rebels would make law at their own will by which everybody would be ruled. Many of the other chroniclers noted the rebels' hostility to lawyers. The Evesham author of the life of Richard II took the view that the killing of the men of law was intended to guarantee that no one would survive who would have knowledge of either the old or the new. These indications of rebel opinion, insofar as the reports of the hostile chroniclers are not to be dismissed as mere hysteria, suggest an unusually radical attitude to existing law, which, as we have seen, was sometimes thought by peasants to be a shield rather than a weapon turned against them. But the rebels' actions in 1381 fit in with these suggestions that some of them were thinking of creating a new law, and that even more of them wanted to destroy all relics of the old. There was widespread destruction of manorial records from Norfolk to Kent; the books and records of the lawyers in the Temple were burnt; lawyers and jurors were killed or their houses pillaged wherever they could be found. It is true that other officials such as tax collectors, escheators, justices of the peace and members of Parliament were also attacked, but these were usually singled out as individuals. The attack on lawyers was indiscriminate, as if in eliminating them the rebels felt they could wipe out the whole legal system.

There could hardly be a clearer indication that the leaders of the rebellion, if not the mass following, were far from thinking in terms of the balanced, tripartite society, than the proposals that were put concerning the organization of the church. It would not be unreasonable to regard Ball as a sort of proto-Lollard, and to expect that naturally he would have radical ideas on the subject which might not be widely shared. The stock of ideas disseminated by Ball, according to the chroniclers (mainly Froissart, Walsingham and the Anonimalle) include commonplaces of the European heretical tradition, the evangelical strand rather than the millenarian. These include the abolition of the ecclesiastical hierarchy, except for one archbishop; the abolition of all monks, except for two houses of religion; the distribution of clerical property among the laity; tithes to be paid only by those richer than the parson, and only to parsons leading better lives than their parishioners. Walsingham declared that Ball held Wycliffe's doctrines, a widely believed accusation which was partly made by the orthodox to discredit Wycliffe. If he had said that Ball was a Lollard he might have been nearer to the truth and in view of the identification of Lollardy with Wycliffism, subsequent confusion is not surprising. There is no evidence, however, that Ball was concerned with doctrinal refinements, such as Wycliffe's doctrine of the Eucharist.

But evidently the religious radicalism had spread beyond Ball, for the proposals made by Wat Tyler at Smithfield included some of the ideas attributed to Ball. These were as follows: No churchmen, whether monastic or secular, were to hold property, but only to be given their reasonable subsistence. The surplus in the parishes, once the parish clergy had received their subsistence, was to be divided among the parishioners. The great property of the possessioners (here the wealthy abbeys must have been envisaged) should be redistributed to the commons. There should only be one bishop at the head of the church. Jack Straw's confession also has its ecclesiastical content. Possessioners were to be exterminated, and the distribution of the sacraments to be done by the friars. There is a different emphasis here. The preference for mendicants as against the secular parish clergy does not ring true, since the clerical supporters of the rising were all seculars, and the friars were by this time the objects of as much popular opprobrium as the monks. There may have been an attempt to link the Franciscans with the rebellion for the same reasons that Wycliffe had been blamed. The Benedictine chroniclers who referred to this confession (Walsingham and the monk of Evesham) loved the friars hardly more than they loved Wycliffe.

Naturally, Walsingham, affronted as an orthodox Christian and as a threatened possessioner, asserted that the rebels aimed to destroy the church and the Christian faith as well as the kingdom itself. Their aims were not as radical as this. Ball was in a long tradition of dissentients who believed in a Christian church and religion, though it was so different from the elaborate hierarchical structure of the existing Catholic church that it is not a matter for surprise that people like Walsingham would think that, if realized, Ball's ideas would spell the end of religion and of the organized society of which it was so intimate a part. It could, of course, be argued that the rebel aims, so largely known to us through the writings of hostile chroniclers, were therefore hopelessly distorted in an extreme direction. Yet there is not only an internal consistency in the reports by different writers about the rising itself but a consistency too with what we know about the ideas which had currency in heretical and rebellious circles in the Europe of this epoch. The rebels' ideas fit in on the one hand with the Christian radical tradition and on the other with the more legalistic tradition which emerged from the conflicts with lords about freedom of tenure and status.

It cannot be said that the rebel leaders of 1381 had a sophisticated or elaborate or well worked out or (above all) realizeable vision of what could be put in the place of the social order they were attacking. Nor can it be said that the mass of their followers shared more than some of their long-term ends, though this is true of rebellious and revolutionary movements at all times. Nevertheless, a not altogether incoherent picture emerges, simple though it is. They seem to have envisaged a people's monarchy (or monarchies) in which there would be no intermediary between the king and his people, that is, no class of landowning nobles and gentry controlling law and administration. Similarly, there would be a people's church whose basic unit would be the parish, again with no intermediate hierarchy between Christians and the single bishop or archbishop who, as head of the church was the ecclesiastical equivalent of the people's king. Somehow the people would make the law and administer justice. In spite of Froissart's version of John Ball's sermon, it is unlikely that it was believed that all things should be held in common. A regime of family ownership of peasant holdings and artisan workshops, with the large scale landed property of the church and the aristocracy divided among the peasants, was probably envisaged. Little emerges as to a rebel programme for the towns. One suspects that it was thought by the rural element among the rebel leaders that they would continue an independent existence as self-governing corporations. There are, however, some hints of suspicion of urban policy. The Evesham chronicler tells us that one of the Mile End demands was for freedom to buy and sell in all cities, boroughs, townships, markets and other places in the kingdom, a provision which would infringe urban monopolies.[20] And John Ball in his letters warned his followers to 'beware of guile in borough'. Whatever the naïveté of this political vision (if we have interpreted the evidence correctly), it can hardly be thought to conform to the tripartite pattern, not even that to which Langland refers.

Within the simple framework of an alternative society, there were certain elements in the rebels' programme concerned with immediate issues, short-term demands, as we would now say. The first of these, with which we have dealt, was the demand for the execution of the traitors, the king's evil advisers, who were held responsible for the poll tax and the maladministration of justice. Certain clauses of the Mile End and Smithfield petitions probably refer to the Statute of Labourers and its enforcement—a major cause of social friction. Thus, at Mile End, it was asked that no man should serve another except voluntarily and by written contract (*covenant taille*). This seems to refer to the compulsion under the statute on all able-bodied persons holding a bovate of land or less to work on demand, and first of all for their lords. The Smithfield demand for an end to outlawry as a process of law may have had a similar reference. Outlawry was the means used by the courts to coerce those who, though summoned, failed to appear after five summonses in the county court. Labourers on the move could very easily be put in this position. According to Henry Knighton, another immediate demand at Smithfield was for all private game reserves in water, park and woods to be made common so that rich and poor alike could take game. This, as we have seen, was a frequent peasant demand, found many centuries earlier, and was the main content of the St Albans charters.

It has been a commonplace of historians since Charles Petit-Dutallis' attack on the views of J. E. Thorold Rogers, that the

[20] *Vita Regis Ricardi II*, p 28. This issue caused trouble among the men of Dunstable who took advantage of the rebellion to gain a charter from the Prior of Dunstable. The charter contained a clause forbidding butchers and fishmongers from neighbouring townships to sell in Dunstable. The Prior discovered that not all the burgesses favoured this clause and so divisions appeared among them (*schisma erat inter eos ita quod alter in alterum vellet ruere*), *Annals of Dunstable*, p 418.

1381 rising had no noticeable effect on the course of social and economic development and in particular that none of the gains that the rebels wished to make were either advanced or retarded by their actions. The latest expression of this view is by R. B. Dobson: 'In general the results of the great revolt seem to have been negative where they were not negligible.'[21] The case is as difficult to prove as to disprove. The economic conjuncture of the late fourteenth and fifteenth centuries was such as to favour a downward trend in rents and an upward trend in wages, though recent investigations into the finance of the Duchy of Cornwall suggest that vigorous estate administrators could periodically revise rents in an upward direction, given the will, the opportunity and no resistance from the tenants.[22] One can say with some certainty that the English government and the English landlords acted with some notable circumspection in the application of repressive measures after the capture and execution of the obvious leaders. There was nothing compared with the aristocratic savagery of the repression of the Jacquerie in 1359, and in view of the behaviour of the English in France during the war this can hardly be attributed to gentlemanliness on their part. The continuation of local revolts for at least a couple of decades after 1381 is well known and this in itself is evidence of the continued self-assertiveness of the English lower classes. The upper class was clearly very apprehensive about popular sedition and it was this fear which gave extra bite to the repression of Lollardy, in spite of the pacific character of most of these heretics of insignificant or even of humble status.[23] If one looks at the 1381 rising, not in isolation but as the most striking manifestation of popular discontent in a century which saw a mass of sporadic local actions by peasants against landowners, it would seem as rash to assert that this 'portentous phenomenon' (as Stubbs called it)[24] had no effect, as to attribute to it all subsequent change in the condition of the working masses. There are in fact good grounds for supposing that the post-Black Death feudal reaction was not only partially

[21] Dobson, p 27.
[22] J. Hatcher, *Rural Economy and Society in the Duchy of Cornwall 1300–1500*, 1970.
[23] M. Aston, 'Lollardy and Sedition', *P & P*, 1960.
[24] W. Stubbs, *Constitutional History of England*, 1891, II, p 471.

responsible for precipitating the rising, but that it faded away as a result of it. In spite of the strengthening of labour legislation in the Statute of Cambridge of 1388, wages went up; and in spite of the threats to intensify the conditions of villeinage these were, in fact, considerably relaxed.

It must be conceded nevertheless that the failure of the rebels to end villeinage and to extend the rights of free tenure to all tenants meant much for the future of the English peasants and rural labourers. The landlord reaction may have been ineffective in the years immediately after 1381; it became very effective from the sixteenth century onwards, when 'despite the development of capitalist farming and the virtual extinction of serfdom the structure of farming society yet remained intensely patriarchal' and continued to be so until comparatively recent times. Concerning the nineteenth-century agricultural labourer (the descendants of the rebels of 1381) J. E. Thorold Rogers wrote: '... scattered and incapable of combined action with his fellows, bowed down by centuries of oppression, hard usage and hard words, with every social force against him, the landlords in league with the farmers and the clergymen in league with both, the latter constantly preaching resignation, the two former constantly enforcing it, he has lived through evil times.'[25] This was not the immediate legacy of the defeat of the rebels in 1381, for the English peasants and artisans kept their end up against the landowner and employer, with varying success, for many years afterwards. But it was the ultimate legacy of the failure of the specific battle for freedom and for the end of villeinage. The noticeable tendency of the English to be self-congratulatory about having given the idea of liberty to the world with Magna Carta could well be modified in the light not merely of the exclusion from its enjoyment of the mass of the population, but of the long-term consequences of that exclusion.

[25] J. Thirsk, ed., *The Agrarian History of England and Wales*, IV, 1966, p 400; J. E. Thorold Rogers, *Six Centuries of Work and Wages*, 1903, p 509.

10 Conclusion

The prevailing theories about the nature of the social order which all medieval thinkers and preachers put forward were in one way realistic, in another quite unrealistic. These theories were realistic in that they recognized the fact of social stratification. No attempt was made to disguise the fact that there was a ruling class which possessed the means of coercion and which depended for its existence on the labours of the classes it ruled, primarily the peasants. It also recognized that a group of intermediaries between man and God, the priests, the prayers, was an essential part of the social fabric and that this group not only mediated between the seen and the unseen worlds, but legitimized the seen social order in terms of its reflection of the unseen order beyond. The theory was unrealistic because it did not allow for social mobility and was uneasy about accepting new social groups which emerged owing to the increasing complexity of the economy. It assumed that certain forms of social behaviour were sinful deviations rather than essential class characteristics, such as peasant acquisitiveness or seigneurial pride in domination. It assumed too that social conflict occurred only because of sinful departure, usually (though not invariably) by the ruled, from obedience in their allotted tasks, rather than because conflict over the distribution of the social product was inevitably built into the landlord–tenant system.

Justificatory social theories are always found as part of any social order. But social historians should not, of course, accept these theories as correct descriptions. Nevertheless, many historians who would not admit that they accept an organic theory of society remain reluctant to see conflict as the principal underlying feature of the relationship between the main classes of medieval society, even though they happily recognize that violence and conflict prevailed in other aspects of medieval life. The survey of peasant movements which is contained in this book goes some way to documenting the element of conflict in the medieval countryside. It is, of course, incomplete. It could be argued that, spread over the whole span of the medieval centuries, the evidence seems thin. That which has been presented has, of course, been a selection. Furthermore, medieval evidence is hardly susceptible of statistical analysis. Nevertheless, as new evidence turns up, it seems to justify rather than to contradict the view put forward here that rural social relationships in the middle ages were characterized by conflict rather than harmony of lord and peasant interests. It hardly needs to be emphasized that to recognize this conflict of interest does not mean that one interprets the life of the medieval village as a constant and open battle. The respect for custom moderated or concealed without eliminating conflict. Conflict could assume many forms, non-violent as well as violent. Resistance and rebellion, if on a small scale and quickly suppressed, could leave no trace in the historical record.

One way of denying the essentially antagonistic nature of lord–peasant relationships, is to demonstrate how futile such antagonisms were, to deny any success to peasant rebellions and consequently to imply that they were irrelevant aberrations from normal social evolution. However illogical such an argument might seem, the problem posed is nevertheless important. Did peasant movements make any difference to peasant conditions? Did the more violent manifestations of this peasant discontent—that is, the peasant wars and rebellions—result in any realization of the aims of either the leaders or the led?

There can be no doubt that some fundamental, though limited, peasant aims were achieved. At various times the level and the nature of rents and services owed by peasants to their lords were altered in a way demanded by peasants. There was a long-term, though occasionally reversed, trend away from labour rent towards money rent. There were periods when the general level of rents declined. It could be argued, and of course it is argued, that these trends had nothing to do with the organized and deliberate action of peasant communities but depended simply on such impersonal factors as the supply of land, population trend, the demand for agricultural products and so on. Of course these factors were most important and perhaps the most that one could claim for peasant actions, in the long run, was that they followed, perhaps reinforced, the existing currents of historical change.

Similar remarks might be made about another important object of peasants' strivings, the abolition of serfdom and the achievement of free status. Here again the trend was towards the freedom of status—with important setbacks. Was the achievement of freedom entirely due to peasant agitation, pressure or rebellion? It would be difficult to deny other factors, such as the use of free status as a bait to colonizers offered in the interests of landlord expansion or emancipation as a means of securing free labour for urban industry in some parts of Italy. Nevertheless, if the aspirations of the peasant class for freedom required certain objective conditions for their realization, that realization also required the organized push of peasant movements. In fact it might be said that the concept of the freeman, owing no obligation, not even deference, to an overlord, is one of the most important if intangible legacies of medieval peasants to the modern world.

The most ambitious of the mass movements of peasants were undoubtedly failures as far as the full achievement of their aims was concerned. The medieval landed aristocracy, supported by the great merchants, was too great and too solid a social force to allow the monarchical governments they had created to be replaced by a political community of peasant proprietors. Such a community might not be inconceivable in primitive economies on the northern fringes of medieval Europe but could no more exist in the urbanized and market-oriented societies which dominated Europe in the later middle ages than in the feudal hegemonies of the Frankish period. It may seem a platitude to say that the only social force emerging from the medieval world which was capable of taking over from the aristocracy was the bourgeoisie; this was not only what did happen, but any examination of the peasantry as an alternative ruling group must show that this was the only development that could happen. The point is all the stronger in that, as we have seen, the leading social force in medieval peasant movements, even the most radical, seems to have been those elements most in contact with the market, those who in suitable circumstances would become capitalist farmers.

If these conclusions are platitudinous, they are perhaps worth emphasizing at the present moment when historians and sociologists are engaged in comparative studies of peasant societies in different epochs. It would be very risky to transfer any generalizations about the peasant societies of medieval Europe to any other time. For example, the capitalist farmers who were to be an important element in the history of early European capitalism emerged in the general environment of small-scale enterprise. What could the fate of peasant societies in the present world of almost world-wide commercial and industrial monopoly capitalism have in common with that of the peasant societies of the late medieval world? Clearly, the tasks of leadership in contemporary peasant society have nothing in common with the tasks of the past, except in the recognition that conflict is part of existence and that nothing is gained without struggle.

Index